664 **ZECC**, Utrecht

264 **Groep Delta**, Zonhoven

320 **Jarmund / Vigsnæs**, Oslo

298 **Herzog & de Meuron**, Leymen

650 **Weber + Hummel**, Erlangen

610 **Jyrki Tasa**, Espoo

272 **Zaha Hadid**, Moscow

292 **Hertl.Architekten**, Luftenberg

174 **Devanthéry & Lamunière**, Evolène
206 **Fuhrimann & Hächler**, Vnà

12 **3LHD**, Zagreb

168 **Deca Architecture**, Antiparos Island

52 **Tadao Ando**, Treviso
508 **Plasma Studio**, Sesto

534 **Search & CMA**, Vals
582 **Philippe Stuebi**, Lucerne
678 **Peter Zumthor**, Jenaz
528 **Laurent Savioz**, Chamoson

570 **Álvaro Siza Vieira**, Mallorca

Gurgit Singh Matharoo, Ahmedabad 420

Jouin Manku, Kuala Lumpur 334

Shigeru Ban, Karuizawa 84
Terunobu Fujimori, Nagano 214
General Design, Minamisaku 242
Kataro Ide, Karuizawa 310
Tezuka Architects, Nagano 626
TNA, Nagano 630

Edge Design Institute, Beijing 188

Zhang Lei, Nanjing 670, 674

90 **Shigeru Ban**, Lake Yamanaka
64 **Atelier Masuda**, Kawaguchi
220 **Sou Fujimoto Architects**, Chiba
70 **Atelier Tekuto**, Tokyo
150 **Curiosity**, Tokyo
402 **Kengo Kuma**, Tokyo
446 **Mount Fuji Architects Studio**, Tokyo
460 **Ryue Nishizawa**, Tokyo
486 **John Pawson**, Tokyo
638 **TNA**, Tokyo
358 **Kamayachi + Harigai**, Yokohama
604 **Masaharu Takasaki**, Nagoya
44 **Tadao Ando**, Kobe
278 **Hiroshi Hara**, Chijiwa

Chris Tate, Titirangi 618

Durbach Block Architects, Sydney 180

Peter Stutchbury, Sydney 590

Sean Godsell, Glenburn 248

Systemarchitects

Casey Brown, Great Mackere

Judd Lysenko Marshall, Daylesford 346

Room 11, Hobart 518

Fearon Hay, Great Barrier Island 200
Herbst Architects, Great Barrier Island 284

Ross Stevens, Owhiro Bay 576

100

CONTEMPORARY HOUSES

IMPRINT

PROJECT MANAGEMENT
Anne Gerlinger and Florian Kobler, Cologne

PRODUCTION
Ute Wachendorf, Cologne

DESIGN
Sense/Net Art Direction, Andy Disl and Birgit Eichwede, Cologne www.sense-net.net

GERMAN TRANSLATION
Caroline Behlen, Berlin; Christiane Court, Frankfurt; Nora von Mühlendahl, Ludwigsburg; Kristina Brigitta Köper, Berlin

FRENCH TRANSLATION
Jacques Bosser, Paris

© VG BILD-KUNST
Bonn 2012, for the works of Patrick Devanthéry, Inès Lamunière, and Ben van Berkel

PRINTED IN CHINA
ISBN
978–3–8365–2330–1

© 2012 TASCHEN GMBH
Hohenzollernring 53 D–50672 Cologne
www.taschen.com

This book is in large part a compilation from TASCHEN's previously published **ARCHITECTURE NOW!**-series

100
CONTEMPORARY HOUSES

100 Zeitgenössische Häuser
100 Maisons Contemporaines
Philip Jodidio

VOL 2

TASCHEN

CONTENT VOLUME I

CONTENT VOLUME II

KAMAYACHI + HARIGAI

Seiji Kamayachi
KIKA/Office of Seiji Kamayachi
502 Honcho Building, 5–49 Honcho Nakaku
Yokohamashi, Kanagawaken 231–0005
Japan

Tel: +81 45 662 0423
Fax: +81 45 650 5584
E-mail: ka-@ki-ka.jp

Masafumi Harigai
Kengo Kuma & Associates
2–24–8 BY-CUBE 2–4F Minamiaoyama
Minato-ku, Tokyo 107–0062
Japan

Tel: +81 3 3401 7721
Fax: +81 3 3401 7778
E-mail: harigai@kkaa.co.jp

SEIJI KAMAYACHI was born in 1979 in Kanagawa Prefecture, Japan. In 2006, he created his office KIKA with Nagisa Kidosaki, obtaining his M.Arch degree from the Graduate School of Engineering, Department of Architecture at Yokohama National University in 2007. **MASAFUMI HARIGAI** was born in Tochigi Prefecture, Japan, in 1980. He also obtained his M.Arch degree from the same school as Kamayachi in 2007. He began work in the office of Kengo Kuma in 2007, having created a temporary partnership with Kamayachi specifically for the design of the G House (Yokohama, Japan, 2005–07, published here). The two say they may work together again in the future, but for the moment, they have no plans to do so.

SEIJI KAMAYACHI wurde 1979 in der Präfektur Kanagawa, Japan, geboren. 2006 gründete er mit Nagisa Kidosaki sein Büro KIKA. Seinen Masterabschluss am Institut für Bauingenieurwesen und Architektur der Nationaluniversität Yokohama absolvierte er 2007. **MASAFUMI HARIGAI** wurde 1980 in der Präfektur Tochigi, Japan, geboren. Seinen M.Arch. absolvierte er 2007 an derselben Hochschule wie Kamayachi. Seit 2007 arbeitet er für Kengo Kuma, nachdem er für die Gestaltung des G House (Yokohama, Japan, 2005–07, hier vorgestellt) eine zeitweilige Partnerschaft mit Kamayachi begründet hatte. Nach eigener Aussage werden die beiden in Zukunft möglicherweise erneut zusammenarbeiten, planen dies derzeit jedoch nicht konkret.

SEIJI KAMAYACHI, né en 1979 dans la préfecture de Kanagawa au Japon, a fondé en 2006 son agence KIKA avec Nagisa Kidosaki, et il a obtenu son master en architecture à l'École supérieure d'ingénierie du département d'architecture de l'université nationale de Yokohama en 2007. **MASAFUMI HARIGAI**, né dans la préfecture de Tochigi au Japon, en 1980, a obtenu son master en architecture dans même école que Kamayachi (2007). Il a commencé à travailler pour l'agence de Kengo Kuma en 2007 et a créé un partenariat temporaire avec Kamayachi pour le projet de la G House (Yokohama, Japon, 2005–07, présentée ici). Les deux architectes pensent retravailler ensemble dans le futur, mais n'ont pas de projet précis pour le moment.

G HOUSE

Yokohama, Kanagawa, Japan, 2005–07

Site area: 309 m². Floor area: 184 m². Client: Noriyoshi Sumiya
Cost: €307 000. Collaborators: Nagisa Kidosaki (garden design), Masato Araya (structure design)

The architects explain this house in terms of a radical critique of suburban housing developments, "In England, in the USA, but also in Japan, the suburban new town landscapes are planned according to a simple rule: the repetition of a flat site, a private garden, and a pitched roof. The project is situated in a 1970s suburban new town. Each house is built on a flat artificial pedestal, and the repetition of this typology creates a landscape, like shortcakes in a display window. This project takes away one of these shortcakes to propose a building with a new system of values." The first thing the architects did was to remove the pedestal, artificially raised to the level of the street. The concrete wall of the resulting embankment defines the living area. They then created a volume with a pitched roof above the real living space, now apparently below grade, that resembles surrounding residences but contains nothing but a void used as a sort of open family space. A sloping garden relates the street level to that of the "basement" residence. The architects conclude that by using the very rules of the town, they created "a building which has completely different values, and spaces where people can have different kinds of life styles. The town can peacefully make its renewal. The creation of one new residence becomes an opportunity to create a new landscape in the suburbs."

Die Architekten beschreiben das Haus als radikale Kritik an der Planung typischer Vorstadtsiedlungen: „In England, in den USA, aber auch in Japan werden neue Siedlungen in den Vorstädten nach einem schlichten Muster geplant: Wiederholung von flachem Baugrundstück, privatem Garten und Satteldach. Das Projekt liegt in einer in den 1970er-Jahren entstandenen Satellitenstadt. Alle Häuser wurden auf einem flachen, künstlichen Sockel errichtet, und die Wiederholung dieser Typologie schafft eine Landschaft wie Teekuchen in einer Ladenauslage. Dieses Projekt entfernt einen dieser Teekuchen und schlägt stattdessen ein Gebäude vor, das auf einem neuen Wertesystem beruht." Als Erstes ließen die Architekten den Sockel entfernen, den man künstlich auf Straßenniveau angehoben hatte. Die so entstandene Stützmauer aus Beton definiert den Wohnbereich. Schließlich errichtete das Team einen Baukörper mit Satteldach über dem tatsächlichen Wohnraum, der scheinbar im Souterrain zu liegen scheint und den Häusern der Nachbarschaft ähnelt, jedoch nichts weiter als einen Leerraum enthält, der als offener Raum für die Familie dient. Ein schräg abfallender Garten stellt die Verbindung zwischen dem Straßenniveau und dem „Keller"-Haus her. Zusammenfassend bemerken die Architekten, dass sie durch Aufgreifen der bestehenden Regeln des Vororts „ein Gebäude geschaffen haben, das vollkommen andere Werte hat und Räume bietet, in denen Menschen alternative Lebensstile finden können. Die Stadt kann sich friedlich erneuern. Die Schaffung eines neuen Hauses bietet die Gelegenheit, in den Vororten eine neue Landschaft entstehen zu lassen".

Les deux architectes présentent cette maison comme une critique radicale des lotissements de banlieue. « En Angleterre, aux États-Unis, mais aussi au Japon, les paysages des nouvelles villes de banlieue sont établis selon une règle simple : la répétition de trois éléments, terrain plat, jardin privé et toit à pignon. Le projet se situe dans une ville nouvelle édifiée dans les années 1970. Chaque maison est construite sur un socle artificiel plat, et c'est la répétition de cette typologie qui crée le paysage, comme des biscuits alignés dans une vitrine. Ce projet s'empare de l'un de ces »biscuits« pour proposer sa construction dans le cadre d'un nouveau système de valeurs. » La première chose a été de supprimer le socle artificiellement relevé au niveau de la rue. Le mur de béton qui résulte de cet enfoncement définit l'aire de séjour. Ils ont ensuite dessiné un volume surmonté d'une toiture à deux pentes au-dessus du séjour, qui ressemble à celle des autres maisons, mais ne contient rien d'autre qu'un vide affecté à l'espace de vie familial. Un jardin en pente relie le niveau de la rue à celui de la résidence en « sous-sol ». Les architectes concluent qu'en utilisant les règles mêmes de la ville, ils ont créé un « bâtiment qui répond à des valeurs entièrement différentes et des espaces dans lesquels les occupants peuvent mener des styles de vie entièrement autres. La ville peut ainsi tranquillement entreprendre son renouveau. La création d'une nouvelle maison devient une opportunité de créer un nouveau paysage de banlieue. »

The house appears extremely simple or even "ordinary" from a certain distance, but its apparent austerity is far from banal.

Aus der Distanz wirkt das Haus extrem schlicht, ja fast „gewöhnlich", dabei ist die scheinbare Strenge alles andere als banal.

La maison paraît extrêmement simple ou même « ordinaire » vue d'une certaine distance, mais son austérité apparente est loin d'être banale.

Elevations of the house show its shed-like form, while the photo above reveals the luminous base set in the excavated bottom of the site.

Aufrisse des Hauses machen die scheunenartige Form anschaulich, doch das Foto oben enthüllt das leuchtende Fundament im ausgehobenen Grundstück.

Les élévations montrent une forme classique de maison à pignon. La photo ci-dessous met en évidence la base éclairée, creusée dans le sol.

A site plan shows that the form of the house is even less differentiated than that of the neighboring structures with more complex roofs.

Ein Lageplan verrät, dass die Form des Hauses noch weniger untergliedert ist, als die Nachbarbauten mit ihren komplexeren Dächern.

Le plan général de l'implantation montre que la forme de la maison est encore plus simple que celle de ses voisines aux toitures plus complexes.

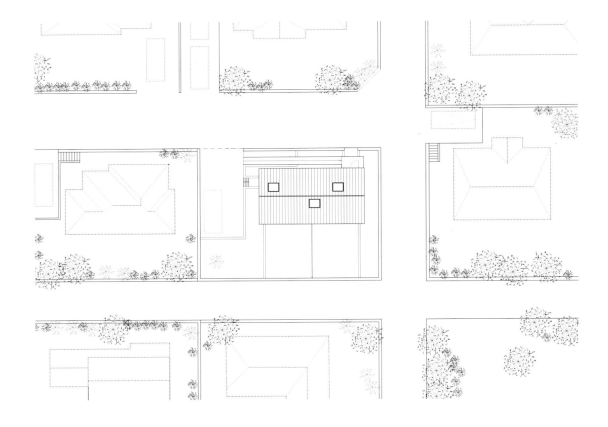

Above, the main area of the house that lies above the normal ground level, and right, the garden sloping down to the spaces that are essentially below grade.

Oben der Hauptbereich des Hauses über dem regulären Erdgeschoss. Rechts ist ein Teil des zu den Räumen unter Straßenniveau hin abgesenkten Gartens zu sehen.

Ci-dessus, le volume principal de la maison surélevé par rapport au niveau normal du sol. À droite, le jardin descend vers les volumes aménagés en sous-sol.

NADER KHALILI

Nader Khalili
Cal-Earth Institute
10177 Baldy Lane
Hesperia, California 92345
USA

Tel: +1 760 956 7533
Fax: +1 760 244 2201
E-Mail: elements@calearth.org
Web: www.calearth.org

NADAR KHALILI was born in 1937 in Iran and trained there as an architect as well as in Turkey and the United States. From 1970 to1975, he practiced architecture in Iran, and has since dedicated himself to research into building with earth. He has been a licensed architect in the State of California since 1970. He has served as a consultant to the United Nations (UNIDO) and a contributor to NASA. Khalili founded the California Institute of Earth Art and Architecture (Cal-Earth) in Hesperia, California in 1986, and has been directing the Architectural Research Program at Sci-Arc in Los Angeles since 1982. He has received awards from organizations such as the California chapter of the American Institute of Architects, for Excellence in Technology; the United Nations and HUD (U. S. Department of Housing and Urban Development), for "Shelter for the Homeless"; and the American Society of Civil Engineers (Aerospace Division), for his work in lunar-base-building technology. He is the author of five published books, including two translations of the work of the thirteenth-century Sufi poet, Jalal-e-Din Mohammad Rumi. Khalili's architectural works include the design of a future-oriented community of 5000 inhabitants (1988); Malekshahr of Isfahan, a community for 20 000 that was partially built before 1979; and more than 100 projects for conventional buildings.

NADER KHALILI, geboren 1937 im Iran, studierte in seinem Heimatland, in der Türkei und in den USA Architektur. Von 1970 bis 1975 arbeitete er im Iran als Architekt; seitdem widmet er sich der Erforschung des Bauens mit Erde. Seit 1970 ist er in Kalifornien zeichnungsberechtigter Architekt. Khalili war als Berater für die Vereinten Nationen (UNIDO) tätig und hat bei Projekten der NASA mitgewirkt. 1986 gründete er das Californian Institute of Earth Art and Architecture (Cal-Earth) in Hesperia, Kalifornien; seit 1982 ist er Leiter des Forschungsprogramms Architektur an der SCI-Arc in Los Angeles. Khalili wurde von verschiedenen Institutionen ausgezeichnet, so z. B. vom kalifornischen Verband des American Institute of Architects für herausragende Leistungen im Bereich Technologie, von den Vereinten Nationen und von HUD (Amerikanische Behörde für Wohnen und Stadtentwicklung) für „Obdach für Obdachlose" sowie von der Amerikanischen Gesellschaft für Bauingenieure (Abteilung Luftfahrt) für seine Arbeit über Bautechnologien auf dem Mond. Nader Khalili hat fünf Bücher geschrieben, darunter zwei Übersetzungen des Sufi-Dichters Jalal-e-Din Mohammad Rumi aus dem 13. Jahrhundert. Zu den architektonischen Arbeiten Khalilis gehören der Entwurf für eine zukunftsorientierte Gemeinde mit 5000 Einwohnern (1988), die Gemeinde Malekshahr in Isfahan für 20 000 Einwohner, die vor 1979 in Teilen realisiert wurde, und mehr als 100 in bautechnischer Hinsicht konventionelle Gebäude.

Né en 1937 en Iran, **NADER KHALILI** y a étudié l'architecture, ainsi qu'en Turquie et aux États-Unis. De 1970 à 1975, il a pratiqué en Iran et s'est, depuis, consacré à la recherche sur la construction en terre. Il est architecte licencié de l'État de Californie depuis 1970. Consultant auprès des Nations Unies (United Nations Industrial Development Organization) et collaborateur de la Nasa, il a fondé le California Institute of Earth Art and Architecture (Cal-Earth) à Hesperia (Californie) en 1986 et dirige l'Architectural Research Program de SCI-Arc à Los Angeles depuis 1982. Il a reçu des prix d'organismes tels que l'antenne californienne de l'American Institute of Architects pour l'excellence en technologie, les Nations Unies et le Département américain du logement et de l'urbanisme (HUD) pour son « Abri pour les sans-abri » et de l'American Society of Civil Engineers (division aérospatiale) pour ses travaux sur les technologies de construction de bases lunaires. Il est l'auteur de cinq ouvrages, dont deux traductions de l'œuvre du poète soufi du XIIIᵉ siècle Jalal-e-Din Mohammad Rumi. Parmi ses réalisations architecturales, on peut citer la conception d'une ville futuriste de 5 000 habitants (Californie, 1988, restée à l'état de prototype) ; Malekshahr d'Isphahan, ville de 20 000 habitants partiellement édifiée vers 1979, et plus de 100 projets de réalisations conventionnelles.

SANDBAG SHELTER PROTOTYPES

Various Locations, 1992–

Floor area: single unit 400 m² or double unit 800 m². Client: Iran office of UNDP/UNHCR and others
Cost: $2300 for a single unit or $2800 for a double unit, 25% extra for each additional unit

A winner of the 2004 Aga Khan Award for Architecture, the Sandbag Shelter Prototypes designed by Nader Khalili were described in the jury citation as follows: "These shelters serve as a prototype for temporary housing using extremely inexpensive means to provide safe homes that can be built quickly and have the high insulation values necessary in arid climates. Their curved form was devised in response to seismic conditions, ingeniously using sand or earth as raw materials, since their flexibility allows the construction of single- and double-curvature compression shells that can withstand lateral seismic forces. The prototype is a symbiosis of tradition and technology. It employs vernacular forms, integrating load-bearing and tensile structures, but provides a remarkable degree of strength and durability for this type of construction, that is traditionally weak and fragile, through a composite system of sandbags and barbed wire." Khalili basically found that stacking sandbags in circular plans to form domed structures, with barbed wire laid between each row to prevent the bags from shifting, was a way of providing readily available and stable housing. Nor is this concept merely theoretical since prototype sandbag shelters have been built in Iran, Mexico, India, Thailand, Siberia, and Chile. The prototypes received California building permits and have also met the requirements of the United Nations High Commission for Refugees (UNHCR) for emergency housing. Both the UNHCR and the United Nations Development Program (UNDP) used the system in 1995 to provide temporary shelters for a flood of refugees coming into Iran from Iraq.

Die Prototypen von Schutzbauten aus Sandsäcken wurden 2004 mit dem Aga-Khan-Preis für Architektur ausgezeichnet. Die Jury beschreibt sie folgendermaßen: „Diese Schutzbauten sind Prototypen von temporären Häusern, die mit extrem preiswerten Mitteln errichtet werden können. Sie stellen sichere Unterkünfte bereit, können schnell gebaut werden und haben einen hohen Wärmedämmwert, der im Wüstenklima notwendig ist. Ihre gekrümmte Form wurde als Antwort auf seismische Bedingungen entwickelt. Auf geniale Weise wird Sand oder Erde als Rohmaterial verwendet, da die Flexibilität dieser Materialien die Konstruktion von einfach und zweifach gekrümmten, auf Druck belasteten Hüllen erlaubt, die seismischen Horizontallasten standhalten können. Der Prototyp ist eine Symbiose von Tradition und Technologie. Er verwendet Formen, die auf dem Land gebräuchlich sind, integriert druck- und zugbelastete Strukturen, bietet aber einen bemerkenswerten Grad an Festigkeit und Haltbarkeit für eine Konstruktion dieser Art, die sonst eher schwach und instabil ist. Dies wird durch eine Kompositsystem aus Sandsäcken und Stacheldraht erreicht." Sandsäcke werden kreisförmig ausgelegt und dann so aufgeschichtet, dass sie eine Kuppel formen. Um ein Verrutschen der Säcke zu verhindern, wird zwischen jede Reihe Stacheldraht gelegt. Auf diese Weise, so fand Khalili heraus, können schnell herzustellende und stabile Unterkünfte gebaut werden. Das Konzept ist nicht theoretischer Natur: Solche Schutzbauten wurden schon im Iran, in Mexiko, Indien, Thailand, Sibirien und Chile errichtet. Die kalifornische Baubehörde genehmigte die Prototypen; sie entsprechen auch den Standards des Hochkommissars für Flüchtlinge der Vereinten Nationen (UNHCR) für Notunterkünfte. Sowohl der UNHCR als auch das Entwicklungsprogramm der Vereinten Nationen (UNDP) benutzte das System 1995, um temporäre Unterkünfte für die Flüchtlinge aus dem Irak in den Iran zu bauen.

Les prototypes d'abris en sacs de sable conçus par Nader Khalili, lauréat du Prix d'architecture Aga Khan 2004, étaient présentés de la façon suivante par le jury : « Ces abris sont des prototypes de logements temporaires créés à l'aide de moyens extrêmement bon marché, afin d'offrir un foyer solide rapidement constructibles et présentant le haut degré d'isolation thermique indispensable dans les climats arides. Leurs formes courbes ont été conçues pour supporter des secousses sismiques, et utilisent ingénieusement comme matières premières le sable et la terre, dont la souplesse permet la construction de coques à simple ou double courbe en compression qui peuvent résister aux forces sismiques latérales. Ces prototypes sont une symbiose de tradition et de technologie. Ils font appel à des formes vernaculaires, intégrant des structures porteuses et en traction, tout en offrant un remarquable niveau de résistance et de durabilité pour ce type de construction, traditionnellement léger et fragile, grâce à un système composite de sacs de sable et de fil de fer barbelé. » À l'origine, Khalili a découvert que le fait d'empiler des sacs de sable en cercle pour former des structures en coupole et de les stabiliser par du fil de fer barbelé intercalé entre chaque strate était un moyen d'obtenir des logements stables et faciles à construire. Son concept n'est pas resté purement théorique, puisque des prototypes ont déjà été construits en Iran, au Mexique, en Inde, en Thaïlande, en Sibérie et au Chili. Ils ont reçu un permis de construire en Californie et sont conformes à la réglementation du Haut Commissariat des Nations Unies aux Réfugiés pour les logements d'urgence. Le HCR et le Programme de développement des Nations Unies (PDNU) ont utilisé ce système dès 1995 pour répondre aux afflux de réfugiés arrivant d'Irak en Iran.

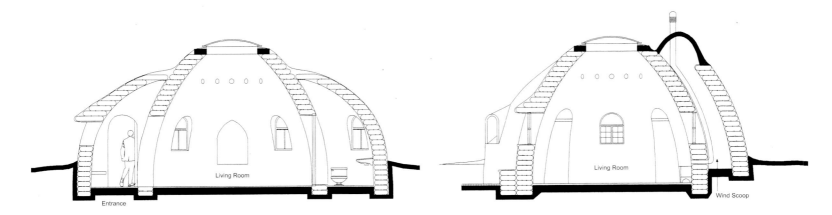

The sandbag shelters can be arranged in various configurations, with a simplicity of construction that can be mastered even by persons who have no knowledge of building.

Aus den Sandsäcken können verschiedene Haustypen gebaut werden. Alle Behausungen sind auch von Menschen, die über keine Baukenntnisse verfügen, einfach herzustellen.

Les abris en sacs de sable peuvent adopter différentes configurations, tout en gardant une simplicité de construction maîtrisable même par des gens qui n'ont aucune connaissance dans ce domaine.

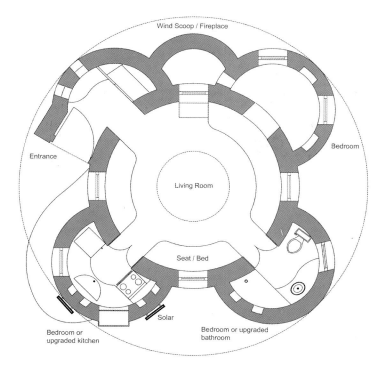

A plan to the right shows how the lobed and domed structures can be adapted to various degrees of sophistication, to include a kitchen or bathroom as well as the central living space. The plentiful raw materials used ensure that this type of shelter could be erected almost anywhere in the world.

Der Grundriss rechts zeigt, dass die kuppelförmigen Konstruktionen aus Sand und Stoff auch höheren Ansprüchen gerecht werden und eine Küche und/oder ein Badezimmer sowie den zentralen Wohnraum aufnehmen können. Aufgrund der reichlich vorhandenen Rohmaterialien kann diese Art der Unterkunft fast überall auf der Welt gebaut werden.

Le plan à droite montre comment ces petites constructions à coupole peuvent acquérir divers degrés de sophistication et comprendre une cuisine, une pièce d'eau ou un séjour central. Le choix de matériaux économiques et abondants fait que ce type d'abri peut être édifié presque n'importe où dans le monde.

Wind Scoop / Fireplace

Entrance

Bedroom

Living Room

Seat / Bed

Bedroom or upgraded kitchen

Solar

Bedroom or upgraded bathroom

KIERANTIMBERLAKE

KieranTimberlake Associates LLP
420 North 20th Street
Philadelphia, PA 19130.3828,

USA

Tel: +1 215 922 6600 / Fax: +1 215 922 4680
E-mail: kta@kierantimberlake.com / Web: www.kierantimberlake.com

Founded in Philadelphia in 1984 by Stephen Kieran and James Timberlake, **KIERANTIMBERLAKE** is comprised of a staff of about 50. Kieran graduated from Yale University and got his M.Arch from the University of Pennsylvania. James Timberlake graduated from the University of Detroit before receiving his M.Arch from the University of Pennsylvania. The firm's projects include programming, planning, and design of all types of new structures and their interiors; and the renovation, reuse, and conservation of existing structures. KieranTimberlake has received over 80 design awards, including the 2008 Architecture Firm Award from the American Institute of Architects. In 2003, the firm developed SmartWrapTM: The Building Envelope of the Future, a mass customizable, high-performance building façade that was initially exhibited at the Smithsonian Institution, Cooper-Hewitt National Design Museum. Structures completed in 2007 include the Sculpture Building Gallery, Yale University (New Haven, Connecticut) and the Suzanne Roberts Theater, Philadelphia Theater Company (Philadelphia, Pennsylvania). Buildings by KieranTimberlake completed in 2008 include the Lower School, Sidwell Friends School (Bethesda, Maryland); and the Multi-Faith Center and Houghton Memorial Chapel Restoration, Wellesley College (Wellesley, Massachusetts). Currently in design are the Northwest Campus Student Housing, University of California (Los Angeles, California); the Center City Building, University of North Carolina at Charlotte (Charlotte, North Carolina); and the Morse and Stiles Colleges, Yale University (New Haven, Connecticut), all in the USA.

KIERANTIMBERLAKE wurde 1984 von Stephen Kieran und James Timberlake in Philadelphia gegründet und hat rund 50 Mitarbeiter. Kieran schloss sein Studium in Yale ab und erhielt seinen M.Arch. an der University of Pennsylvania. James Timberlake machte seinen Abschluss an der University of Detroit und erhielt seinen M.Arch. an der University of Pennsylvania. Das Büro befasst sich mit Programmentwicklung, Planung und Gestaltung von Neubauten aller Art und deren Innenraumgestaltung sowie der Sanierung, Umnutzung und Erhaltung bestehender Bauten. KieranTimberlake erhielt über 80 Designpreise, darunter den Architecture Firm Award 2008 des American Institute of Architects. 2003 entwickelte das Büro SmartWrapTM, die Gebäudehülle der Zukunft, eine technisch ausgeklügelte Gebäudefassade, die sich individualisiert in Massenfertigung herstellen lässt und erstmals im Cooper-Hewitt National Design Museum der Smithsonian Institution präsentiert wurde. Zu den 2007 realisierten Bauten zählen die Sculpture Building Gallery an der Yale University (New Haven, Connecticut) sowie das Suzanne Roberts Theater für die Philadelphia Theater Company (Philadelphia, Pennsylvania). 2008 wurden folgende Bauten bezugsfertig: die Lower School an der Sidwell Friends School (Bethesda, Maryland) sowie das Multi-Faith Center und die Sanierung der Houghton Memorial Chapel am Wellesley College (Wellesley, Massachusetts). In Planung sind derzeit ein Studentenwohnheim für den Northwest-Campus der University of California (Los Angeles, Kalifornien), das Center City Building der University of North Carolina (Charlotte, North Carolina) sowie das Morse und das Stiles College, Yale University (New Haven, Connecticut), alle in den USA.

Fondée à Philadelphie en 1984 par Stephen Kieran et James Timberlake, l'agence **KIERANTIMBERLAKE** emploie 50 collaborateurs. Kieran est diplômé de Yale et a un master en architecture de l'université de Pennsylvanie. James Timberlake, diplômé de l'université de Detroit, a également obtenu son master en architecture à l'université de Pennsylvanie. L'agence propose des services de programmation, d'urbanisme et de conception pour tous types de constructions et leurs intérieurs, ainsi que de rénovation, de réutilisation et de préservation de bâtiments existants. KieranTimberlake a reçu plus de 80 distinctions, dont l'Architecture Firm Award 2008 de l'American Institute of Architects. En 2003, l'agence a mis au point le SmartWrapTM : The Building Envelope of the Future, façade adaptable à hautes performances qui a été exposée initialement au Cooper-Hewitt National Design Museum (Smithsonian Institution). Parmi leurs réalisations achevées en 2007 on compte la Sculpture Building Gallery, Yale University (New Haven, Connecticut), et le Suzanne Roberts Theater, pour la compagnie de théâtre de Philadelphie (Philadelphie, Pennsylvanie). En 2008, KieranTimberlake a réalisé les projets suivants : une école primaire, Sidwell Friends School (Bethesda, Maryland), et la restauration du centre œcuménique et de la Houghton Memorial Chapel de Wellesley College (Wellesley, Massachusetts). Actuellement, ils travaillent sur des logements pour étudiants du Northwest Campus, université de Californie (Los Angeles, Californie), sur le Center City Building, université de Caroline du Nord (Charlotte, Caroline du Nord), et sur les Morse and Stiles Colleges, Yale University (New Haven, Connecticut), tous aux États-Unis.

LOBLOLLY HOUSE

Taylors Island, Maryland, USA, 2007

Floor area: 167 m². Client: Barbara DeGrange. Cost: not disclosed
Team: Stephen Kieran (Design Partner), James Timberlake (Design Partner), David Riz (Associate in Charge)

Lifted up off the ground, with its irregular cladding, folding shades and exterior stairway, the Loblolly House is an original and ecologically responsible realization.

Über dem Boden aufgeständert, mit seiner unregelmäßigen Holzverblendung, den klappbaren Fensterläden und einer Außentreppe ist das Loblolly Haus einmalig und ökologisch ausgerichtet zugleich.

Surélevée, avec ses parements irréguliers, ses volets pliants et son escalier extérieur, la maison Loblolly est une réalisation originale et écologiquement responsable.

This house is named for the pines on its Chesapeake Bay site. The architects have sought to form the house in its context of trees, tall grasses, and the sea. Set up on timber piles "it is a house among and within the trees." It was built with off-site fabricated elements in a period of six weeks using an innovative assembly system. The bathroom and mechanical systems were assembled as modules off-site as well and lifted into place. The methods used allow the house to be disassembled using little more than a wrench, in a particularly effective expression of environmental responsibility. The house won a 2008 AIA Honor Award—the citation read: "The Loblolly House, by the 2008 AIA Architecture Firm Award winner KieranTimberlake, draws inspiration and formal cues from the surrounding coastal flora and landscape: loblolly pines and saltmeadow cordgrass. The 167-m^2 house was modularly constructed with simple tools in only six weeks and is intended to sit lightly on the land." The staggered vertical wood siding of the house gives it an unusual appearance that is far from what one might expect of a residence conceived for easy assembly.

Das Haus, benannt nach den Loblolly-Kiefern auf dem an der Chesapeake Bay gelegenen Grundstück, soll den Architekten zufolge im Kontext der Bäume, Gräser und des Meeres Gestalt annehmen. Auf Kiefernpfählen aufgeständert ist es „ein Haus zwischen und in den Bäumen". Die Montage aus vorgefertigten Bauelementen mithilfe eines innovativen Systems erfolgte in nur sechs Wochen. Die Versorgungsleitungen des Hauses ebenso wie das Bad wurden als Module vorinstalliert und mit einem Kran an Ort und Stelle gehoben. Diese Technik erlaubt zudem, das Haus bei Bedarf mit kaum mehr als einem Schraubenschlüssel zu demontieren, ein besonders überzeugender Beweis für umweltbewusstes Bauen. 2008 wurde das Haus mit einem Sonderpreis der AIA ausgezeichnet, die Begründung lautete: „Das Loblolly House vom Büro KieranTimberlake, das 2008 mit dem AIA Architecture Firm Award geehrt wurde, lässt sich von der Küstenflora und -landschaft seines Umfelds inspirieren und formal anregen: von den Loblolly-Kiefern ebenso wie den Schlickgräsern. Das 167 m^2 große Haus wurde mit einfachen Werkzeugen in nur sechs Wochen aus Modulen montiert und soll leicht auf dem Baugrund stehen." Die vertikal gestaffelte Verschalung aus Holzpaneelen verleiht dem Haus eine ganz eigene Optik, die sich erheblich von dem unterscheidet, was man von einem Leichtmontagebau erwarten würde.

Cette maison tire son nom des pins qui occupent ce terrain en bordure de la baie de Chesapeake. Les architectes ont cherché à lui donner une forme répondant à ce contexte d'arbres, d'herbes hautes et d'océan. Surélevée sur des piles de bois, « c'est une maison parmi et dans les arbres ». Elle a été construite à partir d'éléments préfabriqués en six semaines grâce à un tout nouveau système d'assemblage. La salle de bains et les installations techniques ont été préalablement assemblées en modules et mis en place. Ces méthodes permettent de démonter la maison avec une simple clé à pipes, illustration particulièrement efficace de la responsabilité environnementale. La maison a remporté un AIA Honor Award en 2008 avec le commentaire suivant : « La maison Loblolly de l'agence KieranTimberlake tire son inspiration et ses exemples formels de la flore et du paysage côtier environnant : les pins loblolly et les spartina des prés salés. D'une surface de 167 m^2, elle a été construite selon un principe de modularité et de montage original en six semaines seulement, à l'aide d'outils simples, et n'exerce qu'un impact léger au sol. » Les décalages dans le parement de bois donne à la maison un aspect curieux, différent de ce que l'on pouvait attendre d'une résidence d'assemblage aussi facile.

The irregularity of the cladding of the house makes it blend into the trees that surround it, while allowing those within to fully profit from the view.

Die unregelmäßige Holzverblendung lässt das Haus mit den Bäumen verschmelzen; von innen erlaubt sie, die Aussicht maximal zu genießen.

La composition irrégulière de l'habillage des façades les intègre aux arbres qui l'entourent, tout en laissant ses occupants bénéficier pleinement de la vue.

The house's interior is warm, yet open to views of the water, not at all in the minimalist atmosphere that other architects might have proposed. Right, the window shades fold up to become canopies.

Das Interieur des Hauses ist warm und so offen, dass Ausblick aufs Wasser möglich ist, und doch keineswegs minimalistisch geprägt, wie es andere Architekten vielleicht vorgeschlagen hätten. Rechts, die aufgeklappten Fensterläden.

L'intérieur de la maison, chaleureux tout en restant très ouvert sur l'océan, est très différent de l'atmosphère minimaliste que d'autres architectes auraient pu proposer. À droite, les stores transformés en auvents.

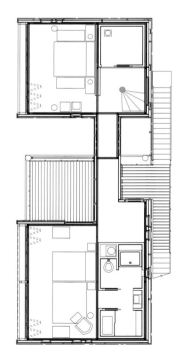

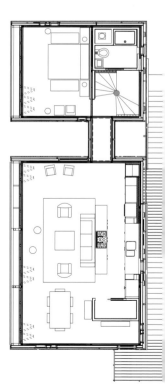

MATHIAS KLOTZ

Mathias Klotz
Los Colonos 0411
Providencia, Santiago
Chile

Tel:+56 2 233 6613
Fax: +56 2 232 2479
E-mail: estudio@mathiasklotz.com
Web: www.mathiasklotz.com

MATHIAS KLOTZ was born in 1965 in Viña del Mar, Chile. He received his architecture degree from the Pontificia Universidad Católica de Chile in 1991. He created his own office in Santiago the same year. He has taught at several Chilean universities and was director of the School of Architecture of the Universidad Diego Portales in Santiago (2001–03). His work has been exhibited at the GA Gallery in Tokyo (Japan); at MoMA in New York, where he was a finalist for the 1998 Mies van der Rohe Prize; and at Archilab (Orléans, France, 2000). He participated in the Chinese International Practical Exhibition of Architecture in Nanjing in 2004, together with such architects as David Adjaye, Odile Decq, Arata Isozaki, and Kazuyo Sejima. Recent work includes the Casa Viejo (Santiago, 2001); the Smol Building (Concepción, 2001); the Faculty of Health, Universidad Diego Portales (Santiago, 2004); the remodeling of the Cerro San Luis House (Santiago, 2004); the Ocho al Cubo House (Marbella, Zapallar, 2005); La Roca House (Punta del Este, Uruguay, 2006); the Techos House (Nahuel Huapi Lake, Patagonia, Argentina, 2006–07, published here); the 11 Mujeres House (Cachagua, 2007, also published here); 20 one-family houses in La Dehesa (Santiago); and the Buildings Department San Isidro (Buenos Aires, Argentina), all in Chile unless stated otherwise.

MATHIAS KLOTZ wurde 1965 in Viña del Mar, Chile, geboren und machte 1991 sein Architekturdiplom an der Pontificia Universidad Católica de Chile. Im gleichen Jahr gründete er in Santiago sein eigenes Büro. Er hat an mehreren chilenischen Universitäten gelehrt und war Direktor der Architekturabteilung an der Universidad Diego Portales in Santiago (2001–03). Seine Arbeiten wurden in der GA Gallery in Tokio, im MoMA in New York, wo er 1998 Finalist für den Mies-van-der-Rohe-Preis war, sowie bei Archilab (Orléans, Frankreich, 2000) ausgestellt. Er war Teilnehmer an der Chinese International Practical Exhibition of Architecture in Nanking 2004, neben so renommierten Architekten wie David Adjaye, Odile Decq, Arata Isozaki und Kazuyo Sejima. Zu seinen neueren Projekten zählen die Casa Viejo (Santiago, 2001), das Edificio Smol (Concepción, 2001), die medizinische Fakultät der Universidad Diego Portales (Santiago, 2004), der Umbau des Hauses Cerro San Luis (Santiago, 2004), das Haus Ocho al Cubo (Marbella, Zapallar, 2005), das Haus La Roca (Punta del Este, Uruguay, 2006), das Haus Techos (Lago Nahuel Huapi, Patagonien, Argentinien, 2006–07, hier veröffentlicht), das Haus 11 Mujeres (Cachagua, 2007, ebenfalls hier veröffentlicht), 20 Einfamilienhäuser in La Dehesa (Santiago) und das Bauamt San Isidro (Buenos Aires, Argentinien), alle in Chile, sofern nicht anders angegeben.

MATHIAS KLOTZ, né en 1965 à Viña del Mar au Chili, a obtenu son diplôme d'architecte de l'université catholique du Chili (1991) et a fondé son agence à Santiago du Chili la même année. Il a enseigné dans plusieurs universités chiliennes et dirigé l'École d'architecture de l'Universidad Diego Portales à Santiago (2001–03). Son travail a été présenté à la GA Gallery à Tokyo (Japon), au MoMA à New York lorsqu'il fut finaliste du prix Mies van der Rohe 1998, et à Archilab (Orléans, France, 2000). Il a participé à l'Exposition internationale pratique chinoise d'architecture à Nankin en 2004 en compagnie d'autres architectes comme David Adjaye, Odile Decq, Arata Isozaki et Kazuyo Sejima. Parmi ses réalisations récentes, toutes au Chili, sauf mention contraire, on peut citer la Casa Viejo (Santiago du Chili, 2001) ; l'immeuble Smol (Concepción, 2001) ; la faculté de santé de l'université Diego Portales (Santiago, 2004) ; le remodelage de la maison Cerro San Luis (Santiago, 2004) ; la maison Ocho al Cubo (Marbella, Zapallar, 2005) ; la maison La Roca (Punta del Este, Uruguay, 2006) ; la maison Techos (lac Nahuel Huapi, Patagonie, Argentine, 2006–07, présentée ici) ; la maison des 11 Femmes (Cachagua, 2007, également présentée ici) ; 20 maisons unifamiliales à La Dehesa (Santiago) et les bâtiments de la Direction de l'équipement San Isidro (Buenos Aires, Argentine).

TECHOS HOUSE

Nahuel Huapi Lake, Patagonia, Argentina, 2006–07

Site area: 2200 m². Floor area: 600 m². Client: not disclosed
Cost: $1.5 million. Collaborator: Alejandro Beals

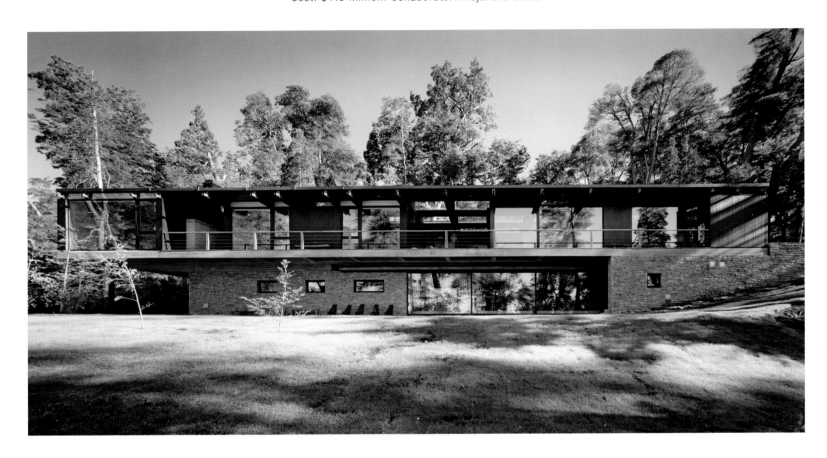

This is a vacation house built on the north shore of Nahuel Huapi Lake in the northern part of Patagonia. The main views from the house are quite naturally turned toward the water. Public and family spaces are located on the larger access level, while guest and service areas are on the lower floor together with a swimming pool that opens out onto the garden. Building regulations in the area require the use of a slightly pitched roof, and it was decided with the client to insert windows in the north facing side of the copper roof. Terraces and patios increase the usable areas of the residence and, as the architect writes, "along with the roof windows, they generate different kinds of relations with the natural surroundings and between the different programmatic elements of the house."

Das Ferienhaus liegt am nördlichen Ufer des Nahuel-Huapi-Sees im Norden Patagoniens. Die Blickrichtung des Hauses geht naturgemäß in Richtung Wasser. Gemeinschafts- und Familienbereiche liegen auf der größer angelegten Zugangsebene des Hauses, während sich Gäste- und Versorgungsbereiche sowie der Pool, der sich zum Garten hin öffnet, auf der unteren Ebene befinden. Die örtlichen Bauvorschriften erforderten ein leicht geneigtes Dach, und so entschied man gemeinsam mit dem Auftraggeber, mehrere Sheddachfenster in das Kupferdach zu integrieren. Terrassen und Veranden erweitern die Nutzfläche des Hauses und, wie der Architekt formuliert, „schaffen ebenso wie die Dachfenster verschiedene Bezüge zur landschaftlichen Umgebung und zwischen den verschiedenen Elementen des Hausprogramms".

Il s'agit d'une maison de vacances construite sur la rive nord du Lac Nahuel Huapi, dans le nord de la Patagonie. Les vues principales de la maison sont naturellement dirigées vers le plan d'eau. Les espaces familiaux et de réception sont situés au niveau de l'entrée, le plus vaste, tandis que les chambres d'amis et pièces de service se trouvent au niveau inférieur, donnant sur la piscine et le jardin. La réglementation régionale de la construction exige des toits légèrement inclinés et il a été décidé avec le client d'ouvrir des fenêtres sur la face nord de la toiture en cuivre. Les terrasses et les patios démultiplient les zones à vivre et, comme l'écrit l'architecte, « avec les fenêtres en toiture, elles génèrent différents types de relations avec l'environnement naturel et entre les divers composants programmatiques de la maison ».

The Techos House appears as two superimposed bands with ample glazing and contrasting materials facing the garden.

Die Casa Techos wirkt wie zwei großzügig verglaste, übereinander liegende Bänder aus kontrastierenden Materialien, die sich zum Garten hin orientieren.

La maison Techos se présente sous forme de deux éléments horizontaux superposés, amplement vitrés, et habillés de matériaux contrastés côté jardin.

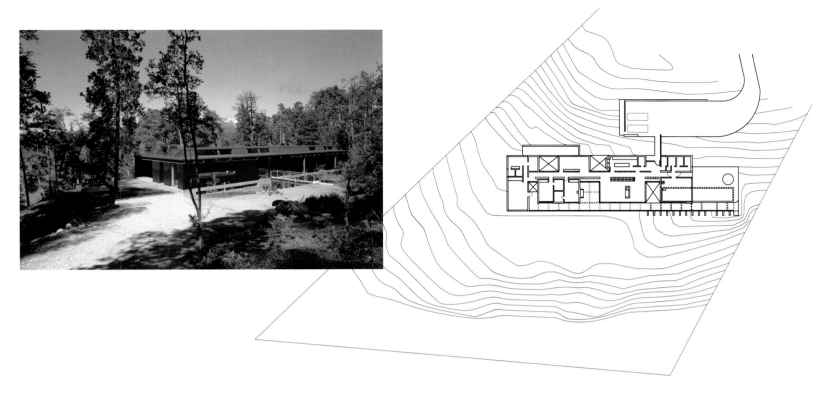

A topographic map of the site shows the way the largely rectangular volume sits on the curving slope.

Eine topografische Karte des Grundstücks veranschaulicht die Hanglage des weitgehend rechteckigen Baukörpers.

Le plan topographique du terrain montre comment la maison de forme essentiellement rectangulaire prend sa place dans la pente.

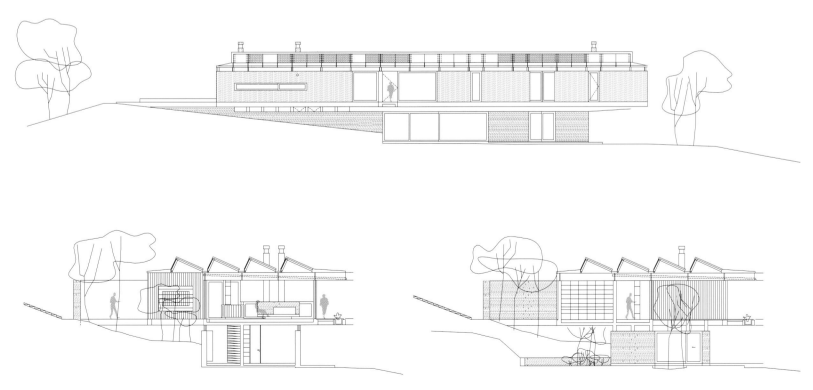

Served by an entrance bridge on the higher side of the slope, the house opens below to the garden, where the hill is lower.

Am oberen Ende des Hangs führt eine Brücke zum Eingang des Hauses, nach unten hin öffnet sich der Bau zum Garten, wo der Abhang abfällt.

Desservie par une passerelle partant du sommet de la pente, la maison s'ouvre en partie inférieure sur le jardin.

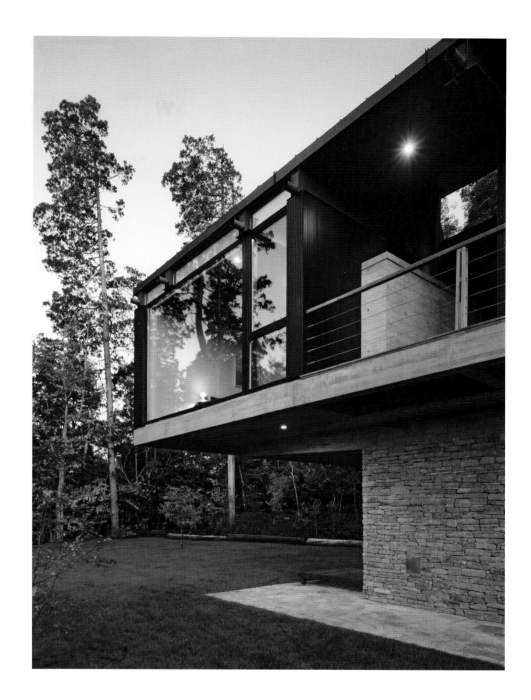

With its sliding glass doors and partitions, the house readily opens out into its natural setting, a design facilitated of course by the local climate.

Mit Glasschiebetüren und -trennwänden öffnet sich das Haus großzügig zur Umgebung, ein Konzept, das natürlich durch das örtliche Klima begünstigt wird.

Grâce à ses portes et cloisons coulissantes, la maison s'ouvre aisément sur son cadre naturel, un concept bien adapté au climat local.

An indoor pool can be opened with sliding glass doors that lead outside.

Das Schwimmbad lässt sich durch Schiebetüren nach außen öffnen.

La piscine intérieure peut s'ouvrir sur le jardin par ses portes coulissantes.

From the bedroom to the living spaces, the house has floor-to-ceiling glazing that permits a veritable inter-penetration of the natural setting with the carefully designed and essentially rectilinear architecture.

Vom Schlafzimmer bis zu den Wohn-räumen ist das gesamte Haus mit raumhohen Fenstern ausgestattet, sodass die Landschaft den einfühl-sam gestalteten und geradlinigen Bau geradezu durchdringen kann.

De la chambre au séjour, la façade est vitrée sur toute la hauteur, ce qui permet à l'architecture soigneuse-ment dessinée et rectiligne pour l'es-sentiel de s'imprégner véritablement du cadre naturel.

11 MUJERES HOUSE

Cachagua, Chile, 2007

Floor area: 700 m². Client: Radovan Kegevic
Cost: $2 million. Collaborator: Baltazar Sanchez

Jutting out from a steep slope above the ocean, the house, like other work by Mathias Klotz, is based on an architecture of right angles composed of rectangles.

Das Haus ragt über einen steilen Abhang am Meer hinaus und ist im Grunde, wie andere Projekte von Mathias Klotz, Architektur, die auf orthogonal angeordneten Rechtecken basiert.

Se projetant d'une pente escarpée au-dessus de l'océan, la maison, comme d'autres réalisations de Mathias Klotz, reprend un principe d'architecture orthogonale composée d'éléments rectangulaires.

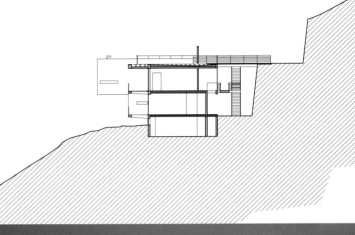

This "house of eleven women" is a vacation residence set on a steeply sloping site that leads down to the Cachagua beach and the Pacific Ocean. It is 140 kilometers north of Santiago, the capital of Chile. The clients have eleven daughters, whence the name of the residence, and the brief called for space for all of them, as well as a master bedroom and spaces for entertaining and guests. The base of the house includes game and TV rooms. The intermediate level contains the bedrooms for the eleven daughters. Since they ranged in age from four to twenty at the time the house was completed, there are two living rooms for the daughters, according to their ages. The upper level of the house has the master bedroom, living, family and dining areas, as well as service spaces. Built essentially of concrete with travertine marble floors, the house adapts to the contours of the site to offer the best possible views from each room. Large terraces encourage outdoor life, while hinged shutters protect the interiors from the sun on the west.

Das „Haus der elf Frauen" ist ein Ferienhaus und liegt auf einem steil abfallenden Grundstück, das zum Cachagua-Strand am Pazifik hinunterführt, 140 km nördlich der chilenischen Hauptstadt Santiago. Die Auftraggeber haben elf Töchter, die dem Haus seinen Namen gaben. Der Auftrag sah Raum für sie alle vor, ebenso Platz für ein Hauptschlafzimmer und Räume für Feste und Gäste. Im untersten Geschoss befinden sich u. a. ein Spiele- und ein Fernsehzimmer. Auf der mittlere Ebene liegen die Schlafzimmer der elf Töchter. Da sie zur Zeit der Fertigstellung des Baus zwischen vier und zwanzig Jahre alt waren, gibt es ihrem Alter entsprechend auch zwei Wohnzimmer für die Töchter. In der obersten Etage liegen das Hauptschlafzimmer, Wohn-, Familien- und Essbereiche sowie die Versorgungsräume. Das überwiegend aus Beton gebaute Haus mit Böden aus Travertin folgt den Konturen des Baugrunds, um optimale Aussicht für alle Räume zu erhalten. Große Terrassen laden ein, Zeit im Freien zu verbringen, während Fensterläden auf der Westseite das Innere des Hauses vor Sonne schützen.

Cette « maison des onze femmes » est une résidence de vacances implantée sur un terrain escarpé qui descend vers la plage de Cachagua et l'océan Pacifique, à 140 kilomètres au nord de la capitale Santiago du Chili. Les clients ont onze filles, d'où le nom de la maison. Le programme prévoyait une chambre pour chacune d'entre elles, une chambre principale, des pièces de réception et des chambres d'amis. La base de la maison comprend des salles de télévision et de jeux. Le niveau intermédiaire contient les chambres des onze jeunes filles. Comme leur âge allait de 4 à 20 ans au moment de l'achèvement du chantier, deux salles de séjour ont été prévues à ce niveau, en fonction de l'âge des enfants. Le niveau supérieur regroupe la chambre principale, les zones de séjour et de repas ainsi que celles réservées à la vie familiale et au service. Essentiellement construite avec des sols en marbre de travertin, la maison s'adapte au profil du terrain pour offrir de chaque pièce la meilleure vue possible. De vastes terrasses incitent à vivre à l'extérieur et des volets articulés protègent l'intérieur du soleil côté ouest.

Given the nature of the site, the house must be entered through a set of steps and a bridge that approach it from roof level. Right, a topographic site plan showing the slope down to the water.

Bedingt durch die Lage des Grundstücks wird das Haus über Treppen und eine Brücke erschlossen, die auf das Dach des Baus führen. Ein topografischer Lageplan, rechts, illustriert die Neigung des Geländes zum Wasser hin.

Étant donné la nature du site, la maison n'est accessible que par un escalier et une passerelle au niveau du toit. À droite, plan topographique montrant la pente par rapport à l'océan.

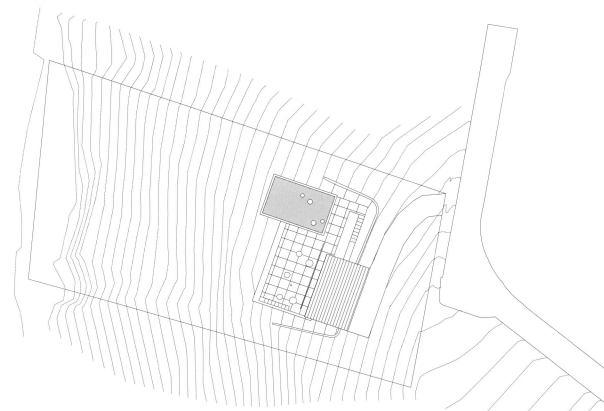

Views from the roof or the inside of the house are spectacular, but the architect also provides the owners with more intimate, enclosed spaces.

Der Ausblick vom Dach oder aus dem Haus ist spektakulär, dennoch bietet der Architekt den Besitzern auch intimere, umbaute Räume an.

Les vues depuis le toit ou l'intérieur de la maison sont spectaculaires, mais l'architecte a également prévu des espaces plus clos et intimes.

The horizontal bands that shape the house are relieved by a cantilevered volume. The house is complemented by a pool located on the slope above the beach.

Die horizontalen Bänder, aus denen das Haus aufgebaut ist, werden vom auskragenden Volumen aufgelockert. Ergänzt wird das Haus um einen Pool auf dem Abhang über dem Strand.

Les éléments horizontaux qui donnent à la maison sa forme sont mis en valeur par le volume en porte-à-faux. La maison est complétée par une piscine nichée dans la pente au-dessus de la plage.

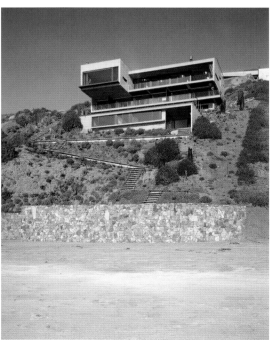

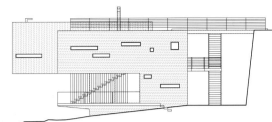

Floor-to-ceiling sliding glass windows
provide uninterrupted views of the
ocean, while interior spaces like the
kitchen or bathroom are shielded
from the bright open vistas present
elsewhere in the house.

Raumhohe Glasschiebetüren bieten
ungestörte Aussicht auf das Meer.
Die im Innern gelegenen Räume hin-
gegen, etwa Küche und Bad, wurden
von den hellen offenen Sichtachsen
im übrigen Haus abgeschirmt.

Les nombreuses baies coulissantes
toute hauteur offrent des vues inin-
terrompues sur l'océan, sauf dans
certains espaces intérieurs comme la
cuisine ou la salle de bains.

Bahia House

MARCIO KOGAN

Marcio Kogan
Studio MK27
Alameda Tietê 505 – Cerqueira César
01417-020 São Paulo, SP
Brazil

Tel: +55 11 3081 3522
Fax: +55 11 3063 3424
E-mail: info@marciokogan.com.br
Web: www.marciokogan.com.br

Born in 1952, **MARCIO KOGAN** graduated in 1976 from the School of Architecture at Mackenzie University in São Paulo. He received an IAB (Brazilian Architects Institute) Award for UMA Stores (1999 and 2002); Coser Studio (2002); Gama Issa House (2002); and Quinta House (2004). He also received the Record House Award for Du Plessis House (2004) and BR House (2005). In 2002 he completed a Museum of Microbiology in São Paulo and in 2003 he made a submission for the World Trade Center Site Memorial. He worked with Isay Weinfeld on the Fasano Hotel in São Paulo. He also participated with Weinfeld in the 25th São Paulo Biennale (2002) with the project for a hypothetical city named Happyland. Kogan is known for his use of boxlike forms, together with wooden shutters, trellises, and exposed stone. Amongst Kogan's recent residential projects are the Cury House (São Paulo, 2004–06); the Primetime Nursery (São Paulo, 2005–07); the E-Home, a "super-technological" house (Santander, Spain, 2007); an "extreme house" on an island in Paraty (Rio de Janeiro, 2007); Warbler House (Los Angeles, California, USA, 2008); a villa in Milan (Italy, 2008); House 53 (São Paulo, 2008); and two other houses in Brasilia, all in Brazil unless stated otherwise. His office is also working on a "green building" in New Jersey (USA, 2008–) and has recently completed Bahia House (Salvador, Bahia, 2010, published here).

Der 1952 geborene **MARCIO KOGAN** beendete 1976 sein Architekturstudium an der Universidade Presbiteriana Mackenzie in São Paulo. Er erhielt einen Preis des brasilianischen Architekturinstituts IAB für seinen Entwurf für die UMA Stores (1999 und 2002), das Coser Studio (2002), die Häuser Gama Issa (2002) und Quinta (2004). Für die Häuser Du Plessis (2004) und BR (2005) wurde ihm der Record House Award verliehen. 2002 stellte er ein Museum für Mikrobiologie in São Paulo fertig, und 2003 reichte er einen Vorschlag für das World Trade Center Site Memorial ein. Mit Isay Weinfeld plante er das Fasano Hotel in São Paulo. Ebenfalls mit Weinfeld nahm er an der 25. Biennale von São Paulo (2002) teil mit einem Projekt für eine hypothetische Stadt namens Happyland. Kogan ist durch seine Kistenformen mit Holzläden, Gittern und Naturstein bekannt geworden. Zu seinen neueren Projekten zählen das Haus Cury (São Paulo, 2004–06), eine Kindertagesstätte (São Paulo, 2005–07), das E-Home, ein „supertechnologisches" Wohnhaus (Santander, Spanien, 2007), ein „extremes Haus" auf einer Insel in Paraty (Rio de Janeiro, 2007), das Haus Warbler (Los Angeles, 2008), eine Villa in Mailand (Italien, 2008), Haus 53 (São Paulo, 2008) sowie zwei weitere Wohnhäuser in Brasília, alle in Brasilien, sofern nicht anders angegeben. Sein Büro arbeitet zurzeit auch an einem umweltfreundlichen Gebäude in New Jersey (USA, 2008–) und hat kürzlich das Haus Bahia (Salvador, Bahia, 2010, hier veröffentlicht) fertiggestellt.

Né en 1952, **MARCIO KOGAN**, diplômé en 1976 de l'École d'architecture de l'université Mackenzie à São Paulo, a reçu en 1983 plusieurs prix de l'IAB (Instituto de Arquitetos do Brazil) pour les magasins UMA (1999 et 2002), le Coser Studio (2002), la maison Gama Issa (2002) et la maison Quinta (2004), tous à São Paulo. Il a également reçu le prix Record House pour la maison Duplessis (2004) et la maison BR (2005). En 2002, il a réalisé le Musée de microbiologie de São Paulo et a participé au concours pour le mémorial du World Trade Center. Il a collaboré avec Isay Weinfeld sur le projet du Fasano Hotel (2001–03) et à l'occasion de la 25e Biennale de São Paulo (2002) pour laquelle ils ont proposé une cité utopique surnommée Happyland. Kogan est connu pour son recours aux formes en boîtes, aux volets en bois, aux treillis et aux pierres apparentes. Parmi ses projets résidentiels récents figurent la maison Cury (São Paulo, 2004–06) ; la crèche Primetime (São Paulo, 2005–07) ; la E-Home, une maison « super-technologique » (Santander, Espagne, 2007) ; une « maison extrême » sur une île face à Paraty (Rio de Janeiro, 2007) ; la maison Warbler (Los Angeles, Californie, 2008) ; une villa à Milan (2008) ; la maison 53 (São Paulo, 2008) et deux autres maisons à Brasília. Son agence travaille actuellement sur le projet d'un « immeuble vert » dans le New Jersey (États-Unis, 2008–) et a récemment achevé la maison Bahia (Salvador, Bahia, 2010, présentée ici).

BAHIA HOUSE
Salvador, Bahia, Brazil, 2010

Client: not disclosed. Cost: not disclosed
Collaboration: Suzana Glogowski and Samanta Cafardo (Coauthors) and
Diana Radomysler (Interior Design Coauthor)

The architect explains that the design of this house comes close to traditional architecture in both plan and materials. "The Bahia House makes use of the old popular knowledge that has been reinvented and incorporated throughout the history of Brazilian architecture. The house was considered for where it is, for the climate of where it is, for Bahia. And for this no 'green' software was used, no equipment and no calculations were made." Local houses with clay roofs and wood ceilings, or wooden mashrabiyyas—a type of Arab screen brought along with Portuguese colonial architecture—serve as an inspiration even as the architect achieves an obviously high degree of modernity. Natural airflow is encouraged through the creation of a central patio, another element frequently present in old, local houses.

Der Architekt gibt an, dass die Gestaltung dieses Hauses sowohl im Grundriss als auch in den Materialien traditioneller Architektur nahekomme. „Das Haus Bahia zieht Nutzen aus dem von alters her verbreiteten Wissen, das in der Geschichte der brasilianischen Architektur weiterentwickelt und angewendet worden ist. Das Haus wurde für seinen Standort und das dort herrschende Klima, eben für Bahia, geplant. Und dafür wurde keine ‚grüne‘ Software verwendet, wurde keine besondere Ausrüstung benötigt und wurden keine Berechnungen angestellt." Örtliche Häuser mit Lehmdächern und Holzdecken oder hölzerne Mashrabiyyas – eine Art arabische Gitterwand, die mit der portugiesischen Kolonialarchitektur ins Land kam – dienten als Inspiration, auch wenn dem Architekten eindeutig ein hohes Maß an Modernität gelungen ist. Natürliche Durchlüftung wird durch die Anlage eines zentralen Innenhofs verstärkt, ein weiteres Element, das häufig in alten Häusern vor Ort anzutreffen ist.

Pour l'architecte, la conception de cette maison se rapproche de celle d'une architecture traditionnelle tant pour son plan que pour ses matériaux. « La Maison Bahia utilise des connaissances populaires anciennes qui ont été réinventées et intégrées tout au long de l'histoire de l'architecture brésilienne. Elle a été pensée pour le lieu où elle se trouve, pour le climat dans lequel elle baigne, pour Bahia. Nous n'avons pas utilisé de logiciel 'vert', ni d'équipements spéciaux, ni de longs calculs. » Les maisons locales à toits d'argile, plafonds de bois et *mashrabiyyas* de bois – un type d'écran arabe importé par l'architecture coloniale portugaise –, ont servi d'inspiration ce qui n'a pas empêché l'architecte d'atteindre avec cette maisonun degré élevé de modernité. La circulation naturelle de l'air est encouragée par la création d'un patio central, autre élément fréquent dans les maisons anciennes de la région.

The long, low form of the house is marked by the geometrically disposed screen running along the entire façade.

Kennzeichen der gestreckten, niedrigen Form des Hauses ist die geometrisch aufgeteilte Gitterwand, die an der ganzen Fassade entlangläuft.

La forme longue et surbaissée de la maison est soulignée par l'écran de trame géométrique qui court tout le long de la façade.

The plan of the house is square with an inner courtyard. The climate of Bahia allows for the house to be opened almost entirely to the exterior, especially given the emphasis on natural air flow.

Der Grundriss des Hauses ist quadratisch und umfasst einen Innenhof. Das Klima von Bahia gestattet es, das Haus fast völlig nach außen zu öffnen, wodurch ein natürlicher Luftaustausch gewährleistet wird.

Le plan de la maison est un simple carré qui contient une cour intérieure. Le climat de la région de Bahia permet de laisser la maison presque entièrement ouverte sur l'extérieur et donc de bénéficier d'une ventilation naturelle.

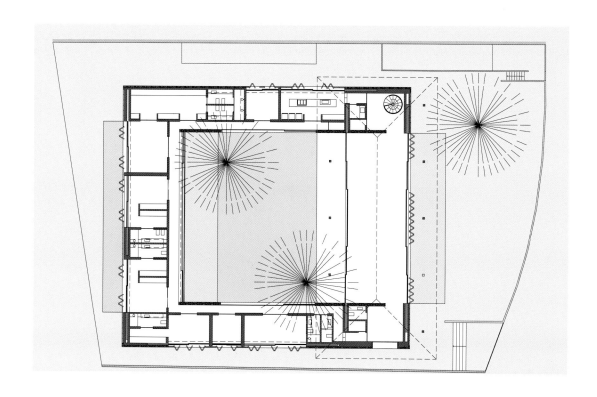

The walls of the house disappear to allow the interior spaces to be entirely open to the garden. Below, the architect contrasts a rough stone wall with a wooden ceiling and a polished floor.

Die Wände des Hauses verschwinden und öffnen die Innenräume vollständig zum Garten. Unten: Der Architekt setzte ein grobe Steinmauer in Kontrast zur hölzernen Decke und zum polierten Fußboden.

Les murs disparaissent pour permettrent aux volumes intérieurs de s'ouvrir entièrement sur le jardin. Ci-dessous: l'architecte fait contraster un mur de pierre brut avec un plafond de bois et un plancher vernis.

Rough stone surfaces are deliberately contrasted with the smooth floor or the screen wall seen above, right.

Raue Steinflächen bilden einen bewussten Gegensatz zum glatten Boden oder zu der Trennwand oben rechts.

Les plans de pierre d'appareillage rustique contrastent délibérément avec les sols en bois poli ou le mur-écran (ci-dessus, à droite).

KENGO KUMA

Kengo Kuma & Associates
2–24–8 BY-CUBE 2–4F Minamiaoyama
Minato-ku / Tokyo 107–0062 / Japan

Tel: +81 3 3401 7721 / Fax: +81 3 3401 7778
E-mail: kuma@ba2.so-net.ne.jp / Web: www.kkaa.co.jp

Born in 1954 in Kanagawa, Japan, **KENGO KUMA** graduated in 1979 from the University of Tokyo with an M.Arch. In 1985–86, he received an Asian Cultural Council Fellowship Grant and was a Visiting Scholar at Columbia University. In 1987, he established the Spatial Design Studio, and in 1991, he created Kengo Kuma & Associates. His work includes the Gunma Toyota Car Show Room (Maebashi, 1989); Maiton Resort Complex (Phuket, Thailand); Rustic, Office Building (Tokyo); Doric, Office Building (Tokyo); M2, Headquarters of Mazda New Design Team (Tokyo), all in 1991; Kinjo Golf Club, Club House (Okayama, 1992); Kiro-san Observatory (Ehime, 1994); Atami Guesthouse, Guesthouse for Bandai Corp (Atami, 1992–95); Karuizawa Resort Hotel (Karuizawa, 1993); Tomioka Lakewood Golf Club House (Tomioka, 1993–96); Toyoma Noh-Theater (Miyagi, 1995–96); and the Japanese Pavilion for the Venice Biennale (Venice, Italy, 1995). He has also completed the Stone Museum (Nasu, Tochigi, 2000); a Museum of Ando Hiroshige (Batou, Nasu-gun, Tochigi, 2000); the Great (Bamboo) Wall Guesthouse (Beijing, China, 2002); One Omotesando (Tokyo, 2003); LVMH Osaka (2004); the Nagasaki Prefecture Art Museum (2005); the Fukusaki Hanging Garden (2005); and the Zhongtai Box, Z58 building (Shanghai, China, 2003–06). Recent work includes the Tobata C Block Project (Kitakyushu, Fukuoka, 2005–07); Steel House (Bunkyo-ku, Tokyo, 2005–07, published here); Sakenohana (London, 2007); Tiffany Ginza (Tokyo, 2008); the Nezu Museum (Tokyo, 2007–09); and the Museum of Kanayama (Ota City, Gunma, 2009), all in Japan unless stated otherwise.

KENGO KUMA wurde 1954 in Kanagawa, Japan, geboren und schloss sein Studium an der Universität Tokio 1979 mit einem M.Arch. ab. 1985–86 erhielt er ein Stipendium des Asian Cultural Council und war Gastdozent an der Columbia University. 1987 gründete er das Büro Spatial Design Studio, 1991 folgte die Gründung von Kengo Kuma & Associates. Sein Werk umfasst den Showroom für Toyota in der Präfektur Gunma (Maebashi, 1989), die Hotelanlage Maiton (Phuket, Thailand), ein Bürogebäude für Rustic (Tokio), ein Bürogebäude für Doric (Tokio), M2, die Zentrale für das neue Mazda-Designteam (Tokio), alle 1991, ein Clubhaus für den Kinjo Golf Club (Okayama, 1992), das Planetarium Kiro-san (Ehime, 1994), das Gästehaus für Bandai (Atami, 1992–95), das Hotel Karuizawa (Karuizawa, 1993), das Tomioka Lakewood Golfclubhaus (Tomioka, 1993–96), das No-Theater in Toyoma (Miyagi, 1995–96) sowie den japanischen Pavillon für die Biennale in Venedig (1995). Darüber hinaus realisierte er das Steinmuseum (Nasu, Tochigi, 2000), ein Ando-Hiroshige-Museum (Batou, Nasu-gun, Tochigi, 2000), das Gästehaus Great (Bamboo) Wall (Peking, China 2002), One Omotesando (Tokio, 2003), LVMH Osaka (2004), das Kunstmuseum der Präfektur Nagasaki (2005), die hängenden Gärten von Fukusaki (2005) sowie die Zhongtai Box, Z58 (Shanghai, China, 2003–06). Jüngere Projekte sind u.a. der Tobata C Block (Kitakyushu, Fukuoka, 2005–07), das Steel House (Bunkyo-ku, Tokio, 2005–07, hier vorgestellt), Sakenohana (London, 2007), Tiffany Ginza (Tokio, 2008), das Nezu Museum (Tokio, 2007–09) und das Museum of Kanayama (Ota City, Gunma, 2009), alle in Japan, sofern nicht anders vermerkt.

Né en 1954 à Kanagawa au Japon, **KENGO KUMA** est diplômé en architecture de l'université de Tokyo (1979). En 1984–86, il bénéficie d'une bourse de l'Asian Cultural Council et devient chercheur invité à l'université de Columbia. En 1987, il crée le Spatial Design Studio et, en 1991, Kengo Kuma & Associates. Parmi ses réalisations, on peut citer le Show Room Toyota de Gunma (Maebashi, 1989) ; le Maiton Resort Complex (Phuket, Thaïlande, 1991) ; l'immeuble de bureaux Rustic (Tokyo, 1991) ; l'immeuble de bureaux Doric (Tokyo, 1991) ; M2, siège du département de design de Mazda (Tokyo, 1991) ; le Kinjo Golf Club Club House (Okayama, 1992) ; l'Observatoire Kiro-San (Ehime, Japon, 1994) ; l'Atami Guest House pour Bandaï Corp (Atami, 1992–95) ; l'hôtel de vacances Karuizawa (Karuizawa, 1993) ; le club house du Tomioka Lakewood Golf (Tomioka, 1993–96) ; le théâtre Nô Toyoma (Miyagi, 1995–96) et le pavillon japonais pour la Biennale de Venise (1995). Il a également réalisé le Musée de la pierre (Nasu, Tochigi, 2000) ; un musée consacré à Ando Hiroshige (Batou, Nasugun, Tochigi, 2000) ; la maison d'hôtes du Great (Bamboo) Wall (Pékin, 2002) ; l'immeuble One Omotesando (Tokyo, 2003) ; l'immeuble LVMH Osaka (2004) ; le Musée d'art de la préfecture de Nagasaki (2005) ; le jardin suspendu de Fukusaki (Osaka, 2005) et la Zhongtai Box, immeuble Z58 (Shanghaï, 2003–06). Plus récemment se sont ajoutés le projet Tobata C Block (Kitakyushu, Fukuoka, 2005–07) ; la maison d'acier (Bunkyo-ku, Tokyo, 2005–07, présentée ici) ; le restaurant Sakenohana (Londres, 2007) ; Tiffany Ginza (Tokyo, 2008) ; le musée Nezu (Tokyo, 2007–09) et le Musée de Kanayama (Ota City, Gunma, 2009), toutes au Japon, sauf mention contraire.

STEEL HOUSE

Bunkyo-ku, Tokyo, Japan, 2006–07

Floor area: 265 m². Client: Professor Hirose. Cost: not disclosed
Structural design: Ejiri Structural Engineers. Construction: Eiger Co. Ltd.

This monocoque design resembling a "freight car," because the client is interested in trains, was made of 3.2-millimeter-thick corrugated steel plates, without any beams or columns. Obviating the need for traditional structure, the steel skin becomes the load-bearing element. The two-story residence is fitted into an L-shaped site. The architect explains that "the basic idea of the architectural structure is to bend the steel plates to gain strength." Kengo Kuma points out that if the steel is not bent, but is painted, it would look like any other material—plaster boards or concrete for example. "The detail created by bending the steel," he states, "establishes communication between the steel and us. Based on these ideas, we have also been creating architecture from materials such as stone and wood." In this instance, the unpainted and bent, or rather folded steel assumes its industrial appearance and stands out in its densely built Tokyo residential neighborhood. The client proudly displays his collection of toy trains within.

Der Schalenbau, der an einen „Güterwaggon" erinnert – der Bauherr ist Eisenbahnliebhaber – wurde ohne jegliche Träger oder Stützen aus 3,2 mm starken Wellblechplatten gefertigt. Die Stahlhaut selbst wird zum tragenden Element und macht ein traditionelles Tragwerk verzichtbar. Das zweistöckige Haus wurde in ein L-förmiges Grundstück eingepasst. Der Architekt erläutert: „Es ist die Grundidee dieser architektonischen Konstruktion, die Stahlplatten zu biegen, um sie tragfähig zu machen." Kengo Kuma weist darauf hin, dass der Stahl, falls er nicht gebogen, sondern nur gestrichen wäre, wie jedes beliebige andere Baumaterial wirken würde – wie Leichtbauplatten etwa oder Beton. „Das Detail, das sich ergibt, wenn man den Stahl biegt", betont er, „schafft eine Verbindung zwischen dem Stahl und uns. Ausgehend von dieser Idee haben wir auch Konstruktionen aus Baumaterialien wie Stein und Holz realisiert." In diesem Fall gewinnt der ungestrichene und gebogene oder vielmehr gefaltete Stahl eine industrielle Anmutung und beginnt, inmitten der dichtbesiedelten Wohngegend Tokios aufzufallen. In den Innenräumen präsentiert der Bauherr stolz seine Modelleisenbahnsammlung.

La forme monocoque de la maison évoque un « wagon de fret », car le client s'intéresse aux trains, est en tôle d'acier ondulé de 3,2 mm d'épaisseur, sans poutres ni colonnes. Contournant la nécessité d'une structure de soutien, la peau d'acier devient ainsi l'élément porteur. Le plan de cette maison sur deux niveaux est adapté au terrain en forme de « L ». L'architecte explique que « l'idée de base de la structure architecturale est de plier les tôles pour gagner en résistance ». Kuma fait également remarquer que, si l'acier n'était pas plié et peint, il ressemblerait à n'importe quel autre matériau, des panneaux de plâtre ou de béton par exemple. « La forme, créée par le pliage de l'acier, établit une communication entre l'acier et nous. À partir de ces idées, nous avons également créé des architectures sur des matériaux comme la pierre et le bois. » Ici, l'acier brut courbé, ou plutôt plié, assume son aspect industriel et se laisse remarquer dans ce quartier résidentiel dense de Tokyo. Le client peut y présenter fièrement sa collection de trains miniatures.

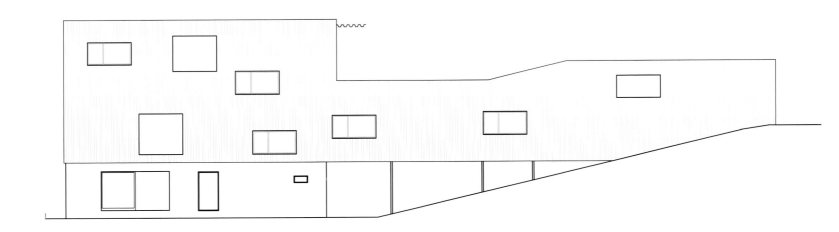

Kengo Kuma uses corrugated steel, a material that might seem rather "industrial", in a sophisticated way, giving this house an undeniable presence in a crowded residential area of Tokyo.

Kengo Kuma arbeitet mit Wellblech, einem Material, das auf anspruchsvolle Weise „industriell" wirkt und dem Haus in der dicht besiedelten Wohngegend Tokios zweifellos Präsenz verleiht.

Kengo Kuma s'est servi de tôle d'acier ondulée – un matériau qui peut sembler assez « industriel » – mais de façon sophistiquée, qui confère à la maison une présence indéniable dans ce quartier résidentiel surpeuplé de Tokyo.

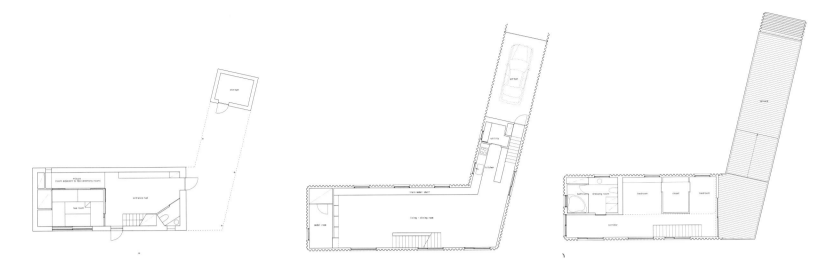

The architect continues the rather industrial vocabulary of the house inside, using chain-link fencing material near the stairway.

Im Innern des Hauses führt der Architekt die industrielle Formensprache fort, etwa indem er an der Treppe mit Maschendraht arbeitet.

L'architecte emploie le même vocabulaire industriel à l'intérieur de la maison, avec, par exemple, le garde-corps en grillage de l'escalier.

Largely closed in on itself, the house nonetheless makes subtle use of natural light throughout. A long curtain covers a wall (right), and a more traditional tea ceremony space is included (below).

Das überwiegend geschlossene Haus nutzt dennoch auf subtile Weise im gesamten Bau Tageslicht. Ein bodenlanger Vorhang kaschiert eine Wand (rechts), auch ein Raum für die Teezeremonie fehlt nicht (unten).

Refermée sur elle-même, la maison n'en utilise pas moins avec subtilité la lumière naturelle dans tous ses volumes. Un long rideau recouvre un mur (à droite) et un espace plus traditionnel pour la cérémonie du thé a été prévu (ci-dessous).

DANIEL LIBESKIND

Studio Daniel Libeskind, Architect LLC
2 Rector Street, 19th Floor / New York, NY 10006 / USA
Tel: +1 212 497 9154 / Fax: +1 212 285 2130
E-mail: info@daniel-libeskind.com / Web: www.daniel-libeskind.com

Born in Poland in 1946 and a US citizen since 1965, **DANIEL LIBESKIND** studied music in Israel and in New York before taking up architecture at the Cooper Union in New York (B.Arch, 1970). He then received a postgraduate degree in the History and Theory of Architecture (School of Comparative Studies, Essex University, UK, 1972). He has taught at Harvard, Yale, Hanover, Graz, Hamburg, and UCLA. Libeskind has had a considerable influence through his theory and his proposals, and more recently with his built work. His work includes the city museum of Osnabrück, the Felix Nussbaum Haus (Germany, 1998); the Jewish Museum in Berlin and extension (Germany, 1989–2001); the Imperial War Museum North (Manchester, UK, 2001); the Danish Jewish Museum (Copenhagen, Denmark, 2003); an extension to the Denver Art Museum (Colorado, USA, 2006); and that to Toronto's Royal Ontario Museum (Canada, 2007). Libeskind's 2003 victory in the competition to design the former World Trade Center site in New York placed him in the forefront of contemporary architecture, despite changes afterwards that caused him to largely withdraw from the project. Carla Swickerath attended the University of Florida (Gainesville, Florida, B.A., 1995) and the University of Michigan (Ann Arbor, M.Arch, 1999). She has worked with Daniel Libeskind since 1999 and is presently CEO and a Principal of the firm. Their recent work includes Westside Shopping and Leisure Center (Bern, Switzerland, 2005–08); Crystals at CityCenter (Las Vegas, Nevada, USA, 2006–09); 18.36.54 House (Connecticut, USA, 2007–10, published here); Zlota 44, a residential high-rise in Warsaw (Poland, 2013 completion); the Military History Museum in Dresden (Germany); and the L Tower and Sony Center for the Performing Arts in Toronto (Canada).

Der 1946 in Polen geborene **DANIEL LIBESKIND** ist seit 1965 Bürger der USA. Er studierte Musik in Israel und New York, bevor der das Studium der Architektur an der Cooper Union in New York aufnahm (B.Arch, 1970). Danach erwarb er einen Postgraduate-Degree für Geschichte und Theorie der Architektur (School of Comparative Studies, Essex University, Großbritannien, 1972). Er hat an den Universitäten Harvard, Yale, Hannover, Graz, Hamburg und an der University of California in Los Angeles gelehrt. Libeskind hat durch sein theoretisches und planerisches Werk beachtlichen Einfluss ausgeübt, in letzter Zeit auch durch seine ausgeführten Bauten. Zu diesen gehören das Museum für die Stadt Osnabrück – Felix-Nussbaum-Haus (1998); das Jüdische Museum in Berlin und dessen Erweiterung (1989–2001, 2007); das Imperial War Museum North (Manchester, Großbritannien, 2001); das Dänische Jüdische Museum (Kopenhagen, Dänemark, 2003); eine Erweiterung des Denver Art Museum (Colorado, USA, 2006) sowie eine weitere des Royal Ontario Museum in Toronto (Kanada, 2007). Der Gewinn des Wettbewerbs für das Gelände des früheren World Trade Center in New York im Jahr 2003 führte Libeskind an die Spitze der zeitgenössischen Architektur, obgleich Veränderungen am Entwurf ihn später veranlassten, sich weitgehend aus dem Projekt zurückzuziehen. Carla Swickerath studierte an der University of Florida (Gainesville, Florida, B.Arch, 1995) und der University of Michigan (Ann Arbor, M.Arch., 1999). Seit 1999 arbeitet sie mit Daniel Libeskind und ist gegenwärtig Geschäftsführerin und Leiterin des Büros. Zu dessen jüngeren Projekten zählen ein Freizeit- und Einkaufszentrum (Bern, Schweiz, 2005–08); Crystals at CityCenter (Las Vegas, Nevada, USA, 2006–09); 18.36.54 House (Connecticut, USA, 2007–10, hier vorgestellt); Zlota 44, ein Wohnhochhaus in Warschau (Polen, Fertigstellung 2013); das Militärhistorische Museum in Dresden und der L Tower sowie das Sony Center for the Performing Arts in Toronto (Kanada).

Né en Pologne in 1946 et devenu citoyen américain en 1965, **DANIEL LIBESKIND** étudie la musique en Israël et à New York avant d'opter pour l'architecture et d'étudier à la Cooper Union à New York (il y obtient son diplôme en 1970). Il est également diplômé d'études supérieures en histoire et théorie de l'architecture (École d'études comparatives, Université de l'Essex, Grande-Bretagne, 1972) et a enseigné à Harvard, Yale, UCLA, Hanovre, Graz et Hambourg. Ses propositions théoriques et ses projets ont exercé une influence considérable et, plus récemment ses réalisations. Son œuvre comprend entre autres le musée municipal d'Osnabrück, la Maison Felix Nussbaum (Allemagne, 1998), le Musée juif de Berlin (1989–2001) et son extension ; le Musée impérial de la guerre Nord à Manchester (Grande-Bretagne, 2001) ; le Musée juif danois (Copenhague, 2003 ; l'extension du Musée d'art de Denver (Colorado, États-Unis, 2006) et celle du Musée royal de l'Ontario (Toronto, 2007). En 2003, sa victoire dans le concours pour le site de l'ancien World Trade Center à New York l'a placé au premier rang des grands créateurs contemporains, même si les changements imposés par la suite l'ont amené à se retirer en grande partie du projet. Carla Swickerath a obtenu son diplôme d'architecture en 1995 à l'université de Floride (Gainesville, Floride) et son master en 1999 à l'université du Michigan (Ann Arbor). Elle travaille avec Libeskind depuis 1999 et est actuellement directrice générale de l'agence. Parmi leurs réalisations récentes, on peut citer le centre commercial et de loisirs Westside (Berne, Suisse, 2005–08) ; le Crystals at CityCenter (Las Vegas, Nevada, 2006–09) ; la maison 18.36.54 (Connecticut, 2007-10, présentée ici) ; Zlota 44, une tour résidentielle à Varsovie (Pologne, achèvement en 2013) ; le musée d'histoire militaire de Dresde (Allemagne) et la L Tower ainsi que le Sony Center for the Performing Arts à Toronto (Canada).

18.36.54 HOUSE

Connecticut, USA, 2007–10

Area: 186 m². Client: not disclosed
Cost: not disclosed

The essential element of this steel, single-family weekend residence is "a spiraling ribbon of 18 planes, defined by 36 points connected by 54 lines" (whence the name of the house). Large glass planes that "virtually disappear within the ribbon" provide for views of neighboring meadows and oak trees on the 22-hectare site. The architect has sought to create a free-flowing space where interior and exterior interact in a "seamless" manner, just as public and private spaces are directly connected. Sitting on the earth as though it might have no foundations, this house is a sculptural object clad in bronze stainless-steel panels that confirms and honors the style of Daniel Libeskind, which he describes as "aggressive and soothing." The clients selected Libeskind as the architect because of their admiration for his Jewish Museum in Berlin. As his firm's description of the project reads: "Challenging both traditional and modern notions of 'the house in the landscape,' this design gives nothing of itself up to its natural setting, but selectively incorporates the elements therein for the enhancement of both house and landscape."

Das wichtigste Element dieses Einfamilien-Wochenendhauses aus Stahl ist „ein spiralförmig aufsteigendes Band aus 18 ebenen Flächen, definiert über 36 Punkte und verbunden durch 54 Linien" (daher der Name des Gebäudes). Große Glasflächen, die "in diesem Band geradezu verschwinden", bieten Ausblicke auf die Wiesen und Eichenbäume des 22 ha großen Geländes. Der Architekt hat versucht, einen frei fließenden Bereich zu gestalten, in dem Außen- und Innenraum „nahtlos" ineinander übergehen; in ähnlicher Weise sind auch die öffentlichen und privaten Räume direkt miteinander verbunden. Dieses Haus, das scheinbar ohne Fundament auf dem Erdboden steht, ist ein skulpturales, mit bronzefarbenen Edelstahlplatten verkleidetes Objekt – ein gelungener Beweis für Daniel Libeskinds Baustil, den er selbst als „aggressiv und sanft" bezeichnet. Die Bauherren entschieden sich für Libeskind als Architekten, weil sie sein Jüdisches Museum in Berlin bewundern. Sein Büro beschreibt dieses Projekt wie folgt: „Dieser Entwurf, der traditionelle wie auch moderne Vorstellungen vom ‚Haus in der Landschaft' herausfordert, gibt nichts von sich selbst an sein natürliches Umfeld preis, sondern betont vielmehr mittels ausgewählter Elemente sowohl das Haus als auch die Landschaft."

L'élément essentiel de cette résidence secondaire familiale, construite en acier, est un « ruban en spirale qui se développe sur 18 plans, définis par 36 points et réunis par 54 lignes » (d'où le nom de la maison). De vastes plans vitrés qui « disparaissent virtuellement dans le ruban » offrent des vues sur les prairies et les chênes environnants de cette propriété de 22 hectares. L'architecte a voulu créer un espace fluide, dans lequel l'intérieur et l'extérieur interagissent « sans rupture visible », de même que les espaces privés et de réception sont directement reliés entre eux. Posée sur le sol comme si elle n'avait pas de fondations, cette maison est une sculpture en panneaux d'acier inoxydable de couleur bronze qui illustre et célèbre le style de Daniel Libeskind, présenté par l'architecte lui-même comme « agressif et apaisant». Les clients l'avaient choisi parce qu'ils admiraient le Musée juif de Berlin. Comme l'indique la description du projet publiée par l'agence de Libeskind : « Mettant en cause à la fois les notions traditionnelles et modernes de 'maison dans le paysage', ce projet ne cède rien de lui-même à son cadre naturel, mais intègre de manière sélective des éléments de celui-ci pour mettre en valeur à la fois la maison et son cadre. »

The astonishing forms of the house seem to rise out of the earth itself, though their geometric rigor contrasts with the gentle countryside. Below, a section drawing reveals the technical complexity of the house.

Die erstaunlichen Formen dieses Hauses scheinen aus der Erde aufzusteigen, obgleich ihre geometrische Strenge im Gegensatz zur lieblichen Landschaft steht. Unten: Der Schnitt offenbart die technische Komplexität des Hauses.

Les formes étonnantes de la maison semblent jaillir du sol, même si leur rigueur géométrique contraste avec la douceur du cadre champêtre. Ci-dessous, un dessin de coupe détaille la complexité technique du projet.

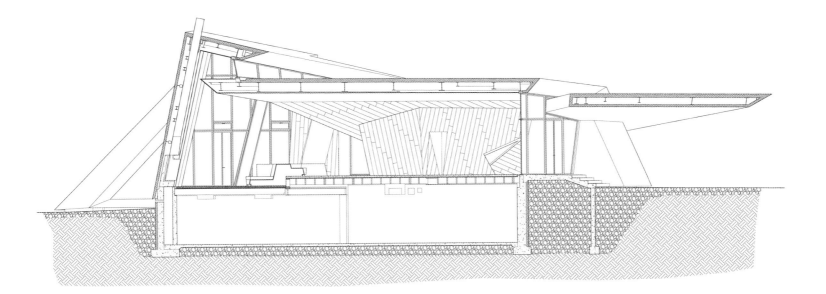

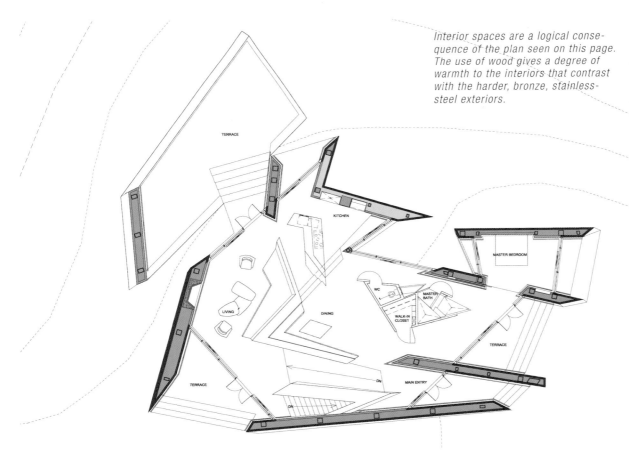

Interior spaces are a logical consequence of the plan seen on this page. The use of wood gives a degree of warmth to the interiors that contrast with the harder, bronze, stainless-steel exteriors.

Der Innenbereich ist eine logische Folgerung des auf dieser Seite gezeigten Planes. Die Verwendung von Holz verleiht den Räumen eine gewisse Wärme, die einen Kontrast zur Außengestaltung mit bronzefarbenem Edelstahl bildet.

Les espaces intérieurs sont la conséquence logique du plan qui figure sur cette page. L'utilisation du bois confère une certaine chaleur à l'intérieur, en contraste avec les extérieurs plus durs en acier inoxydable de couleur bronze.

Furnishings, including the bookshelves seen above, are designed to fit into the spaces but also to continue the overall formal development of the architecture, seen in the folded shapes in the drawing (left).

Die Möblierung einschließlich der oben abgebildeten Bücherregale wurde den Räumen angepasst, aber auch dem gesamten Erscheinungsbild der Architektur, wie sie in den gefalteten Formen auf der Zeichnung (links) zu sehen ist.

Le mobilier, y compris la bibliothèque ci-dessus, est conçu spécialement pour s'intégrer aux espaces, mais aussi pour prolonger le développement entièrement formel de l'architecture, tel qu'il se donne à voir dans les formes pliées sur le dessin ci-contre.

GUILHERME MACHADO VAZ

Guilherme Machado Vaz
Rua Dr. Ramalho Fontes 193, 5º Esq.
4150–630 Porto
Portugal

Tel: +351 91 785 3719
E-mail: gmvarq@gmail.com

GUILHERME MACHADO VAZ was born in 1974 in Porto. In 1999, he graduated from the Faculdade de Arquitectura da Universidade do Porto (FAUP). The buildings of the FAUP were designed by Álvaro Siza (1987–93). Machado Vaz worked with Souto Moura Arquitectos (1997–98), before creating his own office. His main projects are: Valley House (Vieira do Minho, 1998–2004, published here); Primary School (Matosinhos, 2000–03); Grave (Porto, 2003–04); Esplanade (Matosinhos, 2004–05); and Civic Center (Matosinhos, 2002–06), all in Portugal. He is currently working on four houses as a local architect for David Chipperfield in Portugal. He won Second Prize in an international competition for the new Psychology Faculty in Coimbra, Portugal (associated with architect Nuno Graça Moura), in 2004.

GUILHERME MACHADO VAZ wurde 1974 in Porto geboren, wo er 1999 an der Faculdade de Arquitectura da Universidade do Porto (FAUP) sein Studium abschloss. Die Bauten der FAUP (1987–93) entstanden nach Entwürfen Álvaro Sizas. Ehe Machado Vaz sein eigenes Büro eröffnete, arbeitete er 1997 bis 1998 bei Souto Moura Arquitectos. Seine wichtigsten Projekte sind: das hier vorgestellte Valley House (Vieira do Minho, 1998–2004), Grundschule (Matosinhos, 2000–03), ein Grab (Porto, 2003–04), Esplanade (Matosinhos, 2004–05) sowie ein Verwaltungszentrum (Matosinhos, 2002–06), sämtlich in Portugal. Zurzeit arbeitet er als Architekt vor Ort für David Chipperfield an vier Häusern in Portugal. Beim internationalen Wettbewerb für die neue Psychologische Fakultät in Coimbra, Portugal, gewann er 2004 in Zusammenarbeit mit dem Architekten Nuno Graça Moura den zweiten Preis.

GUILHERME MACHADO VAZ, né à Porto en 1974, est diplômé en 1999 de la Faculté d'architecture de l'université de Porto (FAUP) dont les bâtiments ont été conçus par Álvaro Siza en 1987–93. Machado Vaz a travaillé pour Souto Moura Arquitectos (1997–98) avant de créer sa propre agence. Parmi ses principaux projets au Portugal : la maison de la Vallée, Vieira do Minho (1998–2004) présentée ici ; une école primaire à Matosinhos (2000–03) ; une tombe, Porto (2003–04) ; une esplanade (2004–05) et un centre municipal à Matosinhos (2002–06). Il travaille actuellement pour David Chipperfield sur quatre projets de maisons au Portugal en tant qu'architecte local. En 2004, il a remporté le second prix d'un concours international pour la faculté de psychologie de Coimbra (en association avec Nuno Graça Moura).

VALLEY HOUSE
Vieira do Minho, Portugal, 1998–2004

Floor area: 340 m². Client: Prof. Júlio Benfiquista
Cost: €250 000

This house stands out as a concrete, glass, wood, and steel composition in intentional contrast to the natural surroundings. But the architect also anticipates the moment when natural aging of the construction materials will make the residence blend more fully into the site. No less than a total of 82 meters long, 8 meters wide, with a usable floor area of 340 m², the structure appears to echo the form of a nearby natural stone wall. The architect states that the "floor plan obeys a typical regional typology in which all the elements are gathered around a central room, the 'veranda,' that assumes the role of the 'nuclear' part of the building where family and friends congregate. The Valley House," he concludes, "is an isolated shelter that transports us to a place in time where man lived in a purely natural environment due to the lack of technical ability to transform it." Both Álvaro Siza and to an even greater extent Eduardo Souto Moura have also experimented with the close integration of modern houses into their natural settings, an undoubted influence on Guilherme Machado Vaz.

Dieses Haus steht als Komposition aus Beton, Glas, Holz und Stahl in bewusstem Kontrast zu seiner Umgebung. Der Architekt rechnet allerdings auch mit dem Zeitpunkt, wenn das Haus dank der natürlichen Alterung des Baumaterials stärker mit dem Gelände verschmilzt. Der stattliche 82 m lange, 8 m breite Bau mit einer Nutzfläche von 340 m² nimmt scheinbar die Form einer nahe gelegenen Natursteinmauer auf. Der Architekt konstatiert, dass „der Grundriss einer typischen lokalen Form folgt, bei der sich sämtliche Elemente um einen zentralen Raum, die ‚Veranda‘, das Herz des Hauses, gruppieren, in dem Familie und Freunde zusammenkommen. Das Valley House", schließt er, „gleicht einem isolierten Schutzraum, der uns an einen Ort und in eine Zeit versetzt, in der der Mensch, bedingt durch das Fehlen der technischen Fähigkeit, etwas zu verändern, in einer rein naturbelassenen Umgebung lebte." Auch Álvaro Siza und in noch stärkerem Maß Eduardo Souto Moura haben mit der engen Einbindung moderner Häuser in ihre natürliche Umgebung experimentiert und damit zweifellos Guilherme Machado Vaz beeinflusst.

Cette maison est une composition en béton, verre, bois et acier qui se détache de son cadre naturel par contraste. L'architecte a cependant prévu le moment où le vieillissement naturel des matériaux de construction entraînera une intégration plus douce avec le site. De pas moins de 82 mètres de long, 8 mètres de large et de 340 m² de surface, cette résidence semble faire écho à l'ancien mur de pierre voisin. L'architecte précise que « le plan au sol obéit à une typologie régionale typique dans laquelle tous les éléments sont regroupés autour d'une pièce centrale, la « véranda », qui joue le rôle d'un « noyau » dans lequel famille et amis se retrouvent. Cette maison de la vallée, conclut-il, est un abri isolé qui nous transporte dans une période de l'Histoire où l'homme vivait dans un cadre purement naturel par manque de capacité technique à le transformer. » Álvaro Siza et, dans une mesure encore plus forte, Eduardo Souto Moura, qui ont également travaillé sur l'intégration étroite de maisons modernes dans un cadre naturel, ont certainement influencé Guilherme Machado Vaz.

Despite its planar concrete walls, the house is intended to blend in with its natural setting, almost appearing to rise up out of the earth itself.

Ungeachtet seiner ebenen Betonwände soll das Haus mit seiner natürlichen Umgebung verschmelzen, ja sich scheinbar aus der Erde erheben.

Malgré ses murs plans en béton, la maison fusionne avec son cadre naturel, comme si elle sortait de la terre.

The simple lines of the exterior architecture are echoed inside, with a living room wall opening entirely to the outdoors in the image below.

Die einfachen Linien des Außenbaus spiegeln sich im Inneren; unten ist der auf einer Seite nach außen offene Wohnraum zu sehen.

Les lignes simples de l'architecture se retrouvent en écho à l'intérieur. Un mur du séjour s'ouvre entièrement vers l'extérieur (image ci-dessous).

The landscape and swimming pool
are designed in harmony with the
house itself, planar and carefully
integrated into the natural setting.

Grünflächen und Schwimmbecken
sind in Einklang mit dem behutsam in
die natürliche Umgebung eingebette-
ten Haus gestaltet.

Le paysage et la piscine sont conçus
en harmonie avec la maison soigneusement intégrée au cadre naturel.

The plan below shows the very strict
and narrow rectangular design of the
house, corresponding to its insertion
into the existing hillside.

Der Grundriss unten zeigt die sehr
strenge, längsrechteckige Gestaltung
des Hauses, die seiner Stellung zum
vorhandenen Hang entspricht.

Le plan ci-dessous montre l'organisation de la maison sur un rectangle
long et étroit, qui correspond à son
insertion dans le flanc de la colline.

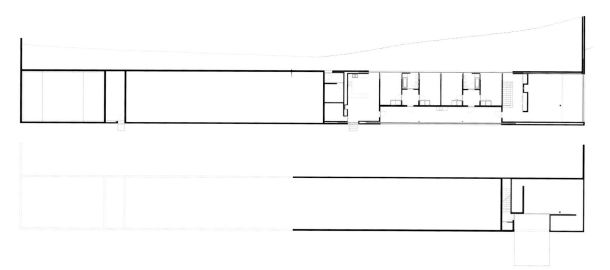

GURJIT SINGH MATHAROO

Matharoo Associates
24-E Capital Commercial Centre, Ashram Road
Ahmedabad
380 009 Gujarat
India

Tel: + 91 79 2657 7757
Mobile: +91 98 7954 3505
E-mail: studio@matharooassociates.com
Web: www.matharooassociates.com

GURJIT SINGH MATHAROO was born in Ajmer (Rajasthan, India), in 1966. He received a diploma in Architecture from the Center for Environmental Planning and Technology (CEPT, Ahmedabad, 1989). He worked for one year in the offices of Michele Arnaboldi and Giorgio Guscetti in Ticino, Switzerland, before creating his own firm, Matharoo Associates, in Ahmedabad in 1991. The firm, which has a strength of 15 people, has projects in the area of architecture, interior design, product design, and structural design. His work includes the Prathama Blood Center (Ahmedabad, 2000); the Dilip Sanghvi House with its award-winning Curtain Door (Surat, 2007); the Net House (Ahmedabad, 2009–10, published here); and the House with Balls (Ahmedabad, 2010), all in India.

GURJIT SINGH MATHAROO wurde 1966 in Ajmer (Rajasthan, Indien) geboren. Er erwarb sein Architekturdiplom am Center for Environmental Planning and Technology (CEPT, Ahmedabad, 1989). Ein Jahr arbeitete er im Büro von Michele Arnaboldi und Giorgio Guscetti im Tessin (Schweiz) und gründete 1991 sein eigenes Büro, Matharoo Associates, in Ahmedabad. Dieses beschäftigt 15 Personen und realisiert Projekte in den Bereichen Architektur, Innenarchitektur, Produktdesign und Baukonstruktion. Zu seinen Arbeiten zählen das Prathama Blood Centre (Ahmedabad, 2000); das Haus Dilip Sanghvi mit der preisgekrönten Curtain Door (Surat, 2007); das Net House (Ahmedabad, 2009–10, hier vorgestellt) sowie das House with Balls (Ahmedabad, 2010), alle in Indien.

GURJIT SINGH MATHAROO, né à Ajmer (Rajasthan, Inde) en 1966, est diplômé d'architecture du Centre de planification et de technologies environnementales (CEPT, Ahmedabad, 1989). Il a travaillé pendant un an dans l'agence de Michele Arnaboldi et Giorgio Guscetti à Ticino (Suisse), avant de créer en 1991 sa propre structure, Matharoo Associates, à Ahmedabad en 1991. L'agence, qui compte 15 collaborateurs, intervient dans les domaines de l'architecture, de l'architecture intérieure, du design produit et de la conception structurelle. Parmi ses réalisations, toutes en Inde, on peut citer le Centre du sang Prathama (Ahmedabad, 2000); la résidence Parag Shah (Surat, 2005); la maison des Parents (Ajmer, Rajasthan, 2010) et la maison Net (Ahmedabad, 2009–10, présentée ici).

NET HOUSE
Ahmedabad, India, 2009–10

Area: 200 m²
Client: Dr. Urmish Chudgar. Cost: $560 400

The architect uses the word "Net" in the sense of "clear of all else, subject to no further deductions." The house provides a 12-meter, square space without columns and has a monolithic 90-ton concrete slab set on an elaborate steel frame. The skin of the house is made up of net shutters, providing a play on the different meanings of the name of the house. The sliding mosquito nets, roll-up blinds, and folding glass panels allow residents to adjust their level of privacy or the openness to nature of each space. A thin (15-centimeter) pipe surrounded by a glass stairway draws monsoon rainwater from the roof into a fountain that empties into a 1.4-million-liter underground storage tank. The net-enclosed space on the upper floor has a gazebo, and allows for sunbathing or the practice of yoga.

Der Architekt verwendet das Wort „Netz" im Sinne von „ohne alles andere, nicht weiter reduzierbar". Das Haus besteht aus einem 12 m langen, quadratischen, stützenfreien Raum mit einer monolitischen, 90 t schweren Betonplatte, die auf ein sorgfältig ausgearbeitetes Stahlskelett gesetzt wurde. Die Außenhaut besteht aus netzbespannten Rahmen, die ein Spiel mit den verschiedenen Bedeutungen des Hausnamens bilden. Diese verschiebbaren Moskitonetze sowie aufrollbare Jalousien und aufklappbare Glastafeln ermöglichen es den Bewohnern, in jedem Raum selbst das gewünschte Maß an Abschirmung oder Öffnung zur Natur zu regeln. Ein enges Rohr von 15 cm Durchmesser leitet im verglasten Treppenhaus das Wasser der Monsunregen vom Dach in einen Brunnen, der sich in einen unterirdischen, 1,4 Mio. l fassenden Tank entleert. In dem von Netzen umgebene Bereich im Obergeschoss befindet sich auch eine Laube, wo man Sonnenbäder nehmen oder sich seinen Yogaübungen widmen kann.

L'architecte utilise le terme anglais de « net » (filet, réseau) au sens de « libre de toute chose, soumis à aucune autre déduction ». La maison offre un espace carré de 12 mètres de côté sans colonnes et repose sur une dalle monolithique de béton de 90 tonnes appuyée sur une structure en acier. La peau de la maison est faite de grands volets tendus d'un maillage fin, un filet (jouant ainsi avec les différents sens du nom de la maison). Des moustiquaires coulissantes, des stores enroulables et des volets de verre repliables permettent aux habitants de régler comme ils le souhaitent le niveau d'intimité ou d'ouverture sur la nature de chaque espace. Un petit tuyau de 15 centimètres de diamètre entouré d'un escalier en verre récupère l'eau des pluies de la mousson de la toiture et la conduit à une fontaine qui se dévere ensuite un réservoir souterrain de 140 mètres cubes. Au niveau supérieur se trouve un belvédère sur lequel on peut prendre des bains de soleil ou pratiquer le yoga.

The strict geometric forms of the building and the use of netting appear to borrow something from the vocabulary of industrial architecture, contrasting here with the natural setting.

Die strengen geometrischen Formen des Gebäudes und die Verwendung von Netzen stammen offenbar aus dem Vokabular der Industriearchitektur; hier bilden sie einen Gegensatz zum natürlichen Umfeld.

Les formes strictement géométriques de la construction et l'utilisation d'un maillage fin semblent tirées du vocabulaire de l'architecture industrielle et contrastent ici avec le cadre naturel.

A colorful plan of the house shows the various layers of protection ranging from folding glass to the slide-up nets and roll-up bamboo screens.

Ein farbenfroher Plan des Hauses zeigt die verschiedenen Schutzschichten, die von ausklappbarer Verglasung bis zu verschiebbaren Netzelementen und aufrollbaren Bambusjalousien reichen.

Le plan très coloré de la maison montre les différentes strates de protection : volets en verre repliables, écrans de bambou enroulables, écrans en maillage coulissants.

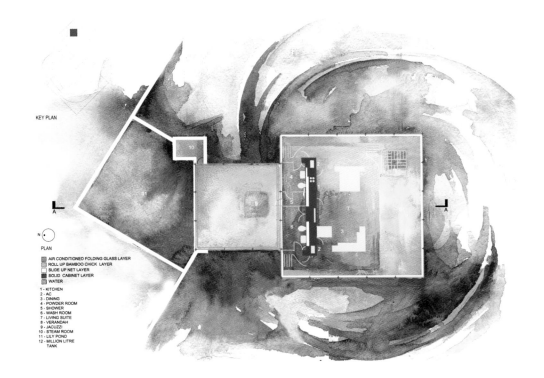

KEY PLAN

N

PLAN

☐ AIR CONDITIONED FOLDING GLASS LAYER
☐ ROLL UP BAMBOO CHICK LAYER
☐ SLIDE UP NET LAYER
■ SOLID CABINET LAYER
■ WATER

1 - KITCHEN
2 - AC
3 - DINING
4 - POWDER ROOM
5 - SHOWER
6 - WASH ROOM
7 - LIVING SUITE
8 - VERANDAH
9 - JACUZZI
10 - STEAM ROOM
11 - LILY POND
12 - MILLION LITRE
     TANK

RICHARD MEIER

Richard Meier & Partners
475 Tenth Avenue
New York, NY 10018
USA

Tel: +1 212 967 6060 / Fax: +1 212 967 3207
E-mail: mail@richardmeier.com / Web: www.richardmeier.com

RICHARD MEIER was born in Newark, New Jersey, in 1934. He received his architectural training at Cornell University, and worked in the office of Marcel Breuer (1960–63), before establishing his own practice in 1963. In 1984, he became the youngest winner of the Pritzker Prize, and he received the 1988 RIBA Gold Medal. His notable buildings include the Atheneum (New Harmony, Indiana 1975–79); High Museum of Art (Atlanta, Georgia, 1980–83); Museum of Decorative Arts (Frankfurt, Germany, 1979–84); Canal Plus Headquarters (Paris, France, 1988–91); Barcelona Museum of Contemporary Art (Barcelona, Spain, 1988–95); City Hall and Library (The Hague, The Netherlands, 1990–95); and the Getty Center (Los Angeles, California, 1984–97). Recent work includes the US Courthouse and Federal Building (Phoenix, Arizona, 1995–2000); Yale University History of Art and Arts Library (New Haven, Connecticut, 2001); Jubilee Church (Rome, Italy, 1996–2003); Crystal Cathedral International Center for Possibility Thinking (Garden Grove, California, 1998–2003); 66 Restaurant in New York (New York, 2002–03); Ara Pacis Museum (Rome, Italy, 1995–2006); 165 Charles Street (New York, New York, 2003–06); and Arp Museum (Rolandseck, Germany, 1997–2007). More recent and current work includes the ECM City Tower (Pankrác, Prague, Czech Republic, 2001–08); Rickmers Residence (Hamburg, Germany, 2005–08); and On Prospect Park (Brooklyn, New York, USA, 2003–09).

RICHARD MEIER wurde 1934 in Newark, New Jersey, geboren. Seine Ausbildung zum Architekten erhielt er an der Cornell University und arbeitete anschließend bei Marcel Breuer (1960–63), ehe er 1963 sein eigenes Büro gründete. 1984 wurde er als jüngster Preisträger mit dem Pritzker-Preis ausgezeichnet und erhielt 1988 die RIBA-Goldmedaille. Zu seinen bekanntesten Bauten gehören das Atheneum (New Harmony, Indiana, 1975–79), das High Museum of Art (Atlanta, Georgia, 1980–83), das Museum für Angewandte Kunst (Frankfurt am Main, 1979–84), die Hauptverwaltung von Canal Plus (Paris, 1988–91), das Museum für Zeitgenössische Kunst in Barcelona (1988–95), Stadthaus und Bibliothek in Den Haag (1990–95) sowie das Getty Center (Los Angeles, 1984–97). Zu seinen jüngeren Projekten zählen das Bundesgerichtsgebäude in Phoenix (Arizona, 1995–2000), die Bibliothek für Kunst und Kunstgeschichte der Universität Yale (New Haven, Connecticut, 2001), die Kirche Dio Padre Misericordioso in Rom (1996–2003), das Crystal Cathedral International Center for Possibility Thinking (Garden Grove, Kalifornien, 1998–2003), das Restaurant 66 in New York (2002–03), das Museum Ara Pacis (Rom, 1995–2006), 165 Charles Street (New York, 2003–06) sowie das Arp-Museum (Rolandseck, Deutschland, 1997–2007). Aktuellere Projekte sind u. a. der ECM City Tower (Pankrác, Prag, 2001–08), das Haus Rickmers (Hamburg, 2005–08) und das Haus On Prospect Park (Brooklyn, New York, USA, 2003–09).

RICHARD MEIER, né à Newark (New Jersey) en 1934, a fait ses études à l'université Cornell, puis a travaillé dans l'agence de Marcel Breuer (1960–63), avant de fonder sa propre structure en 1963. En 1984, il a été le plus jeune titulaire du prix Pritzker, et a reçu en 1988 la médaille d'or du RIBA. Parmi ses réalisations les plus connues, on peut citer l'Atheneum (New Harmony, Indiana 1975–79) ; le High Museum of Art (Atlanta, Georgie, 1980–83) ; le Musée des arts décoratifs (Francfort, Allemagne, 1979–84) ; le siège de Canal Plus (Paris, 1988–91) ; Le Musée d'art contemporain de Barcelone (MACBA, Barcelone, Espagne, 1988–95) ; l'hôtel de ville et bibliothèque municipale de La Haye (Pays-Bas, 1990–95) ; et le Getty Center (Los Angeles, 1984–97). Parmi ses réalisations récentes, on compte le tribunal et immeuble fédéral (Phoenix, Arizona, 1995–2000) ; la bibliothèque des arts et d'histoire de l'art de l'université Yale (New Haven, Connecticut, 2001) ; l'église du Jubilé (Rome, 1996–2003) ; la cathédrale de cristal, l'International Center for Possibility Thinking (Garden Grove, Californie, 1998–2003) ; le Restaurant 66 à New York (2002–03) ; le musée de l'Ara Pacis (Rome, 1995–2006) ; l'immeuble d'appartements du 165 Charles Street (New York, 2003–06) ; le musée Arp (Rolandseck, Allemagne, 1997–2007) ; la City Tower ECM (Pankrác, Prague, République tchèque, 2001–08) ; la résidence Rickmers (Hambourg, 2005–08) ; et l'immeuble d'appartements On Prospect Park (Brooklyn, New York, 2003–09).

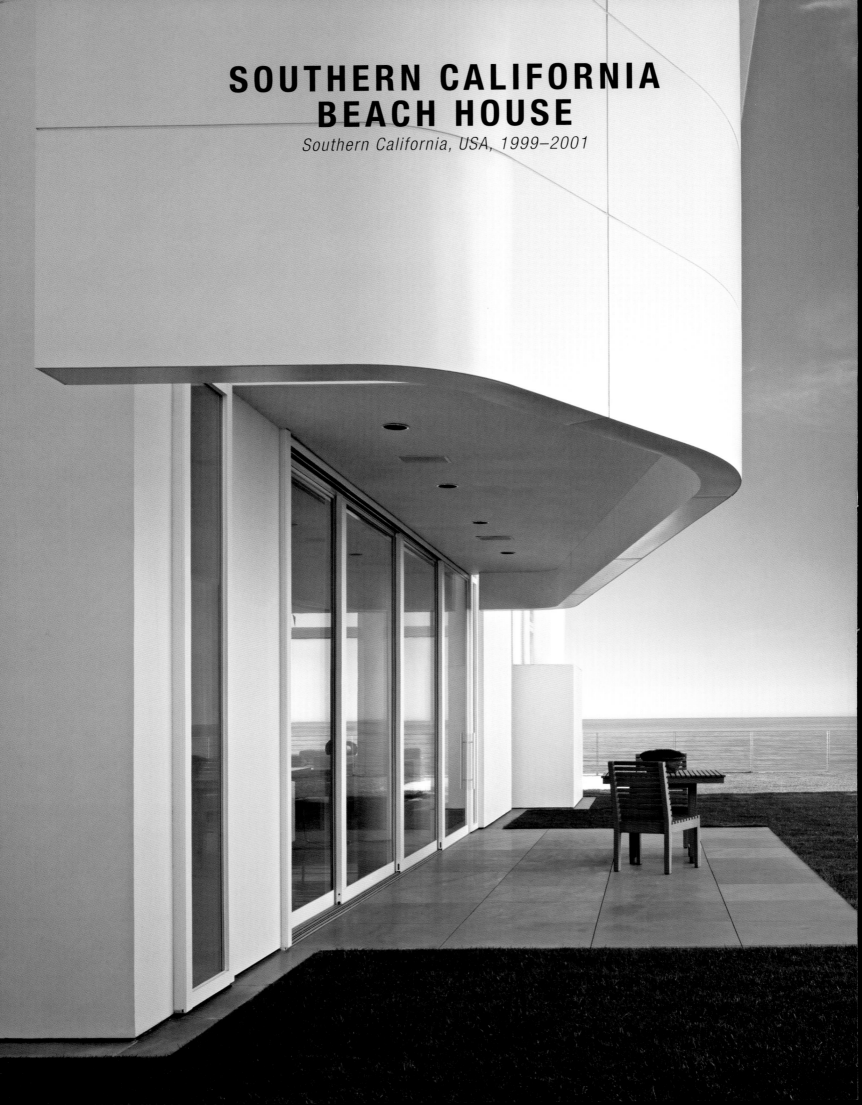

SOUTHERN CALIFORNIA
BEACH HOUSE

Southern California, USA, 1999–2001

The Pacific Coast Highway runs from Dana Point to Oxnard in southern California. Notable sections such as that running past Santa Monica are lined on the oceanside with remarkable residences. Meier's own Ackerberg House is near the Pacific Coast Highway in Malibu. This Beach House is located directly on the beach with magnificent open vistas of the Pacific Ocean. A glazed, translucent entry in the center of the house on the roadside reveals a grass courtyard and a single tree planted within the perimeter of the residence. The two-story entrance hall immediately offers visitors the view of the water. A double-height glazed living room prolonged by a wooden deck look out onto the beach. Sliding glass doors create a tangible continuity between exterior and interior. Although the climate of southern California does not really recall that of Japan, the fundamental ambiguity between inside and outside is very much a part of Japanese architectural tradition. As the architect explains the structure, "The beams at the roof level, located above the fenestration, express the structural rhythm and layering of the components. This cadence is echoed in the pattern of the painted aluminum wall panels and modular windows. Elsewhere, the external plaster walls are juxtaposed with the transparent glazed façades, creating a mosaic of layered materials. This use of layered wall elements, intersected by transparent surfaces, dissolves the separation between inside and outside throughout the house."

Der Pacific Coast Highway führt von Dana Point zum südkalifornischen Oxnard. An schönen Streckenabschnitten – etwa bei Santa Monica – reihen sich auf der Pazifikseite ansehnliche Privathäuser aneinander. Auch Richard Meiers Ackerberg House in Malibu befindet sich in der Nähe des Pacific Coast Highway. Das Beach House steht direkt am Wasser und bietet eine eindrucksvolle Aussicht auf den Pazifischen Ozean. Straßenseitig ist in der Mitte des Hauses ein transluzent verglaster Eingang angeordnet. Daran schließt ein Rasenhof mit einem Baum an. Der zweigeschossige Eingangsbereich öffnet sofort den Blick auf den Pazifik. Ein zweigeschossiger verglaster Wohnraum, der sich im Außenbereich als holzgedeckte Terrasse fortsetzt, bietet Ausblicke auf den Strand. Glasschiebetüren schaffen eine Kontinuität zwischen innen und außen. Das Klima in Südkalifornien hat zwar mit dem in Japan nicht viel gemein, dennoch prägt die grundsätzliche Mehrdeutigkeit der Beziehung zwischen innen und außen auch die japanische Architekturtradition. Der Architekt erläutert die Konstruktion des Hauses: „Die Dachträger oberhalb der Verglasung zeigen den konstruktiven Rhythmus und die Schichtung der Elemente. Dieser Rhythmus findet sich im Raster der äußeren Wandverkleidung mit den weißen Aluminiumplatten und in den modularen Fenstern wieder. An anderer Stelle kontrastieren die verputzten Außenwände mit den transparenten Glasfassaden und schaffen ein mehrschichtiges Mosaik. Geschichtete Wandelemente und transparente Oberflächen lösen die Trennung zwischen innen und außen im gesamten Haus auf."

La Pacific Coast Highway est un important axe routier de Californie du Sud qui va de Dana Point à Oxnard. Certaines sections, notamment celle qui longe Santa Monica, sont bordées du côté de l'océan par de remarquables résidences. La maison Ackerberg dessinée par Meier se trouve à Malibu, au bord de cette route. Cette résidence balnéaire se dresse vraiment au bord de l'eau et bénéficie donc de remarquables perspectives sur le Pacifique. Côté route, au milieu de la maison, une entrée vitrée translucide donne sur une cour gazonnée animée par un unique arbre. Le hall d'entrée, sur une hauteur double, offre une vue directe sur l'océan. Le séjour, également double-hauteur, est prolongé par une terrasse en bois donnant sur la plage. Des portes coulissantes en verre créent une continuité entre l'intérieur et l'extérieur. Bien que le climat de la Californie du Sud ne soit pas vraiment celui du Japon, cette ambiguïté dedans/dehors se retrouve dans la tradition architecturale japonaise. Meier explique ainsi son projet : « Les poutres de la toiture, au-dessus du fenêtrage, soulignent le rythme structurel et la stratification des divers éléments de la composition. Ce tempo se retrouve en écho dans le calepinage des panneaux muraux en aluminium peint et des fenêtres modulaires. Ailleurs, les murs extérieurs plâtrés alternent avec des façades vitrées transparentes, pour créer une mosaïque de matériaux ordonnée. Ce maillage d'éléments muraux coupés par des surfaces transparentes estompe dans la maison tout entière la séparation entre intérieur et extérieur. »

Richard Meier's rich articulation of the white surfaces of the house gives it an animation that goes far beyond what the geometric rigor of the plans (below) might imply.

Richard Meiers vielfältige Gliederung der weißen Flächen des Hauses verleiht ihm eine Lebendigkeit, welche die geometrische Strenge der Grundrisse (unten) nicht vermittelt.

La riche articulation des plans immaculés de la maison conçue par Richard Meier crée une animation qui dépasse de loin la rigueur géométrique du projet (ci-dessous).

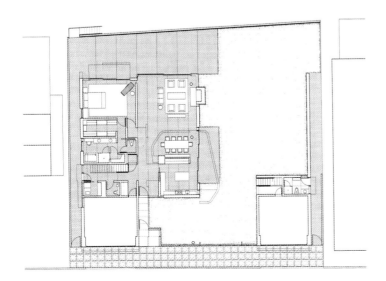

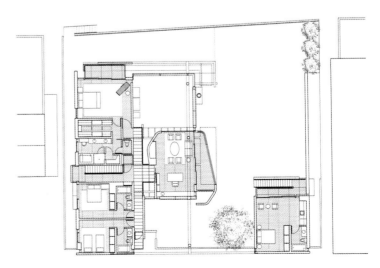

TOSHIKO MORI

Toshiko Mori Architect
180 Varick Street, Suite 1322
New York, NY 10014
USA

Tel: +1 212 337 9644 / Fax: +1 212 337 9647
E-mail: info@tmarch.com / Web: www.tmarch.com

TOSHIKO MORI attended the Cooper Union School of Art, and School of Architecture (1970–76), and received an Honorary M.Arch degree from the Harvard GSD in 1996. From 2002 to 2008, she was Chair of the Department of Architecture at the Harvard GSD, where she has taught since 1995. Prior to joining the faculty at Harvard, Toshiko Mori taught for more than a decade at Cooper Union. She has served as a visiting faculty member at Columbia University and Yale University, where she was the Eero Saarinen Visiting Professor in 1992. Toshiko Mori has worked on numerous institutional projects, such as the addition to Syracuse University's Link Hall (Syracuse, New York, 2008); the renovation of Brown University's Pembroke Hall (Providence, Rhode Island, 2008); the Syracuse Center of Excellence in Environmental and Energy Systems Headquarter Building (Syracuse, New York, 2009); and a master plan for New York University. She has built houses in Maine (2001, 2004); Florida (2005); Connecticut (1994, 2009); New York (2008, 2009); and designed the Visitor Center for Frank Lloyd Wright's Darwin D. Martin House (Buffalo, New York, 2008–09). The firm created the design for the Cooper-Hewitt National Design Museum's exhibition *Fashioning Felt* (New York, March 6 to September 7, 2009). In March 2009, Toshiko Mori won the competition to design a pavilion for the Penobscot Marine Museum in Searsport (Maine), all in the USA.

TOSHIKO MORI studierte an der Cooper Union School of Art und School of Architecture (1970–76) und erhielt 1996 einen Honorary M.Arch. an der Harvard Graduate School of Design. Von 2002 bis 2008 hatte sie den Vorsitz der Architekturabteilung an der Harvard School of Design inne, wo sie seit 1995 lehrt. Davor lehrte sie über ein Jahrzehnt an der Cooper Union. Sie war Gastfakultätsmitglied an den Universitäten Columbia und Yale, an letzterer hatte sie 1992 die Eero-Saarinen-Gastprofessur inne. Toshiko Mori hat an zahlreichen öffentlichen Projekten gearbeitet, wie dem Anbau der Link Hall an der Syracuse University (Syracuse, New York, 2008), der Sanierung der Pembroke Hall der Brown University (Providence, Rhode Island, 2008), dem Hauptgebäude des Syracuse Center of Excellence in Environmental and Energy Systems (Syracuse, New York, 2009) und einem Generalbebauungsplan für die New York University. Sie hat Häuser in Maine (2001, 2004), Florida (2005), Connecticut (1994, 2009) und New York (2008, 2009) gebaut und das Besucherzentrum für Frank Lloyd Wrights Haus Darwin D. Martin (Buffalo, New York, 2008–09) geplant. Ihr Büro gestaltete auch die Ausstellung *Fashioning Felt* im Cooper-Hewitt National Design Museum (New York, 6.3.–7.9.2009). Im März 2009 gewann Toshiko Mori den Wettbewerb für eine Erweiterung des Penobscot Marine Museum in Searsport (Maine), alle in den USA.

TOSHIKO MORI a étudié à la Cooper Union School of Art and School of Architecture (1970–76). Elle est M.Arch honoraire de l'Harvard University Graduate School of Design (1996). De 2002 à 2008, elle a présidé le Département d'architecture de l'Harvard School of Design, où elle enseigne depuis 1995. Auparavant, elle avait déjà enseigné pendant plus de dix ans à la Cooper Union. Elle a aussi été professeur invité à la Columbia University et à la Yale University (Eero Saarinen Visiting Professor en 1992). Elle a travaillé à de nombreux projets institutionnels, comme l'extension du Syracuse University's Link Hall, (Syracuse, New York, 2008) ; la rénovation du Pembroke Hall de Brown University (Providence, Rhode Island, 2008) ; l'immeuble du siège du Syracruse Center of Excellence in Environmental and Energy Systems (Syracuse, New York, 2009) et un plan directeur pour la New York University. Elle a construit des maisons dans le Maine (2001, 2004) ; en Floride (2005) ; dans la Connecticut (1994, 2009) ; dans l'État de New York (2008, 2009) et a conçu le centre d'accueil des visiteurs de la maison Darwin D. Martin de Frank Lloyd Wright (Buffalo, New York, 2008–09). Son agence a créé la mise en scène de l'exposition *Fashioning Felt* du Cooper Hewitt National Design Museum (New York, 6 mars–7 septembre 2009). En mars 2009, Toshiko Mori a remporté le concours pour le pavillon du Penobscot Marine Museum à Searsport (Maine).

ADDITION TO HOUSE ON THE GULF OF MEXICO I

Casey Key, Florida, USA, 2004–05

Floor area: 186 m². Client: not disclosed. Cost: not disclosed

Toshiko Mori was called on to create an addition to a house designed by the respected architect Paul Rudolph in 1957. The site, in Casey Key, Florida, to the south of Sarasota, is on a narrow sand bar. The older house is located to the south of the site, and a guest house, also designed by Toshiko Mori, is on the northern end of the plot. The new addition is set on the southeast corner of the site, and is connected to the existing house by a translucent canopy. A kitchen and dining area occupy the ground floor of the addition and open out onto a swimming pool. A master bedroom, bath, and terrace are on the upper floor. The addition, designed with glass, concrete and steel, has a fiberglass and carbon fiber exterior stairway, materials chosen "because of their resistance to the extreme climatic conditions on the site." The large glazed surface of the addition affords generous views of the garden with its large trees.

Toshiko Mori erhielt den Auftrag, einen Anbau für ein Haus zu konzipieren, das der renommierte Architekt Paul Rudolph im Jahr 1957 entworfen hatte. Der Baugrund auf Casey Key südlich von Sarasota befindet sich auf einer schmalen Sandbank. Das ältere Haus liegt im Süden des Geländes und ein ebenfalls von Toshiko Mori entworfenes Gästehaus am nördlichen Ende des Grundstücks. Der neue Anbau steht an der südwestlichen Ecke des Baugrunds und ist mit dem bestehenden Haus durch ein lichtdurchlässiges Schutzdach verbunden. Im Erdgeschoss des Anbaus sind Küche und Essbereich untergebracht, durch eine Öffnung gelangt man zum Schwimmbecken. Im Obergeschoss finden Hauptschlafraum, Bad und Terrasse Platz. Der aus Glas, Beton und Stahl errichtete Anbau verfügt über eine Außentreppe aus Fiberglas und Karbonfaser, Materialien, die „wegen ihrer Beständigkeit angesichts der hier herrschenden extremen klimatischen Bedingungen" gewählt wurden. Der großflächig verglaste Anbau erlaubt zahlreiche Ausblicke in den mit hohen Bäumen bestandenen Garten.

Toshiko Mori avait été appelée pour créer l'extension d'une maison conçue en 1957 par le très respecté Paul Rudolph. Casey Key, en Floride au sud de Sarasota, est une étroite bande de sable. La maison existante se trouve en partie sud du site et une maison d'amis, également due à Toshiko Mori, au nord. La nouvelle extension occupe l'angle sud-est du terrain et se rattache à la maison existante par un auvent translucide. La cuisine et la salle des repas se trouvent au rez-de-chaussée, ouvert sur une piscine. Une chambre principale, une salle de bains et une terrasse constituent l'étage. L'extension, en verre, béton et acier, possède un escalier extérieur en fibre de verre et de carbone, matériaux choisis « pour leur résistance aux conditions climatiques extrêmes que connaît cet endroit ». De vastes plans vitrés permettent de généreuses perspectives sur le jardin et ses grands arbres.

Toshiko Mori's elevated addition has an unobtrusive presence and is well adapted to its natural surroundings.

Toshiko Moris erhöhter Anbau scheint sich mit einer der natürlichen Umgebung angepassten, leichtgewichtigen Präsenz in die Gartenlandschaft einzufügen.

L'extension surélevée de Toshiko Mori semble s'insérer avec facilité dans le cadre du jardin. La légèreté de sa présence est adaptée à son environnement.

Seen at night near the swimming pool, the addition is largely transparent, and is formed through a strong contrast between its vertical column elements and the horizontal floor and roof planes.

Nachts am Swimmingpool aufgenommen, wirkt der Anbau weitgehend transparent und ist durch den starken Kontrast zwischen seinen vertikalen Stützen und den horizontalen Geschoss- und Dachflächen geprägt.

Vue la nuit, près de la piscine, l'extension est en grande partie transparente, et présente de forts contrastes entre ses colonnes verticales et les plans horizontaux des sols et de la toiture.

Reflecting the garden and blending into it, the rectilinear forms of the addition are softened by the close presence of vegetation.

Die rechtwinkligen Formen des Anbaus, die den Garten reflektieren und mit ihm verschmelzen, werden durch die nahe Vegetation gemildert.

Reflétant le jardin et fusionnant avec lui, les formes orthogonales de l'extension sont adoucies par la présence de la végétation.

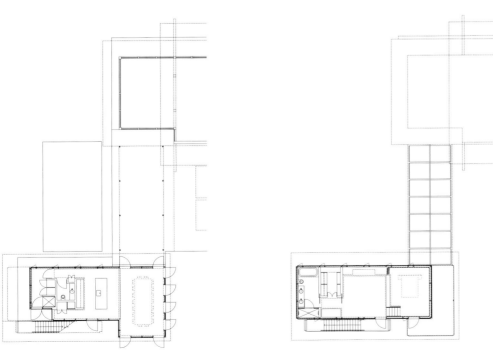

The crisp lines of the architecture are complemented by a sober choice of modern furniture. The floor to ceiling glazing means that nature is omnipresent.

Die scharfen Linien der Architektur werden durch klug gewähltes modernes Mobiliar ergänzt. Die deckenhohe Verglasung führt zur ständigen Präsenz der Natur überall im Haus.

Les lignes tendues de l'architecture sont complétées par un choix de mobilier moderne et sobre. Les vitres toute hauteur s'ouvrent sur la nature qui entoure la maison.

MOS

MOS
92 William Street
New Haven, CT 06511
USA

Tel: +1 646 797 3046
Fax: +1 866 431 3928
E-mail: info@mos-office.net
Web: www.mos-office.net

Michael Meredith was born in New York in 1971. He received his B.Arch degree from Syracuse University (1989–94) and his M.Arch from the Harvard University Graduate School of Design (1998–2000). He completed a residency at the Chinati Foundation (Marfa, Texas) in 2000. He is presently an Assistant Professor of Architecture at the Harvard GSD. Hilary Sample was born in Pennsylvania in 1971 and also attended Syracuse University (B.Arch), receiving her M.Arch from Princeton (2003). She worked in the offices of Skidmore, Owings & Merrill in New York (1997–99); and at OMA in Rotterdam (2000–02) as a project architect. She is an Assistant Professor at the Yale University School of Architecture. Michael Meredith and Hilary Sample created their present firm, **MOS**, in 2003. Their projects include the Hill House (Rochester, New York, 2003); the Huyghe + Le Corbusier Puppet Theater, Harvard University Art Museums (Cambridge, Massachusetts, 2004); the Floating House (Lake Huron, Ontario, Canada, 2006–07, published here); and the Winters Studio (Columbia County, New York, 2007, also published here), all in the USA unless stated otherwise.

Michael Meredith wurde 1971 in New York geboren. Er machte seinen B.Arch. an der Syracuse University (1989–94) und seinen M.Arch. an der Harvard University Graduate School of Design (1998–2000). 2000 folgte ein Gastaufenthalt an der Chinati Foundation (Marfa, Texas). Gegenwärtig ist Meredith Juniorprofessor für Architektur an der Harvard GSD. Hilary Sample wurde 1971 in Pennsylvania geboren und studierte ebenfalls an der Syracuse University (B.Arch.), ihren M.Arch. erhielt sie in Princeton (2003). Sie arbeitete für Skidmore, Owings & Merrill in New York (1997–99) sowie als Projektarchitektin für OMA in Rotterdam (2000–02). Sie ist Juniorprofessorin an der Architekturfakultät in Yale. Michael Meredith und Hilary Sample gründeten 2003 ihr Büro **MOS**. Zu ihren Projekten zählen u. a. das Hill House (Rochester, New York, 2003), das Huyghe + Le Corbusier Puppentheater, die Harvard University Art Museums (Cambridge, Massachusetts, 2004), das Floating House (Huronsee, Ontario, Kanada, 2006–07, hier vorgestellt) sowie das Studio Winters (Columbia County, New York, 2007, ebenfalls hier vorgestellt), alle in den USA, sofern nicht anders vermerkt.

Michael Meredith, né à New York en 1971, est B.Arch de Syracuse University (1989–94) et M.Arch de la Harvard University GSD (1998–2000). Il a bénéficié d'une résidence à la Chinati Foundation (Marfa, Texas) en 2000. Il est actuellement professeur assistant d'architecture à la Harvard GSD. Hilary Sample, née en Pennsylvanie en 1971, a également étudié à Syracuse University (B.Arch), et a passé son M.Arch à Princeton (2003). Elle a travaillé chez Skidmore, Owings & Merrill à New York (1997–99) et à l'OMA à Rotterdam (2000–02) en qualité d'architecte de projet. Elle est professeur assistant à l'école d'architecture de Yale University. Michael Meredith et Hilary Sample ont créé leur agence actuelle, **MOS**, en 2003. Parmi leurs réalisations, on peut citer la maison Hill (Rochester, New York, 2003) ; le théâtre de marionnettes Huyghe + Le Corbusier, Harvard University Art Museums (Cambridge, Massachusetts, 2004) ; la maison flottante (Lac Huron, Ontario, Canada, 2006–07, présentée ici) et le Winters Studio (comté de Columbia, New York, 2007, également présenté ici).

FLOATING HOUSE

Lake Huron, Pointe du Baril, Ontario, Canada, 2006–07

Floor area: 204 m². Client: Doug Worple. Cost: $350 000

The architects intentionally used a "vernacular house typology" with cedar siding for an unusual site, an island on Lake Huron. Since the water levels of the lake vary considerably from season to season, the house is set up on steel pontoons that allow it to move up or down with the water level. The most was made of water transport, given the remote location of the site. Thus the steel platform with its pontoons attached was towed to the lake outside the builder's workshop. The house was then brought to the site and anchored—causing it to be moved a total of 80 kilometers on the water. The architects explain that "a 'rainscreen' envelope of cedar strips condense to shelter interior space and expand to either filter light entering interior spaces or screen and enclose exterior spaces giving a modulated yet singular character to the house, while performing pragmatically in reducing wind load and heat gain." The house includes a small boat dock and an upper-floor bridge linking it to the rocky coast.

Die Architekten entschieden sich bei diesem ungewöhnlichen Grundstück, einer Insel im Huronsee, ganz bewusst für ein mit Zedernholz verblendetes „regionaltypisches Haus". Da der Wasserstand des Sees je nach Jahreszeit stark wechselt, wurde das Haus auf Stahlpontons installiert, die sich dem Wasserstand anpassen. Angesichts der abgelegenen Lage profitierte man so weit wie möglich vom Wasser als potenziellem Transportweg. So wurde die auf den Pontons montierte Stahlplattform über den See geschleppt. Schließlich wurde das Haus vor Ort gebracht und dort verankert – zu diesem Zeitpunkt hatte es bereits 80 km auf dem Wasser zurückgelegt. Die Architekten beschreiben, dass sich die „hinterlüftete Fassade aus Zedernholzlatten verdichtet, um den Innenraum zu schützen und sich öffnet, um den Lichteinfall nach innen zu regulieren. Sie dient auch zur Abschirmung bzw. Einfriedung der Außenbereiche, wodurch das Haus einen ebenso modulierten wie unverwechselbaren Charakter gewinnt und zugleich ganz pragmatisch Windlasten und Wärme reduziert". Zum Haus gehören ein kleiner Bootsanleger und eine Brücke, die die obere Etage mit der felsigen Küste verbindet.

Les architectes ont intentionnellement fait appel à une « typologie de maison vernaculaire » qu'ils ont habillée de cèdre pour ce terrain très inhabituel, une île sur le lac Huron. Comme le niveau des eaux varie considérablement d'une saison à l'autre, la maison repose sur des pontons en acier qui lui permettre de suivre ces variations. Le transport s'est fait principalement par voie d'eau, étant donné la situation reculée du terrain. La plate-forme en acier et ses pontons ont été remorqués sur le lac à partir des ateliers du constructeur. La maison a ensuite été amenée sur place et ancrée après un parcours lacustre de 80 kilomètres. Les architectes expliquent qu'« une enveloppe » écran de pluie « en lattes de cèdre protège le volume intérieur, et se dilate pour filtrer la lumière ou enclore et protéger les espaces extérieurs, ce qui confère à la maison un caractère modulaire mais singulier, tout en permettant de réduire concrètement la pression des vents et le gain solaire. » La maison intègre un petit ponton pour un bateau et une passerelle supérieure qui la relie à la côte rocheuse.

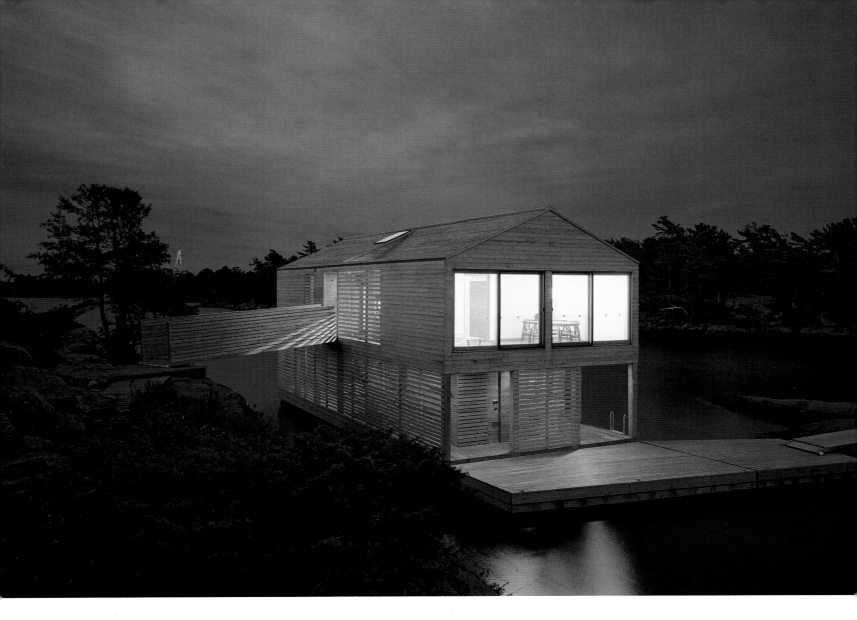

As its name implies, the Floating House, which was brought by water to its remote site, could rather easily be moved somewhere else. It is set on pontoons to compensate for varying lake levels.

Wie schon der Name sagt, wurde das Floating House auf dem Wasserweg an seinen entlegenen Standort gebracht und ließe sich ebenso problemlos an einen anderen Ort transportieren. Wegen des variierenden Wasserpegels schwimmt das Haus auf Pontons.

Comme son nom l'indique, la « maison flottante » a été transportée par voie d'eau jusqu'à son site reculé et pourrait facilement se transférer ailleurs. Elle est posée sur des pontons pour compenser les changements de niveau du lac.

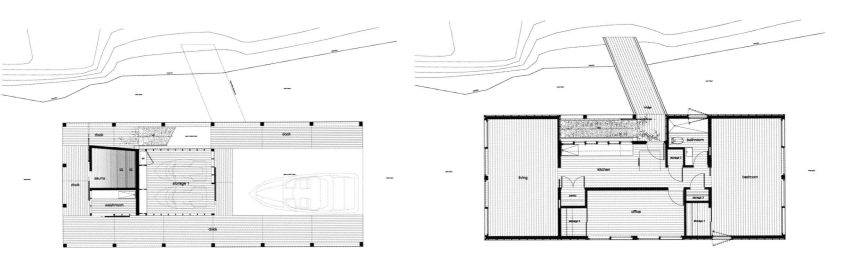

WINTERS STUDIO

Columbia County, New York, USA, 2007

Floor area: 511 m². Client: Terry Winters
Cost: not disclosed

"This project explores the idea of creating a space for both painting and drawing set against an intense landscape of shale cliffs, forest, and ponds," say the architects. Zinc panels are used for all exterior cladding, with the ends of the structure fully glazed to permit views to the hills of Taconic State Park. An angle in the glass wall allows for a covered exterior porch area. Intended for both painting and drawing, the interior is column free and allows for free movement between the disciplines of the owner. A kitchen, archives, and washroom are contained in a centrally positioned gray box with sliding panels. A concrete floor inside gives way to a ring of shale around the exterior.

Den Architekten zufolge „beschäftigt sich das Projekt mit der Idee, einen Raum zum Malen und Zeichnen zu schaffen, der in ein bemerkenswertes natürliches Umfeld aus Schieferkliffs, Wald und Teichen eingebunden ist". Die Verkleidung des Außenbaus besteht aus Zinkpaneelen, während die Kopfseiten des Baus vollständig verglast sind, um Ausblick auf die Hügellandschaft des Taconic State Park zu ermöglichen. Durch die schräge Positionierung der Glaswand entsteht eine überdachte Veranda. Der sowohl zum Malen als auch Zeichnen vorgesehene Innenraum ist stützenfrei und erlaubt dem Hausherren, sich frei zwischen den beiden Disziplinen zu bewegen. In einer zentral positionierten grauen „Box" mit Schiebetüren befinden sich Küche, Archiv und ein kleines Bad. Um den Betonfußboden im Inneren des Hauses zieht sich außen ringförmig ein Bodenbelag aus Schiefer.

« Ce projet explore l'idée d'un espace pour peindre et dessiner face à un paysage d'une grande intensité, composé de falaises de schistes, de forêts et d'étangs », expliquent les architectes. L'habillage extérieur est en panneaux de zinc tandis que les extrémités de la structure ont été entièrement vitrées pour dégager des vues sur les collines du parc d'État de Taconic. Le retrait en biais du mur de verre dégage l'emplacement d'un porche extérieur couvert. Conçu pour un artiste, l'intérieur de cet atelier sans colonnes permet à son propriétaire d'exercer ses diverses pratiques artistiques. La cuisine, les archives et une salle d'eau occupent une boîte centrale de couleur grise, fermée par des panneaux coulissants. La transition entre le sol intérieur en béton et l'extérieur se fait par une gouttière de schiste autour de la maison.

The rather simple and slightly asymmetric volume of the studio does not suggest a precise function from the exterior.

Das vergleichsweise schlichte und leicht asymmetrische Volumen des Atelierhauses verrät seine genaue Funktion von außen nicht.

Vu de l'extérieur, le volume assez simple et légèrement asymétrique ne suggère aucune fonction précise.

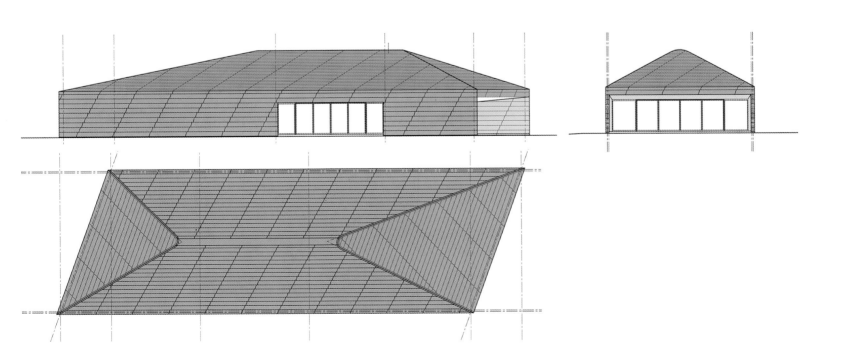

Inside the large open volume, the artist is free to dispose of his working environment as he sees fit. Ceiling lights complement the lateral natural light.

Im Innern des großen offenen Baus steht es dem Künstler frei, seinen Arbeitsraum nach Belieben einzuteilen. Deckenleuchten ergänzen das seitlich einfallende Tageslicht.

Dans ce vaste volume ouvert, l'artiste est libre d'organiser son cadre de travail comme il le souhaite. Les spots complètent l'éclairage naturel latéral.

The gray box (left) contains a washroom, kitchen and archives. Furnishings are kept to a strict minimum and, in these images, even works of art are not made readily visible.

In der grauen „Box" (links) sind ein Bad, eine Küche und ein Archiv untergebracht. Die Möblierung wurde auf das absolute Minimum reduziert und selbst Kunstwerke sind auf diesen Abbildungen kaum zu sehen.

Le bloc de couleur grise vu à gauche contient une salle d'eau, une cuisine et des archives. La présence du mobilier est minimale et, sur ces images, même les œuvres d'art sont pratiquement invisibles.

MOUNT FUJI ARCHITECTS STUDIO

Mount Fuji Architects Studio
2–44–8–801 Den-En-Chofu
Ohta-ku
Tokyo 145–0071
Japan

Tel/Fax: +81 3 3721 1018
E-mail: fuji-s@rmail.plala.or.jp
Web: www14.plala.or.jp/mfas/fuji.htm

Masahiro Harada was born in Yaidu, Shizuoka Prefecture, Japan, in 1973. He graduated with a Master's in Architecture from the Shibaura Institute of Technology, Department of Architecture, in 1997. He worked as an architect in the office of Kengo Kuma in Tokyo (1997–2000), in the office of José Antonio Martinez Lapeña and Elias Torres in Barcelona, Spain (2001–02, Japanese Government Scholarship), and finally in the office of Arata Isozaki in Tokyo as a Project Manager (2003), before establishing **MOUNT FUJI ARCHITECTS STUDIO** in 2004. He has taught since 2007 at the Shibaura Institute of Technology as an associate professor. Harada Mao was born in Sagamihara, Kanagawa Prefecture, Japan, in 1976 and graduated from the Department of Architecture, Faculty of Engineering at the Shibaura Institute of Technology in 1999, before working in the editorial office of the Workshop for Architecture and Urbanism (2000–03) and establishing Mount Fuji Architects Studio with Masahiro Harada. They have worked on the M3/KG Residence (Meguro-ku, Tokyo, 2006); the T House (Chofu-shi, Tokyo, 2006); the Sakura House (Meguro-ku, Tokyo, 2006, published here); the Okinawa Football Stadium (Okinawa Prefecture, 2006–); the E and K Houses (Tokyo, 2007–); and the Clover Building (Yokohama, 2008–), all in Japan.

Masahiro Harada wurde 1973 in Yaidu, Präfektur Shizuoka, Japan, geboren. Sein Architekturstudium schloss er 1997 am Department of Architecture des Shibaura Institute of Technology mit einem Master ab. Als Architekt war er bei Kengo Kuma in Tokio (1997–2000), im Büro von José Antonio Martinez Lapeña und Elias Torres in Barcelona, Spanien (2001–02), und schließlich bei Arata Isozaki in Tokio als Projektmanager tätig (2003), bevor er 2004 **MOUNT FUJI ARCHITECTS STUDIO** gründete. Seit 2007 lehrt er am Shibaura Institute of Technology. Harada Mao wurde 1976 in Sagamihara, Präfektur Kanagawa, Japan, geboren und schloss ihr Architekturstudium 1999 am Shibaura Institute of Technology ab, bevor sie im Verlagsbüro des Workshop for Architecture and Urbanism arbeitete (2000–03) und mit Masahiro Harada das Büro Mount Fuji Architects Studio gründete. Gemeinsam arbeiteten sie an der M3/KG Residence (Meguro-ku, Tokio, 2006), am T House (Chofu-shi, Tokio, 2006), am Sakura House (Meguro-ku, Tokio, 2006, hier vorgestellt), am Fußballstadion von Okinawa (Präfektur Okinawa, 2006–), am E House und am K House (Tokio, 2007–) sowie am Clover Building (Yokohama, 2008–), alle in Japan.

Masahiro Harada est né à Yaidu, préfecture de Shizuoka, Japon, en 1973. Il a obtenu un master en architecture au département d'architecture du Shibaura Institute of Technology, en 1997. Il a d'abord travaillé dans l'agence Kengo Kuma à Tokyo (1997–2000), puis chez José Antonio Martinez Lapeña et Elias Torres à Barcelone, Espagne (2001–02, bourse du gouvernement japonais), et finalement chez Arata Isozaki à Tokyo, comme chef de projets (2003), avant de créer **MOUNT FUJI ARCHITECTS STUDIO** en 2004. Il enseigne comme professeur associé depuis 2007 au Shibaura Institute of Technology. Harada Mao, né à Sagamihara, préfecture de Kanagawa, Japon, en 1976, est diplômé du département d'architecture de la faculté d'ingénierie du Shibaura Institute of Technology en 1999, avant d'entrer dans le bureau d'édition du Workshop for Architecture and Urbanism (2000–03) et de fonder Mount Fuji Architects Studio avec Masahiro Harada. Ils ont réalisé ensemble la résidence M3/KG (Meguro-ku, Tokyo, 2006) ; la maison T (Chofu-shi, Tokyo, 2006) ; la maison Sakura (Meguro-ku, Tokyo, 2006, présentée ici) ; le stade de football d'Okinawa (préfecture d'Okinawa, 2006–) ; les maisons E et K (Tokyo, 2007–) et le Clover Building (Yokohama, 2008–), tous au Japon.

SAKURA HOUSE

Meguro-ku, Tokyo, Japan, 2006

Site area: 131 m². Floor area: 279 m². Client: a couple
Cost: not disclosed

The annual blossoming of the cherry trees (sakura) remains an important ritual in Japan despite its congested urban environments. This house is largely closed to its environment, though the patterned openings recall cherry blossom time.

Die alljährliche Kirschblüte (sakura) bleibt in Japan trotz der drangvollen Enge der Städte ein entscheidendes Ritual. Dieses Haus verschließt sich zwar weitgehend seinem Umfeld, doch die Lochstanzungen erinnern an die Kirschblüte.

La floraison annuelle des cerisiers (sakura) reste un rituel important au Japon malgré l'expansion des villes. Autour de cette grande maison très fermée sur elle-même, les perforations rappellent le temps des cerisiers en fleurs.

This four-story home and office has a footprint of 75 m^2 and is 8.48 meters high. It is located in one of the most expensive and densely built residential areas of Tokyo. Built with reinforced concrete and a partial steel frame, it makes use of stainless-steel cladding panels on the exterior and chestnut wood flooring within. Masahiro Harada says that he thought of the "classic Glass Houses by Mies (Farnsworth House) and Philip Johnson" in conceiving Sakura (cherry blossom). Since the forested land used by Mies van der Rohe and Johnson was not available, the architect sought to replace nature with a pair of freestanding walls. Respectively 7.5 and 5 meters tall, and made with elaborately pierced 3-millimeter steel plates, these walls "filter light like sunshine through foliage, with holes punched out in a floral pattern depicting cherry blossoms, a traditional Ise paper stencil pattern." The Japanese await the blossoming of the cherry trees with great anticipation and the use of this pattern is thus a symbolic recreation of a natural setting not available in Tokyo.

Das vierstöckige Wohnhaus mit Büro hat eine Grundfläche von 75 m^2 und ist 8,48 m hoch. Es liegt in einer der teuersten und dichtest besiedelten Gegenden Tokios. Der teils als Stahlbeton- und teils als Stahlrahmenkonstruktion realisierte Bau ist außen mit Stahlplatten verblendet, innen wurden Holzböden aus Kastanie verlegt. Masahiro Harada gibt an, dass er beim Entwurf von Sakura (Kirschblüte) an die „klassischen Glasbauten von Mies (Farnsworth House) und Philip Johnson" dachte. Da ihnen die Waldlandschaften, in denen Mies van der Rohe und Johnson gebaut hatten, nicht zur Verfügung standen, entschieden sich die Architekten, die Natur durch freistehende Wände zu ersetzen. Die jeweils 7,5 m bzw. 5 m hohen Wände wurden aus 3 mm starken Stahlplatten mit Ausstanzungen gefertigt; die Wände „filtern das Licht wie Sonnenschein, der durch Laub fällt. Die Löcher wurden als florales Muster gestanzt, das Kirschblüten symbolisiert, ein traditionelles Papierschablonenmuster aus Ise." Die Japaner erwarten die Kirschblüte jedes Jahr sehnsüchtig, und so kommt die Wahl dieses Motivs der symbolischen Nachbildung einer natürlichen Umgebung gleich, die es in Tokio nicht gibt.

Ce bâtiment de 8,48 mètres de haut, comprenant une maison et un bureau répartis sur quatre niveaux, présente une emprise au sol de 75 m^2. Il se trouve dans l'un des quartiers résidentiels les plus recherchés et les plus construits de Tokyo. Édifiée en béton armé sur ossature partielle en acier, elle est habillée à l'extérieur d'un parement d'acier inoxydable et ses sols intérieurs sont en châtaignier. Masahiro Harada avoue avoir pensé aux « classiques maisons de verre de Mies (Farnsworth House) et de Philip Johnson » en concevant cette maison Sakura (fleurs de cerisier). Le cadre boisé des réalisations de Mies van der Rohe et de Johnson n'étant pas disponible, l'architecte a cherché à remplacer la nature par un couple de murs autoporteurs. Mesurant respectivement 5 et 7,5 mètres de haut, ces murs percés en tôle d'acier de 3 millimètres d'épaisseur, « filtrent la lumière comme le feuillage filtre le soleil, leurs perforations reprenant un motif floral de fleurs de cerisiers utilisé dans les pochoirs traditionnels en papier Ise ». Les Japonais attendent chaque année avec impatience l'apparition des fleurs de cerisiers et l'utilisation de ce motif recrée ainsi symboliquement le cadre naturel qui n'était pas accessible à Tokyo.

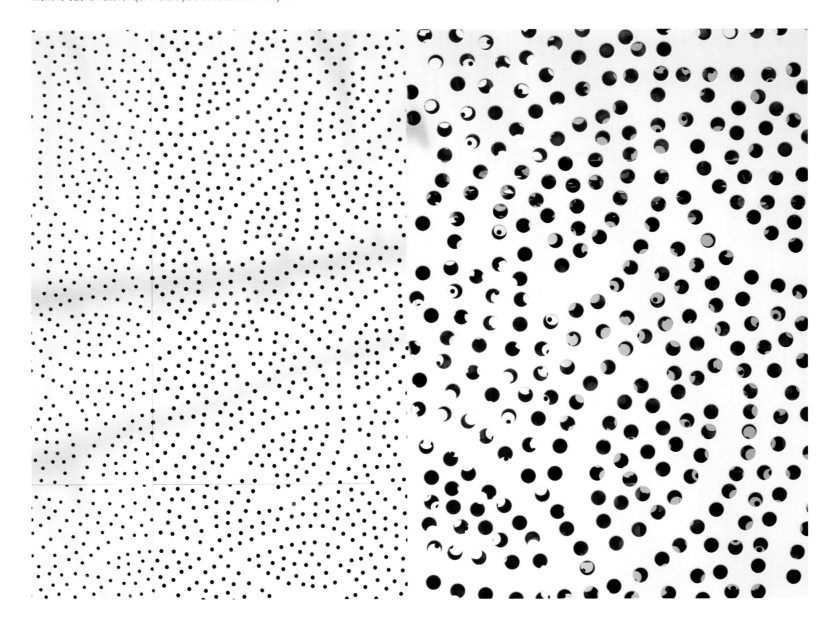

The complex perforation of the screen makes for varied light patterns, while interior spaces are lighter and more open to sky light.

Die komplexe Perforation der Wände erzeugt wandelbare Lichtmuster. Die Innenräume sind heller und lassen Licht von oben ein.

Les perforations complexes de l'écran sont de motifs variés. Les volumes intérieurs sont plus lumineux et plus ouverts vers le ciel.

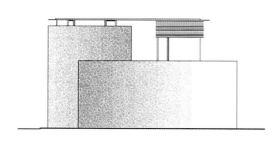

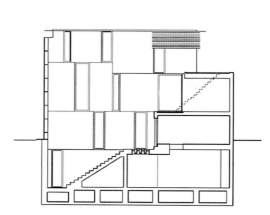

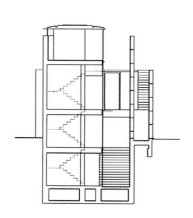

The interior of the house adapts an austere Japanese minimalism in its décor, but light is everywhere present in different forms.

Die Ausstattung der Innenräume orientiert sich am nüchternen japanischen Minimalismus, doch Licht ist überall in verschiedener Form präsent.

Pour son décor, l'intérieur de la maison a adopté un minimalisme austère, très japonais. Sous différentes formes, la lumière est omniprésente.

NIALL MCLAUGHLIN ARCHITECTS

Niall McLaughlin Architects / 39–51 Highgate Road
London NW5 1RS / UK

Tel: +44 20 74 85 91 70 / Fax: +44 20 74 85 91 71
E-mail: info@niallmclaughlin.com / Web: www.niallmclaughlin.com

NIALL MCLAUGHLIN was born in Geneva, Switzerland, in 1962. He was educated in Dublin, Ireland, and received his architectural degree from University College Dublin in 1984. He worked for Scott Tallon Walker in Dublin and London between 1984 and 1989, before establishing his own practice in 1991. He won the Young British Architect of the Year award in 1998. He is a visiting professor of architecture at University College London. **EMMA GUY** was born in Yorkshire, UK, in 1974 and studied at Magdalene College, Cambridge, and the Bartlett, University College London. She joined Seth Stein Architects in 1999 and has been at Niall McLaughlin Architects since 2001. **TIM ALLEN-BOOTH** was born in Sheffield, UK, in 1974 and studied at the University of Nottingham. After graduating in 1996 he moved to London and joined Niall McLaughlin Architects in 2006. **ANNE SCHROELL** was born in Luxembourg in 1977 and studied architecture at the Bartlett, University College London. In her "year out" she worked for Bartenbach Lichtlabor, a lighting designer in Innsbruck, Austria. After graduating from the Bartlett, she joined Tonkin Lui and then worked for De Matos Storey Ryan Architects on several private houses. In 2006 she joined Niall McLaughlin Architects. Their recent work includes Castleford Forum Museum and Library (Wakefield, 2005); a House at Piper's End (Hertfordshire, 2006–08, published here); the Café-Bar on Deal Pier (Deal, Kent, 2008); a House at Anglesea Road (Dublin, Ireland, 2008); TQ2 Bridge (Bristol, 2008); Student Accommodation and Library Buildings, Somerville College, Oxford University (Oxford, 2010); and the Alzheimer's Respite Center (Dublin, Ireland, 2009), all in the UK unless stated otherwise.

NIALL MCLAUGHLIN wurde 1962 in Genf, Schweiz, geboren. Er wuchs in Dublin auf und machte 1984 seinen Abschluss in Architektur am University College Dublin. Danach arbeitete er von 1984 bis 1989 bei Scott Tallon Walker in Dublin und London; 1991 gründete er sein eigenes Büro. 1998 wurde ihm der Young British Architect of the Year Award verliehen. McLaughlin ist Gastprofessor für Architektur am University College London. **EMMA GUY** wurde 1974 in Yorkshire geboren und studierte am Magdalene College, Cambridge, und am Bartlett University College, London. Sie arbeitete ab 1999 bei Seth Stein Architects, seit 2001 ist sie bei Niall McLaughlin Architects tätig. **TIM ALLEN-BOOTH** wurde 1974 in Sheffield geboren und studierte an der University of Nottingham. Nach seinem Abschluss 1996 zog er nach London und trat 2006 bei Niall McLaughlin Architects ein. **ANNE SCHROELL** wurde 1977 in Luxemburg geboren und studierte Architektur am Bartlett University College, London. In einem Jahr „Auszeit" arbeitete sie bei Bartenbach Lichtlabor, einer Firma für Lichtplanung in Innsbruck. Nach ihrem Abschluss am Bartlett war sie bei Tonkin Liu und dann bei De Matos Storey Ryan Architects an der Planung mehrerer privater Wohnhäuser beteiligt. 2006 trat sie bei Niall McLaughlin Architects ein. Zu den neueren Werken dieses Büros zählen Castleford Forum Museum und Bibliothek (Wakefield, 2005), ein Wohnhaus in Piper's End (Hertfordshire, 2006–08, hier veröffentlicht), ein Café mit Bar am Deal Pier (Deal, Kent, 2008), ein Wohnhaus in der Anglesea Road (Dublin, 2008), die TQ2-Brücke (Bristol, 2008), Studentenwohnungen und Bibliothek des Somerville College, Oxford University (Oxford, 2010), sowie ein Pflegeheim für Alzheimerpatienten (Dublin, 2009), alle in Großbritannien, sofern nicht anders angegeben.

Né à Genève en 1962, **NIALL MCLAUGHLIN** a grandi à Dublin. Il sort diplômé du University College à Dublin en 1984. Il a travaillé pour Scott Tallon Walker à Dublin et Londres de 1984 à 1989, avant de créer son agence en 1991. Il a remporté le prix du Jeune architecte britannique de l'année en 1998. Il est professeur d'architecture invité au University College à Londres. **EMMA GUY**, née dans le Yorkshire (Grande-Bretagne) en 1974, a étudié au Magdalene College à Cambridge et au Bartlett, University College à Londres. Elle a rejoint Seth Stein Architects en 1999, puis Niall McLaughlin Architects en 2001. **TIM ALLEN-BOOTH**, né à Sheffield (Grande-Bretagne) en 1974, a étudié à l'université de Nottingham. Après son diplôme (1996), il s'est installé à Londres et est entré chez Niall McLaughlin Architects en 2006. **ANNE SCHROELL**, née à Luxembourg en 1977, a étudié l'architecture au Bartlett, University College à Londres. Lors une année sabbatique, elle a travaillé pour Bartenbach Lichtlabor, un designer de luminaires d'Innsbruck en Autriche. Une fois diplômée du Bartlett, elle a rejoint Tonkin Lui puis De Matos Storey Ryan Architects, intervenant sur plusieurs résidences privées. En 2006, elle est entrée chez Niall McLaughlin Architects. Parmi leurs réalisations récentes : le musée et la bibliothèque du Castleford Forum (Wakefield, 2005) ; une maison à Piper's End (Hertfordshire, 2006–08, présentée ici) ; le café-bar sur Deal Pier (Deal, Kent, 2008) ; une maison à Anglesea Road (Dublin, 2008) ; le pont TQ2 (Bristol, 2008) ; des logements pour étudiants et une bibliothèque pour le Somerville College (Oxford University, 2010) ainsi qu'un Centre pour le traitement de la maladie d'Alzheimer (Dublin, 2009).

HOUSE AT PIPER'S END

Hertfordshire, UK, 2006–08

Area: 175 m²
Client: not disclosed. Cost: €600 000

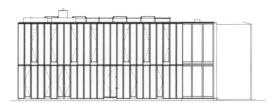  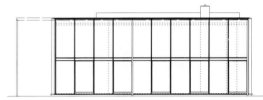

The unusual canopy poised above the house stands apart from the broadly glazed, wooden volume.

Das ungewöhnliche Vordach, das über dem Hause schwebt, hebt sich vom großzügig verglasten, hölzernen Baukörper ab.

Le curieux auvent dont la hauteur dépasse celle de la maison est détaché du volume en grande partie vitré de celle-ci.

The architects demonstrated that this house was more sustainable than refurbishing an existing building would have been. Built between an orchard and an open paddock, the structure is organized as a series of volumes: a "wooden box," a "vitrine" with the main rooms opening from a double-height space, and a steel canopy over a terrace contained by a concrete pool. The house is broadly glazed for the most part and is marked by the high, light canopy. The mixture of wood, steel, and glass makes for a very modern, transparent appearance, though shading from the sun is provided without reducing this openness.

Die Architekten haben gezeigt, dass dieses Wohnhaus zu einem viel nachhaltigeren Gebäude geworden ist, als wenn man ein bestehendes Haus modernisiert hätte. Der zwischen einer Obstplantage und einer freien Koppel errichtete Bau ist als Raumfolge angelegt: eine „hölzerne Kiste", eine „Vitrine", in der die wichtigen Räume Doppelgeschosshöhe haben, und ein Vordach aus Stahl über einer Terrasse mit dem Swimmingpool aus Beton. Das Haus ist zum großen Teil großzügig verglast, das hohe, leichte Vordach wird zu seinem Wahrzeichen. Die Verbindung von Holz, Stahl und Glas sorgt für ein sehr modernes, transparentes Erscheinungsbild, wobei ausreichend Sonnenschutz vorhanden ist, ohne diese Offenheit einzuschränken.

Les architectes ont démontré que réaliser cette maison était au final une démarche plus durable que de rénover une construction ancienne. Construite entre un verger et un paddock ouvert, la maison s'organise en une succession de volumes : « une boîte en bois », une « vitrine » organisée autour d'un volume double hauteur et un auvent en acier qui protège une terrasse bordée par une piscine en béton. La maison est généreusement vitrée dans sa plus grande partie et personnalisée par un auvent léger de grande hauteur. Le mélange de bois, d'acier et de verre lui confèrent un aspect moderne et transparent. Les protections solaires ne nuisent pas au sentiment d'ouverture.

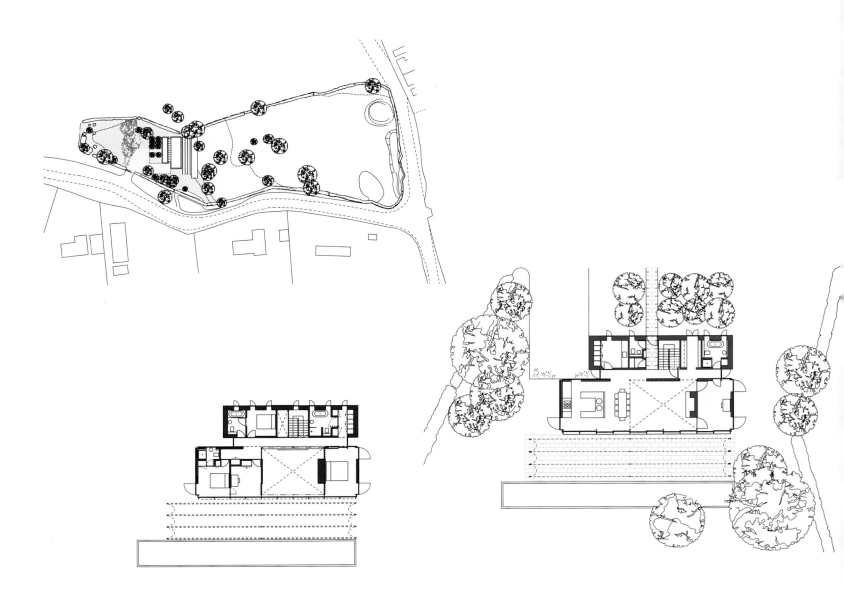

Seen in its site, and in plans, the house is composed of a staggered succession of rectangular volumes. The double-height living space has a wood-framed and fully glazed façade.

Lageplan und Grundrisse zeigen, dass das Haus aus einer gestaffelten Folge rechtwinkliger Baukörper besteht. Der doppelgeschosshohe Wohnbereich hat eine Holzrahmenkonstruktion und eine voll verglaste Fassade.

Comme le montrent les plans au sol et le plan du site, la maison se compose d'une succession de volumes rectangulaires échelonnés. Le séjour double-hauteur s'étend derrière une façade à ossature en bois entièrement vitrée.

RYUE NISHIZAWA

Office of Ryue Nishizawa
2-2-35-6B, Higashi-Shinagawa
Shinagawa-ku
Tokyo 140-0002
Japan

Tel: +81 3 3450 0117
Fax: +81 3 3450 1757
E-mail: office@ryuenishizawa.com
Web: www.ryuenishizawa.com

RYUE NISHIZAWA was born in Tokyo in 1966. He graduated from Yokohama National University with an M.Arch in 1990, and joined the office of Kazuyo Sejima & Associates in Tokyo the same year. In 1995, he established SANAA with Kazuyo Sejima, and two years later his own practice, the Office of Ryue Nishizawa. He has worked on all the significant projects of SANAA and has been a visiting professor at Yokohama National University (2001–), the University of Singapore (2003), Princeton (2006), and the Harvard GSD (2007). His work outside of SANAA includes a Weekend House (Gunma, 1998); the N Museum (Kagawa, 2005); the Moriyama House (Tokyo, 2006, published here); House A (East Japan, 2006); and the Towada Art Center (Aomori, 2006–08), all in Japan.

RYUE NISHIZAWA wurde 1966 in Tokio geboren und erhielt seinen M.Arch. 1990 an der Staatlichen Universität von Yokohama. Im gleichen Jahr trat er in das Büro Kazuyo Sejima & Associates, Tokio, ein. 1995 gründete er zusammen mit Kazuyo Sejima die Firma SANAA und zwei Jahre später ein eigenes Büro, das Office of Ryue Nishizawa. Er hat an allen bedeutenden Projekten von SANAA mitgearbeitet und war Gastprofessor an der Staatlichen Universität Yokohama (seit 2001), den Universitäten Singapur (2003), Princeton (2006) und der Harvard Graduate School of Design (2007). Von seinen Arbeiten bei SANAA abgesehen, zählen zu seinen Bauten ein Wochen-endhaus (Gunma, 1998), das Museum N (Kagawa, 2005), das Haus Moriyama (Tokio, 2006, hier veröffentlicht), das Haus A (Ostjapan, 2006) und das Kunstzentrum Towada (Aomori, 2006–08), alle in Japan.

RYUE NISHIZAWA, né à Tokyo en 1966, obtient son master d'architecture à l'université nationale de Yokohama en 1990 et rejoint l'agence de Kazuyo Sejima & Associates à Tokyo la même année. En 1995, il fonde SANAA avec Kazuyo Sejima, et deux ans plus tard sa propre agence, l'office of Ryue Nishizawa. Il a travaillé sur tous les projets importants de SANAA et a été professeur invité de l'université nationale de Yokohama (2001–), de l'université de Singapour (2003), de Princeton (2006), et la Graduate School of Design de Harvard GSD (2007). Son œuvre, en dehors de SANAA, est entièrement réalisée au Japon et comprend une résidence secondaire (Gunma, 1998) ; le N Museum (Kagawa, 2005) ; la maison Moriyama (Tokyo, 2006, présentée ici) ; la maison A (Japon oriental, 2006) et le centre artistique Towada (Aomori, 2006–08).

MORIYAMA HOUSE

Tokyo, Japan, 2002–06

Floor area: 263 m². Client: Mr. Moriyama. Cost: not disclosed
Principal Architect: Ryue Nishizawa. Associates: Ippei Takahashi, Yusuke Ohi, Kimihiko Okada

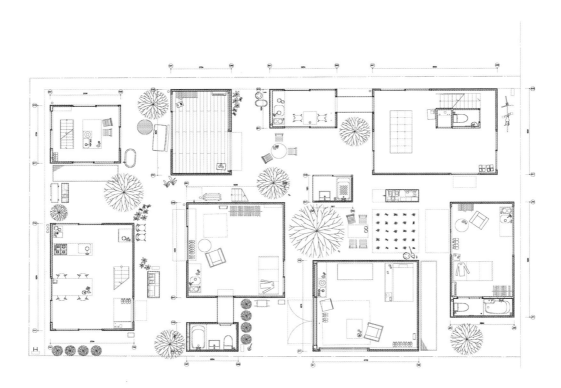

Although it is set in a rather traditional area of Tokyo, the Moriyama House is certainly not typical. Rather than a single structure, the "house" consists of a series of 10 white boxes installed on a 290-m² site. Connected individual gardens occupy the spaces between the blocks. If the structures were to be identified by letters, "A, B, C, D are occupied by the client. More specifically, A is bedrooms and a study, B the kitchen and pantry, C the living room, and D the bathroom. E is the maid's quarters. F, G + H, I, J are rental units of varying size." In an interesting play on Japanese tradition, the bathroom unit can be entered only by going outside, and it has an open glass wall. Ryue Nishizawa says of the Moriyama House, "In this house, the client is given the freedom to decide which part of this cluster of rooms is to be used as a residence or as rental rooms. He may switch among the series of living and dining rooms or use several rooms at a time according to the season or other circumstances. The domain of the residence changes in accordance with his own life." Like a small city rather than an individual residence, the Moriyama House seems likely to be occupied entirely by its owner as soon as his circumstances permit. As the architects write, "All of the buildings might some day be used by Mr. Moriyama. Currently some are rented, creating a small community of little dwellings. This group of individually proportioned buildings creates a kind of new atmosphere and a landscape in and of itself."

Obwohl es in einem eher traditionellen Viertel Tokios steht, ist dieses „Haus" alles andere als typisch. Anstelle eines einzelnen Baukörpers besteht es aus zehn weißen Kästen auf einem 290 m² großen Grundstück. Die Zwischenräume werden von miteinander verbundenen einzelnen Gartenflächen eingenommen. Wenn man die Kästen zum besseren Verständnis mit Buchstaben bezeichnet, werden „A, B, C und D vom Auftraggeber genutzt. Genauer gesagt enthält A Schlafräume und ein Arbeitszimmer, B Küche und Speisekammer, C den Wohnraum und D das Bad. In E wohnt die Hausangestellte. F, G + H, I und J sind vermietete Einheiten unterschiedlicher Größe." Das nur von außen zu betretende Bad mit einer offenen Glaswand stellt eine interessante Variante japanischer Traditionen dar. Nishizawa sagt zum Haus Moriyama:„In diesem Haus hat der Besitzer die Freiheit zu entscheiden, welcher Teil der Raumgruppen als Wohnhaus und welche als vermietete Flächen genutzt werden sollen. Er kann zwischen verschiedenen Gruppen von Wohn- und Esszimmern wechseln oder, abhängig von der Jahreszeit oder anderen Gegebenheiten, mehrere Räume gleichzeitig nutzen. Der Wohnbereich verändert sich in Einklang mit seinem eigenen Leben." Es ist anzunehmen, dass das Haus Moriyama, das eher einer kleinen Stadt als einem Einzelhaus ähnelt, ganz von ihrem Besitzer selbst bewohnt werden wird, sobald seine Verhältnisse dies erlauben. Dazu der Architekt: „Sämtliche Gebäudeteile könnten eines Tages von Herrn Moriyama genutzt werden. Zurzeit sind einige vermietet und so entstand eine begrenzte Kommune kleiner Häuser. Diese Gruppe individuell gestalteter Bauten schafft eine neue Atmosphäre und aus sich heraus eine eigene Landschaft."

Atypique bien que réalisé dans un quartier traditionnel de Tokyo, la « maison » ne se compose pas d'un seul élément mais d'une série de 10 boîtes blanches disposées sur un terrain de 290 m². Des jardins individuels occupent les espaces vides entre ces blocs et les relient. Si l'on devait identifier ces boîtes par une lettre, « A, B, C et D sont occupés par le client. A contient les chambres et un bureau, B la cuisine et le bureau, C le séjour et D la salle de bains. E est un bloc réservé à l'employée. F, G + H, I et J sont des espaces à louer de dimensions diverses ». Jeu intéressant avec la tradition japonaise, la salle de bains à mur de verre n'est accessible qu'en passant par l'extérieur. Selon Nishizawa : « Dans cette maison, le client a la liberté de décider quelle partie de cet ensemble de pièces il utilise pour y habiter ou pour louer. Il peut intervertir les pièces de séjour ou de repas ou utiliser plusieurs pièces à la fois, selon la saison ou les circonstances. Le domaine de sa résidence change en fonction de sa manière de vivre. » Davantage petite ville que maison individuelle, la maison Moriyama sera sans doute bientôt entièrement occupée par son propriétaire dès que les circonstances le permettront. Comme le précise l'architecte : « Tous les bâtiments pourraient un jour être utilisés par Mr. Moriyama. Actuellement, certains sont loués, ce qui crée une petite communauté répartie dans ces petits logements. Ce groupe d'immeubles individuellement proportionnés crée une atmosphère nouvelle, un paysage en soi. »

The Moriyama House is not a house in the traditional sense at all, but rather a series of related pavilions.

Das Haus Moriyama ist keineswegs ein Haus im herkömmlichen Sinn, sondern eher eine Abfolge miteinander verbundener Pavillons.

La maison Moriyama n'est pas une maison au sens traditionnel du terme, mais plutôt une série de pavillons reliés entre eux.

The architect refers to the size or basic form of nearby buildings, while remaining in a strictly modern gamut of shapes and finishes. White opacity is contrasted with large, glazed openings.

Der Architekt nimmt Bezug auf Größe und Grundform benachbarter Gebäude, bleibt jedoch bei einer strikt modernen Auswahl von Formen und Oberflächen. Weiße Opazität kontrastiert mit großflächigen, verglasten Öffnungen.

L'architecte se réfère aux dimensions ou formes des constructions voisines, tout en utilisant une gamme de formes et de finitions strictement modernes. Le blanc opaque contraste avec les grandes ouvertures vitrées.

NO.MAD ARQUITECTOS
EDUARDO ARROYO

Eduardo Arroyo
NO.MAD Arquitectos, S.L.P.
C/ Pez, 27–1° Izda.
28004 Madrid
Spain

Tel: +34 91 532 70 34
Fax: +34 91 522 88 47
E-mail: nomad@nomad.as
Web: www.nomad.as

EDUARDO ARROYO was born in 1964 in Bilbao and graduated from the ETSA Madrid in 1988. He was a professor in the same school from 1996 to 2002. He has also taught in universities in Seoul, Teheran, Paris, Lausanne, Eindhoven, Graz, Ferrara, Porto, Lisbon, Oslo, Brussels, Buenos Aires, Barcelona, Alicante, Valencia, and Seville. His work includes the Euskotren Headquarters (Durango, 2003); Visitors Center and Elica Hotel (Fabriano, Italy, 2003); Kaleido Restaurant (Madrid, 2004); Musée des Beaux-Arts (Lausanne; NMBA, competition entry; 2004); Housing Tower (Durango, 2004); Housing and Sports Center (Valencia, 2004); and the Estonian National Museum (Tartu, Estonia, 2005). He has also worked on urban design at El Torico Plaza (Teruel, 2005); and the access and plaza for Etxebarria Park (Bilbao, 2005). His more recent work includes Social Housing for IVVSA (Valencia, 2006); Social Housing for EMVS (Madrid, 2006); a Single-Family House (Calas, 2006); Scenic Art Center (Zarautz, 2007); Environment Improvement Systems for EDAR (Galindo, 2007); University of Economy (Vienna, Austria, 2008); Head Office for EPSA (Seville, 2008); Zafra-Uceda House (Aranjuez, 2008–09); and a Civic Center (Sestao, 2009), all in Spain unless stated otherwise.

EDUARDO ARROYO wurde 1964 in Bilbao geboren und schloss sein Studium 1988 an der ETSA Madrid ab. Von 1996 bis 2002 war er als Professor an derselben Hochschule tätig. Darüber hinaus lehrte er an Universitäten in Seoul, Teheran, Paris, Lausanne, Eindhoven, Graz, Ferrara, Porto, Lissabon, Oslo, Brüssel, Buenos Aires, Barcelona, Alicante, Valencia und Sevilla. Zu seinen Projekten zählen die Zentrale von Euskotren (Durango, 2003), das Besucherzentrum und Hotel Elica (Fabriano, Italien, 2003), das Restaurant Kaleido (Madrid, 2004), ein Wettbewerbsbeitrag für das Musée des Beaux-Arts in Lausanne (NMBA, 2004), ein Apartmenthochhaus (Durango, 2004), ein Wohn- und Sportkomplex (Valencia, 2004) sowie das Estnische Nationalmuseum (Tartu, Estland, 2005). Darüber hinaus war er an der städtebaulichen Planung der Plaza El Torico beteiligt (Teruel, 2005) sowie an der Erschließung und Platzgestaltung des Etxebarria Parks (Bilbao, 2005). Jüngste Arbeiten sind u. a. soziale Wohnbauprojekte für IVVSA (Valencia, 2006), Sozialwohnungen für EMVS (Madrid, 2006), ein Einfamilienhaus (Calas, 2006), das Centro de Artes Escenicas (Zarautz, 2007), umwelttechnische Optimierungssysteme für EDAR (Galindo, 2007), die Wirtschaftsuniversität Wien (Österreich, 2008), das Hauptkatasteramt (EPSA) in Sevilla (2008), das Haus Zafra-Uceda (Aranjuez, 2008–09) sowie ein Bürgerzentrum in Sestao (2009), alle in Spanien, soweit nicht anders angegeben.

EDUARDO ARROYO est né en 1964 à Bilbao, et a obtenu son diplôme d'architecte de l'ETSA à Madrid en 1988. Il a enseigné dans cette même école de 1996 à 2002, ainsi que dans les universités de Séoul, Téhéran, Paris, Lausanne, Eindhoven, Graz, Ferrare, Porto, Lisbonne, Oslo, Bruxelles, Buenos Aires, Barcelone, Alicante, Valence et Séville. Parmi ses réalisations : le siège d'Euskotren (Durango, Espagne, 2003) ; le centre des visiteurs et l'Elica Hotel (Fabriano, Italie, 2003) ; le restaurant Kaleido (Madrid, 2004) ; le Musée des beaux-arts (Lausanne, Suisse, NMBA, participation au concours, 2004) ; une tour de logements (Durango, 2004) ; le Musée national de l'Estonie (Tartu, Estonie, 2005). Il est également intervenu comme urbaniste sur le projet de la place d'El Torico (Teruel, 2005) ; l'accès et la place du Parc Etxebarria (Bilbao, 2005). Ses projets actuels, pratiquement tous en Espagne, comprennent des logements sociaux pour l'IVVSA (Valence, 2007) et pour l'EMVS, Madrid (2006) ; une maison familiale (Calas, 2006) ; un Centre des arts de la scène (Zarautz, 2007) ; des systèmes pour l'amélioration de l'environnement pour l'EDAR (Galindo, 2007) ; l'Université d'économie (Vienne, Autriche, 2008) ; le siège de l'EPSA (Séville, 2008) ; la maison Zafra-Uceda (Aranjuez, 2008-09) ; un Centre municipal (Sestao, 2009), tous en Espagne sauf mention contraire.

LEVENE HOUSE
San Lorenzo de El Escorial, Spain, 2002–05

Floor area: 400 m². Client: Richard Levene. Cost: €1.2 million
Collaborators: Francesco Monaco, Javier Tamer Elshiekh, Cristina Fidalgo

The astonishing forms of the house
are integrated into the existing
forest. A plan to the right shows the
complexity of the design.

*Die ungewöhnlichen Formen des Hau-
ses arrangieren sich mit den vorhandenen Bäumen. Ein Grundriss rechts
zeigt die Komplexität des Entwurfs.*

*Les formes étonnantes de la maison
s'intègrent à leur environnement
arboré. Le plan de droite expose la
complexité du projet.*

In a somewhat polemical vein, Eduardo Arroyo writes, "For the concept of this home, we asked ourselves whether we were capable of building something while maintaining the utmost respect for the natural surroundings, avoiding speaking about sustainability, alternative energy or ecology as a veneer for modernity and political correctness." The volume of the house was thus integrated into the forest and the topography. Arroyo divided the general volume into what he calls "specialized fingers," or specific programmatic elements. Two of these fingers are intended for family rooms, another for an indoor pool, another for a kitchen-dining room, and so forth. The entrance from the highest level leads down to the lowest space, the master bedroom, a gym, and sauna. Openings in the façades of the house were also determined by the presence of trees. The density of the glazing, transparent, etched, or translucent, depends on the type of light in each space, thus affirming "the influence of the forest on this strange object that has invaded the tranquility of its territory." Amber resin with wooden slats is used for floors, walls, and ceilings. "A strange feature," concludes Arroyo, "slides along the upper floors, a reflection of the owner's collector behavior. Its polycarbonate structure with iridescent sheens holds a mass of tiny inhabitants whose presence filters the boring collective exterior in a personal, non-transferable interior." The tiny inhabitants referred to are the owner's collection of Action Man toy figures.

Etwas polemisch schreibt Eduardo Arroyo: „Bei der Konzeption dieses Hauses fragten wir uns, ob wir in der Lage sein würden, etwas zu bauen und dabei den größtmöglichen Respekt für die umgebende Natur zu bewahren; außerdem wollten wir die Erwähnung von Nachhaltigkeit, alternativer Energie oder Ökologie als Fassade für Modernität und ‚political correctness' vermeiden." Also wurde die Größe des Hauses dem Wald und der Topografie angepasst. Arroyo unterteilte den Baukörper in, wie er das nennt, „spezialisierte Finger" oder spezifische programmatische Elemente. Zwei dieser Finger sind für Wohnräume vorgesehen, ein anderer für ein Schwimmbecken, ein weiterer für eine Kombination aus Küche und Esszimmer usw. Vom Eingang auf der obersten Ebene gelangt man hinunter zu den tiefliegendsten Räumlichkeiten, dem Elternschlafzimmer, einem Fitnessraum und der Sauna. Auch die Öffnungen in der Fassade wurden von der Präsenz besonderer Bäume bestimmt. Von der Dichte des Glases, ob klar, geätzt oder halb durchscheinend, hängt die Art des Lichts in jedem Raum ab und bestätigt „den Einfluss des Waldes auf dieses fremdartige Objekt, das in die Stille seines Hoheitsgebiets eingedrungen ist". Bernsteinfarbenes Harz und Holzbohlen wurden für Böden, Wände und Decken verwendet. „Eine Besonderheit", berichtet Arroyo abschließend, „bewegt sich entlang der Obergeschosse und ist Ausdruck der Sammlertätigkeit des Eigentümers. Die Struktur aus Polykarbonat mit irisierendem Glanz enthält eine große Menge winziger Bewohner, deren Präsenz das langweilige Äußere insgesamt in ein individuelles, nichtübertragbares Interieur filtert." Bei den erwähnten winzigen Bewohnern handelt es sich um des Hausherren Sammlung von Action-Man-Spielzeugfiguren.

De façon assez polémique, Eduardo Arroyo écrit : « Pour le concept de cette maison, nous nous sommes demandés si nous étions capables de construire quelque chose dans le plus grand respect pour l'environnement naturel, en évitant de parler de développement durable, d'énergies alternatives ou d'écologie, ce vernis de modernité et du politiquement correct. » Le volume de cette maison a ainsi été intégré dans la forêt et la topographie. Arroyo a divisé le volume en ce qu'il appelle des « doigts spécialisés » ou éléments programmatiques spécifiques. Deux de ces « doigts » sont destinés aux pièces familiales, un autre à une piscine intérieure, un quatrième à une cuisine-salle à manger, etc. De l'entrée, qui se fait par le haut, on descend vers le niveau inférieur, la chambre principale, une salle de gymnastique et un sauna. Les ouvertures dans les façades ont également été déterminées par la présence des arbres. La densité du verre, transparent, sablé ou translucide dépend du type de lumière nécessaire à chaque espace affirmant ainsi « l'influence de la forêt sur cet étrange objet qui a envahi la tranquillité de son territoire ». Les sols, murs et plafonds sont recouverts d'une résine ambrée et de lattes de bois. « Un élément étrange, conclut Arroyo, se glisse le long des niveaux supérieurs et illustre la passion de collectionneur du propriétaire. Cette structure en polycarbonate aux luisances iridescentes contient une foule de petits habitants dont la présence transforme cet aspect extérieur collectif et ennuyeux en un autre, intériorisé, très personnel et unique. » Ces « petits habitants » sont une collection de poupées-jouets Action-Man.

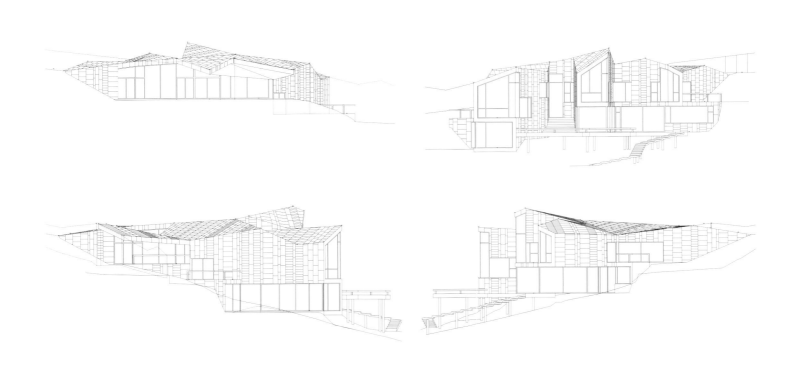

Sections reveal the density of the design and its integration into the sloped site.

Schnitte zeugen von der Kompaktheit der Bebauung und von der Art, wie sie in das Gelände integriert ist.

Coupes montrant la densité du projet et son insertion dans la pente.

Interior views demonstrate the continuity between the outside and the inside of the house and show the frequent openings to the forest setting.

Innenansichten vermitteln die Kontinuität zwischen dem Äußeren und Inneren des Hauses und zeigen insbesondere die zahlreichen Öffnungen zur bewaldeten Umgebung.

Ces vues de l'intérieur montrent la continuité entre l'extérieur et l'intérieur de la maison et, en particulier, les nombreuses ouvertures donnant sur le cadre boisé.

OLSON KUNDIG ARCHITECTS

Olson Kundig Architects
159 South Jackson Street, Suite 600
Seattle, WA 98104
USA

Tel: +1 206 624 5670
Fax: +1 206 624 3730
E-mail: newinquiry@olsonkundigarchitects.com
Web: www.olsonkundigarchitects.com

Tom Kundig received his B.A. in Environmental Design (1977) and his M.Arch (1981) from the University of Washington. He was a Principal of Jochman/Kundig (1983–84) before becoming a Principal of **OLSON KUNDIG ARCHITECTS** (since 1986). Tom Kundig is the recipient of the 2008 National Design Award in Architecture Design, awarded by the Smithsonian's Cooper-Hewitt National Design Museum. Olson Sundberg Kundig Allen Architects received the 2009 National AIA Architecture Firm Award. Aside from the Montecito Residence (Montecito, California, 2006–08) and Rolling Huts (Mazama, Washington, 2007, published here), the firm's work includes Chicken Point Cabin (Northern Idaho, 2002); the widely published Delta Shelter (Mazama, Washington, 2005); and the Hong Kong Villa (Shek-O, China, lead architect Jim Olson, 2008). Current projects include the 1900 First Avenue Hotel and Apartments (Seattle, Washington, in progress) and the T. Bailey Offices (Anacortes, Washington, in progress), all in the USA unless stated otherwise.

Tom Kundig erhielt seinen B. A. in Umweltplanung (1977) ebenso wie seinen M. Arch. (1981) an der University of Washington. Er war leitender Architekt bei Jochman/Kundig (1983–84) und ist seit 1986 Chefarchitekt bei **OLSON KUNDIG ARCHITECTS.** Tom Kundig wurde 2008 mit dem National Design Award für Architektur ausgezeichnet, der vom zur Smithsonian Institution gehörenden Cooper-Hewitt National Design Museum verliehen wird. 2009 wurde das Team mit dem Preis der AIA für Architekturbüros ausgezeichnet. Projekte des Büros sind neben der Montecito Residence (Montecito, Kalifornien, 2006–08) und den Rolling Huts (Mazama, Washington, 2007, hier vorgestellt) auch die Chicken Point Cabin (Northern Idaho, 2002), das vielfach publizierte Delta Shelter (Mazama, Washington, 2005) sowie die Hong Kong Villa (Shek-O, China, leitender Architekt Jim Olson, 2008). Zu den aktuellen Projekten zählen u. a. 1900 First Avenue Hotel and Apartments (Seattle, Washington, in Bau) sowie Büros für T. Bailey (Anacortes, Washington, in Arbeit), alle in den USA, soweit nicht anders angegeben.

Tom Kundig a obtenu son diplôme en conception environnementale (1977) et son master d'architecture (1981) de l'université de Washington. Il a été associé et dirigeant de Jochman/Kundig (1983–84), avant de devenir le dirigeant d'**OLSON KUNDIG ARCHITECTS** (depuis 1986). Tom Kundig a reçu le Prix national de conception architecturale 2008 du Smithsonian's Cooper-Hewitt National Design Museum. Olson Sundberg Kundig Allen Architects a reçu en 2009 le Prix national de l'agence d'architecture de l'année de l'AIA. En dehors de la résidence de Montecito (Montecito, Californie, 2006–08) et des huttes roulantes (Rolling Huts, Mazama, Washington, 2007, présentées ici), l'agence a également construit, entre autres, le chalet de Chicken Point (Chicken Point Cabin, nord de l'Idaho, 2002) ; l'abri du Delta , qui a fait l'objet d'un grand nombre de publications (Delta Shelter, Mazama, Washington, 2005) ; et une villa à Hong-Kong (Shek-O, Chine, architecte de projet : Jim Olson, 2008). Parmi leurs projets actuels figurent le 1900 First Avenue Hotel and Apartments (Seattle, Washington, en chantier) et les bureaux T. Bailey (Anacortes, Washington, en chantier).

ROLLING HUTS

Mazama, Washington, USA, 2007

Area: 19 m² (interior); 41 m² (interior plus deck)
Client: Michal Friedrich. Cost: not disclosed

A number of the Rolling Huts set in a former Washington camping ground. With their slanted roofs and light structures, these rolling residences address numerous ecological concerns.

Eine Gruppe von Rolling Huts auf einem ehemaligen Campingplatz im Staat Washington. Mit ihren geneigten Dächern und der leichten Konstruktion werden die rollenden Domizile gleich mehreren ökologischen Anliegen gerecht.

Quelques huttes roulantes dans un ancien terrain de camping de l'État de Washington. Ces maisonnettes sur roues de structure légère et toiture à simple pente répondent à de nombreuses préoccupations écologiques.

Intended as guest housing for friends and family, these structures are described by the architect as being "several steps above camping, while remaining low-tech and low-impact in their design." Installed on a former camping site, the Rolling Huts are meant to allow the mountain meadow where they are located to return to its natural state. Raised up on wheels, the structures are little more than steel-clad boxes set on steel and wood platforms. Double-paned sliding glass doors provided access to the small interior space where cork and plywood are the main materials. Facilities such as showers and parking space are located in a nearby barn. Tom Kundig states: "The huts evoke Thoreau's simple cabin in the woods; the structures take second place to nature."

Die als Gästehäuser für Freunde und Verwandte gedachten Hütten liegen laut Architekt „ein paar Klassen über Campingniveau, sind aber dennoch mit nur minimaler Technik ausgestattet und auf minimalen Umwelteingriff ausgelegt". Die Rolling Huts (rollende Hütten) befinden sich auf einem ehemaligen Campingplatz und sollen sicherstellen, dass sich die Bergwiese, auf der sie stehen, in ihren ursprünglichen Zustand zurückentwickeln kann. Die auf Rädern montierten Hütten sind kaum mehr als stahlverkleidete Boxen und ruhen auf einer Plattform aus Stahl und Holz. Schiebetüren mit Isolierverglasung bieten Zugang zum kleinen Innenraum, der überwiegend mit Kork und Sperrholz ausgebaut wurde. Einrichtungen wie Duschen und Parkplätze befinden sich in einer nahe gelegenen Scheune. Tom Kundig erklärt: „Die Hütten lassen an Thoreaus schlichte Hütte im Wald denken; diese Bauten ordnen sich der Natur unter."

Prévues pour des amis ou la famille du client, ces petites constructions sont présentées par les architectes comme « plusieurs niveaux au-dessus d'un camping, mais techniquement simples et sans beaucoup d'impact sur l'environnement grâce à leur conception ». Implantées sur un ancien terrain de camping, ces « huttes » devraient permettre le retour de la prairie à son état naturel si elles devaient être déplacées. Ce sont essentiellement des boîtes habillées de tôle d'acier, reposant sur des plates-formes en bois et acier montées sur roues. Des portes à double vitrage coulissantes donnent accès au volume intérieur où règnent le contreplaqué et le liège. Les installations comme les douches ou les emplacements de parking sont regroupées dans une grange voisine. « Ces huttes évoquent la cabane dans les bois de Thoreau. La construction vient en second plan par rapport à la nature », explique Tom Kundig.

In a summer setting, the wheels of the Rolling Huts are visible, making clear their minimal impact on the site.

Im Sommer sind auch die Räder der Rolling Huts zu sehen, anhand derer der minimale Eingriff in die Landschaft deutlich wird.

Dispersées dans un cadre estival, les huttes roulantes dévoilent leurs roues, qui limitent leur impact sur le sol.

The Rolling Huts have a rather sophisticated, mountain cabin feeling about them inside, with large, glazed surfaces and a wood-burning stove, as seen in the image below.

Der Innenraum einer Rolling Hut mit seinen großen Glasfronten und einem Holzofen lässt an eine eher anspruchsvolle Berghütte denken (Foto unten).

L'intérieur bénéficie d'une atmosphère assez sophistiquée de chalet de montagne. Elles sont équipées de grandes baies vitrées et d'un poêle à bois (ci-dessous).

PATKAU ARCHITECTS

Patkau Architects
1564 West 6th Avenue
Vancouver, BC, V6J 1R2
Canada

Tel: + 1 604 683 7633
Fax: + 1 604 683 7634
E-mail: info@patkau.ca
Web: www.patkau.ca

Patkau Architects was founded by **JOHN AND PATRICIA PATKAU** in 1978. John Patkau received a Bachelor of Environmental Studies (University of Manitoba, Canada, 1969), and his M.Arch degree from the same institution in 1972. Patricia Patkau holds a Bachelor of Interior Design (University of Manitoba, 1973), and an M.Arch degree from Yale University (1978). In addition to the practice, she is a Professor Emerita in the School of Architecture at the University of British Columbia, where she has taught since the 1980s. The firm also has three associates—David Shone, Peter Suter, and Greg Boothroyd. Completed projects include the Aquatic Ecosystems Research Laboratory (University of British Columbia, Vancouver, British Columbia, 2002–05); the Winnipeg Centennial Library Addition (Winnipeg, Manitoba, 2002–05); Mishrifah Villa (Ad'Diriyyah, Saudi Arabia, 2007); the Beaty Biodiversity Center (University of British Columbia, Vancouver, British Columbia, 2005–09); and the Linear House (Salt Spring Island, British Columbia, 2006–09, published here). Their current projects include the Goldring Center for High Performance Sport at the University of Toronto (Toronto, 2010); the School of Art Building at the University of Manitoba (Winnipeg, Manitoba, 2011); Fort York National Historic Site Visitor Center (Toronto, 2012 completion); and Cottages at Fallingwater (Bear Run, Pennsylvania, USA, 2011–), all in Canada unless stated otherwise.

Das Büro Patkau Architects wurde 1978 von **JOHN UND PATRICIA PATKAU** gegründet. John Patkau erwarb 1969 einen Bachelor of Environmental Studies (University of Manitoba, Kanada) und 1972 den M.Arch an derselben Universität. Patricia Patkau hat einen Bachelor of Interior Design (University of Manitoba, 1973) und einen M.Arch. von der Yale University (1978). Außer der praktischen Tätigkeit hat sie eine Professur an der School of Architecture der University of British Columbia, wo sie seit den 1980er Jahren lehrt. Drei weitere Architekten – David Shone, Peter Suter und Greg Boothroyd – sind mit dem Büro assoziiert. Zu dessen ausgeführten Projekten zählen: das Aquatic Ecosystems Research Laboratory (University of British Columbia, Vancouver, British Columbia, 2002–05); der Neubau der Winnipeg Centennial Library (Winnipeg, Manitoba, 2002–05); das Beaty Biodiversity Center (University of British Columbia, Vancouver, British Columbia, 2005–09) und das Linear House (Salt Spring Island, British Columbia, 2006–09, hier veröffentlicht). Aktuelle Projekte sind: das Goldring Center for High Performance Sport an der University of Toronto (Toronto, Ontario), das School of Art Building an der University of Manitoba (Winnipeg, Manitoba), die Villa Mishrifah (Ad'Diriyyah, Saudi- Arabien); das Besucherzentrum auf dem Fort York National Historic Site (Toronto) sowie Ferienhäuser in Fallingwater (Bear Run, Pennsylvania, USA), alle in Kanada, sofern nicht anders angegeben.

L'agence Patkau Architects a été fondée par **JOHN ET PATRICIA PATKAU** en 1978. John Patkau est titulaire d'un diplôme en études environnementales (Université du Manitoba, Canada, 1969) et d'un master en architecture de la même institution (1972). Patricia Patkau est diplômée en architecture intérieure (Université du Manitoba, 1973) et a un master en architecture de l'université de Yale (1978). Elle est également professeure à l'École d'architecture de l'université de Colombie britannique depuis les années 1980. L'agence a trois autres associés : David Shone, Peter Suter et Greg Boothroyd. Parmi leurs réalisations figurent le laboratoire de recherches sur les écosystèmes aquatiques (Université de Colombie britannique, Vancouver, 2002–05) ; l'extension de la Bibliothèque du centenaire de Winnipeg (Winnipeg, Manitoba, 2002–05) ; Le Centre sur la biodiversité Beaty (Université de Colombie britannique, Vancouver, 2005–09) et la maison lineaire (Salt Spring Island, Colombie britannique, 2006–09, présentée ici). Leurs projets actuels, tous au Canada sauf mention contraire, comprennent : le Centre Golding pour les sports de haute performance à l'Université de Toronto (Toronto) ; le bâtiment de l'École d'art de l'Université du Manitoba (Winnipeg, Manitoba) ; la villa Mishrifah (Ad'Diriyyah, Arabie saoudite) ; le Centre des visiteurs du site historique national de Fort York (Toronto) et les cottages à Fallingwater (Bear Run, Pennsylvanie, États-Unis).

LINEAR HOUSE

Salt Spring Island, British Columbia, Canada, 2006–09

Area: 340 m²
Cost: not disclosed. Client: not disclosed

Salt Spring Island is located in the Strait of Georgia between Vancouver and the mainland of British Columbia. The site of the house is a 6.5-hectare farm with a large row of Douglas fir trees in the middle and an orchard with fruit trees. A barn, garage, and studio built previously on the site were maintained. The low, 84-meter-long structure is located to the south of the fir trees. A covered walkway marks the side of the house that faces the orchard. The architects explain that the "full extent of the house is never directly experienced from the exterior. That experience is of a dark stealth-like figure sliding in and out behind the screens of trees on either side." Charcoal-colored fiber-cement panels contribute to the "invisibility" of the structure against the background of the trees. Translucent acrylic panels are used as a cladding material for the interior, and more than 40 skylights bring natural light into the house. Roof canopies reach out as much as 8.5 meters over the facades while glazed openings reach a length of nearly 24 meters. Glazed door panels can be retracted in summer, opening the house fully to its environment.

Salt Spring Island liegt in der Strait of Georgia zwischen Vancouver und dem Festland von British Columbia. Das Haus steht auf dem Gelände einer 6,5 Hektar großen Farm mit einer zentralen, langen Reihe von Douglastannen und einem Obstgarten. Eine bereits früher errichtete Scheune, eine Garage und ein Atelier blieben erhalten. Der niedrige, 84 Meter lange Neubau liegt im Süden der Baumreihe. Die zum Obstgarten orientierte Fassade kennzeichnet ein überdachter Gang. Die Architekten erklären, dass "das ganze Ausmaß des Hauses von außen gar nicht ablesbar ist. Vielmehr wirkt es wie eine dunkle, verborgene Figur, die auf beiden Seiten hinter der Wand aus Bäumen auftaucht". Anthrazitfarbige Faserzementplatten erhöhen die "Unsichtbarkeit" des Gebäudes vor dem Hintergrund der Bäume. Die Innenräume sind mit licht-durchlässigen Acrylplatten verkleidet, und durch über 40 Oberlichter fällt natürliches Licht in das Haus. Das Dach kragt bis zu 8,5 Meter über die Fassaden aus, während die verglasten Öffnungen eine Länge bis zu 24 Metern erreichen. Die Glastüren lassen sich im Sommer aufschieben und öffnen das Haus total zu seiner Umgebung.

L'île de Salt Spring est située dans le détroit de Géorgie entre l'île de Vancouver et le continent (Colombie britannique). Le site de la maison est un terrain agricole de 6,5 hectares traversé en son centre par une rangée de majestueux pins Douglas et possédant un verger. Une grange, un garage et un atelier déjà existants ont été conservés. La construction sur un seul niveau de 84 mètres de long est implantée au sud de l'alignement de pins. Un passage couvert longe le côté de la maison face au verger. Selon les architectes : « De l'extérieur on n'appréhende jamais la maison dans toute sa dimension. On découvre seulement une sombre présence fantomatique qui apparaît et disparait des deux côtés derrière des écrans d'arbres. » Des panneaux en fibrociment de couleur carbone contribuent à « l'invisibilité » du bâtiment sur le fond des arbres. Des panneaux en acrylique translucide habillent l'intérieur éclairé par plus de 40 verrières zénithales. Les auvents atteignent jusqu'à 8,5 mètres de profondeur tandis que les immenses baies vitrées mesurent près de 24 mètres de long. Des portes vitrées peuvent être repliées en été pour ouvrir totalement la maison sur son environnement.

As seen from a distance, the residence fully deserves the reference to a "linear" design in its name. The thick roof bar appears to hover over fully glazed surfaces.

Wie aus der Entfernung zu sehen, trifft die Bezeichnung „lineare" Planung für dieses Wohnhaus absolut zu. Das schwere Dachelement scheint über den voll verglasten Flächen zu schweben.

Vue d'une certaine distance, la maison mérite pleinement son nom de « linéaire ». L'épaisse toiture semble flotter au-dessus de pans de verre.

The powerful, cantilevered forms of the ends of the house give it a sculptural resonance that is not readily apparent in plan or even elevation (below).

Die kraftvollen, seitlich auskragenden Formen geben dem Hause eine plastische Wirkung, die weder im Grundriss noch in der Ansicht (unten) klar erkennbar ist.

Les puissants porte-à-faux des deux extrémités de la maison lui confèrent un style sculptural qui n'apparaît pas vraiment dans le plan, ni même dans les élévations (ci-dessous).

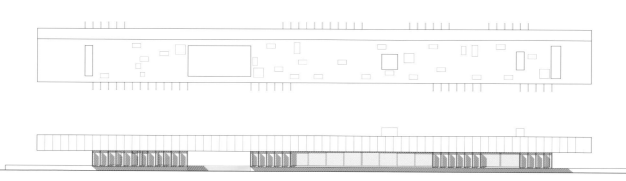

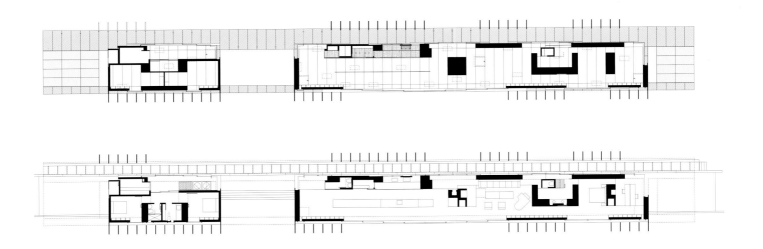

Revealing the spectacular natural setting like a low, flat arch, the house plays on a willful contrast of opaque solidity and airy transparency.

Das Haus erschließt sein spektakuläres natürliches Umfeld wie ein niedriger, flacher Bogen und spielt mit dem bewusst angestrebten Kontrast von undurchlässiger Geschlossenheit und luftiger Transparenz.

Sorte d'arc surbaissé tendu dans un cadre naturel spectaculaire, la maison joue sur un contraste harmonieux entre solidité opaque et transparence aérienne.

Glazed surfaces or sliding panels
allow the house to be transformed
from a more closed and protected
configuration to an open one in
summer.

Mittels verglaster Flächen oder verschiebbarer Tafeln lässt sich das
Haus im Sommer von einer geschlossenen und geschützten Form in eine
offene verwandeln.

Des baies vitrées et des panneaux
coulissants permettent à la maison de
passer d'une configuration assez fermée et protégée à une autre plus
ouverte, pour l'été.

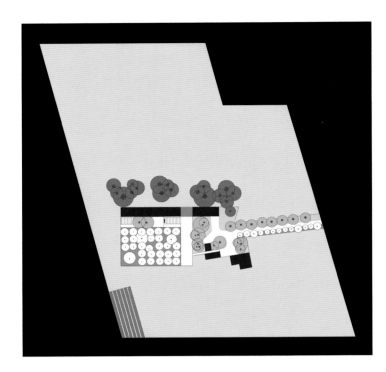

Strict interior design allows even areas like the kitchen space, seen below, to benefit from a spectacular opening onto the natural setting, provided for by folding panels. Left, a site plan including trees.

Die strenge Innenarchitektur macht es möglich, dass auch Bereiche wie die unten gezeigte Küche von der spektakulären Öffnung durch Klapptafeln zum natürlichen Umfeld profitieren.

La rigueur de l'aménagement intérieur offre à toutes les pièces, et même à la cuisine, des perspectives spectaculaires sur le cadre naturel, grâce à des panneaux coulissants. À gauche, un plan du terrain incluant les arbres.

Kitchen space transitions seamlessly into an area that can be used as a desk and bookshelf area, the whole opening directly onto the outdoors.

Die Küche geht nahtlos in einen Raum über, der zum Schreiben oder zur Unterbringung von Büchern genutzt werden kann; der gesamte Bereich ist direkt nach außen geöffnet.

L'espace de la cuisine se transforme sans heurts en un espace qui peut servir de bureau et de bibliothèque, le tout s'ouvrant directement sur l'extérieur.

JOHN PAWSON

John Pawson
Unit B
70–78 York Way
London N1 9AG
UK

Tel: +44 20 7837 2929
Fax: +44 20 7837 4949
E-mail: email@johnpawson.co.uk
Web: www.johnpawson.com

Born in Halifax in central England in 1949, **JOHN PAWSON** attended Eton and worked in his own family's textile mill before going to Japan for four years. On his return, he studied at the Architectural Association (AA) in London and set up his own firm in 1981. He has worked on numerous types of project, including the flagship store for Calvin Klein in New York, airport lounges for Cathay Pacific Airlines at the Chek Lap Kok Airport in Hong Kong, and a small apartment for the author Bruce Chatwin. Pawson may be even better known to the general public because of his 1996 book *Minimum,* which focused on such essential subjects as light, structure, ritual, landscape, and volume. Because of this book, but also for his style, Pawson has come to be considered an essential figure in the minimalist style of recent years. Some of his recent work includes: Tetsuka House (Tokyo, 2003–06, published here); Monastery of Novy Dvûr (Touzim, Czech Republic, 2004); Lansdowne Apartments (London, 2004); Baron House (Skane, Sweden, 2005); Sackler Crossing, Royal Botanic Gardens, Kew (Surrey, UK, 2006); Klein Apartment (New York, 2006); 50 Gramercy Park North (New York, 2007). He also worked on the Hotel Puerta America in Madrid.

Der 1949 in Halifax, England, geborene **JOHN PAWSON** besuchte Eton und arbeitete in der Textilfabrik seiner Familie, ehe er für vier Jahre nach Japan ging. Nach seiner Rückkehr studierte er an der AA in London und eröffnete 1981 sein eigenes Büro. Er war mit vielgestaltigen Projekten befasst, darunter der Flagship Store von Calvin Klein in New York, Flughafenlounges für Cathay Pacific am Flughafen Chek Lap Kok in Hongkong sowie ein kleines Apartment für den Schriftsteller Bruce Chatwin. Der Allgemeinheit ist Pawson besser bekannt wegen seines 1996 erschienenen Buchs *Minimum,* in dem er sich mit solch grundsätzlichen Themen wie Licht, Struktur, Ritual, Landschaft und Raum beschäftigt. Wegen dieses Buchs, aber auch wegen seines Stils gilt Pawson inzwischen als wesentlicher Vertreter des Minimalismus der letzten Jahre. Zu seinen neueren Projekten gehören: Haus Tetsuka (Tokio, 2003–06, hier publiziert); Kloster Novy Dvûr (Touzim, Tschechische Republik, 2004); Lansdowne Apartments (London, 2004); Haus Baron (Skane, Schweden, 2005); Sackler Crossing, Royal Botanic Gardens, Kew (Surrey, Großbritannien, 2006); Apartment Klein (New York, 2006); 50 Gramercy Park North (New York, 2007). Darüber hinaus arbeitete er am Hotel Puerta America in Madrid.

Né à Halifax en Angleterre en 1949, **JOHN PAWSON**, après des études à Eton, travaille dans l'usine textile familiale avant de séjourner quatre ans au Japon. À son retour, il étudie à l'Architectural Association de Londres et crée son agence en 1981. Il est intervenu sur de nombreux types de projets dont le principal magasin de Calvin Klein à New York, les salons de l'aéroport de Chek Lap Kok à Hongkong pour Cathay Pacific ou un petit appartement pour l'écrivain Bruce Chatwin. Il est peut-être surtout connu du grand public à travers le succès de son livre *Minimum* (1996) sur les thèmes de la lumière, de la structure, du rituel, du paysage et du volume. À la suite de ce livre, mais aussi parce que c'est son style, il a été considéré comme une figure essentielle du minimalisme contemporain. Parmi ses réalisations récentes : la maison Tetsuka, Tokyo (2003–06) présentée ici ; le monastère de Novy Dvûr, Touzim, République Tchèque (2004) ; Lansdowne Apartments, Londres (2004) ; la maison Baron, Skane, Suède (2005) ; passerelle Sackler, Royal Botanic Gardens, Kew, Surrey, Grande-Bretagne (2006) ; appartement Klein, New York (2006) ; 50 Gramercy Park North, New York (2007). Il a également participé aux aménagements de l'Hotel Puerta America à Madrid.

TETSUKA HOUSE

Tokyo, Japan, 2003–06

Floor area: 181 m². Client: Tetsuka
Cost: not disclosed

Located in the Setagaya area of Tokyo on a 195-m² site, the Tetsuka House is described by the architect as a "pristine box" containing a Japanese tearoom and double-height open courtyard as well as living space. Concrete with two different gray tints was used to underline the internal division between the ground and upper floors. The windows are carefully placed to offer very specific views. Cooking, dining, and relaxation spaces are "incorporated within three functionally distinct but spatially fluid zones." The tearoom, located alongside the courtyard, also serves as guest space. Pawson chose not to adhere strictly to all aspects of conventional teahouse design in this instance, but he affirms that it "stays true to its essence." The main bedroom includes an outdoor terrace. A traditional Japanese bathtub was used, creating another link between Pawson's minimal design aesthetic and Japanese culture. The architect seems quite at ease in this environment because his form of modernity has its roots in the architecture of Japan.

Das auf einem 195 m² großen Grundstück im Setayaga-Viertel von Tokio stehende Haus Tetsuka wird vom Architekten als ein »unverfälschter Kasten« beschrieben, der einen japanischen Teeraum, einen zweigeschossigen, offenen Innenhof sowie Wohnräume enthält. Zur Unterstreichung der inneren Trennung zwischen Erdgeschoss und Obergeschossen wurde Beton in zwei verschiedenen Grautönen verwendet. Die Fenster sind überlegt platziert, um ganz bestimmte Ausblicke zu bieten. Räumlichkeiten zum Kochen, Essen und Entspannen wurden „in drei funktional unterschiedliche, gleichwohl räumlich fließende Zonen integriert". Der am Innenhof gelegene Teeraum dient darüber hinaus als Gästezimmer. In diesem Fall entschied Pawson, sich nicht streng an alle Regeln konventioneller Teehausgestaltung zu halten, versichert jedoch, dass der Raum „seinem Wesen treu bleibe". Zum Hauptschlafzimmer gehört eine Außenterrasse. Im Haus befindet sich eine traditionelle japanische Badewanne, durch die eine weitere Verbindung zwischen Pawsons minimaler Designästhetik und japanischem Brauchtum entsteht. Augenscheinlich fühlt sich der Architekt in diesem Umfeld ganz zu Hause, wohl weil seine Ausprägung der Moderne viele Wurzeln in der Architektur Japans hat.

Située dans le quartier de Setagaya à Tokyo sur un terrain de 195 m², la maison Tetsuka est décrite par l'architecte comme une « pure boîte » contenant une maison de thé japonaise, une cour ouverte double hauteur et des espaces de vie. Le béton en deux tons de gris différents souligne la division interne entre le rez-de-chaussée et l'étage. Les fenêtres sont implantées avec soin selon des vues très calculées. La cuisine, les repas et les espaces de détente sont « intégrés dans trois zones spatialement fluides mais fonctionnellement distinctes ». La maison de thé, le long de la cour, sert également d'espace de réception. Pawson a choisi de ne pas respecter strictement toutes les règles de la conception traditionnelle d'une maison de thé, mais affirme « qu'elle est authentique dans son essence ». La chambre principale se prolonge sur une terrasse extérieure. Une baignoire japonaise traditionnelle crée un lien supplémentaire entre l'esthétique minimaliste de l'architecte et les coutumes nippones. Pawson est très à l'aise dans cet environnement car sa forme de modernité trouve de multiples racines dans l'architecture du Japon.

John Pawson is known for his minimalist aesthetic. In the case of Japan, there is a natural continuity between this form of modernity and local building traditions.

Pawson ist bekannt für seine minimalistische Ästhetik. In Japan besteht eine natürliche Kontinuität zwischen dieser Ausprägung der Moderne und heimischen Traditionen.

John Pawson est connu pour son esthétique minimaliste. Pour ce qui est du Japon, on observe une continuité naturelle entre cette modernité et les traditions locales.

The external appearance of the house is as minimalist as its interior, providing privacy for the residents, while admitting ample natural light.

Das äußere Erscheinungsbild des Hauses ist ebenso minimalistisch wie sein Interieur, das den Bewohnern ihre Privatsphäre bietet und doch zugleich reichlich Tageslicht einfallen lässt.

L'aspect extérieur de la maison est aussi minimaliste que ses aménagements intérieurs. Elle assure une grande intimité à ses occupants tout en laissant pénétrer généreusement la lumière naturelle.

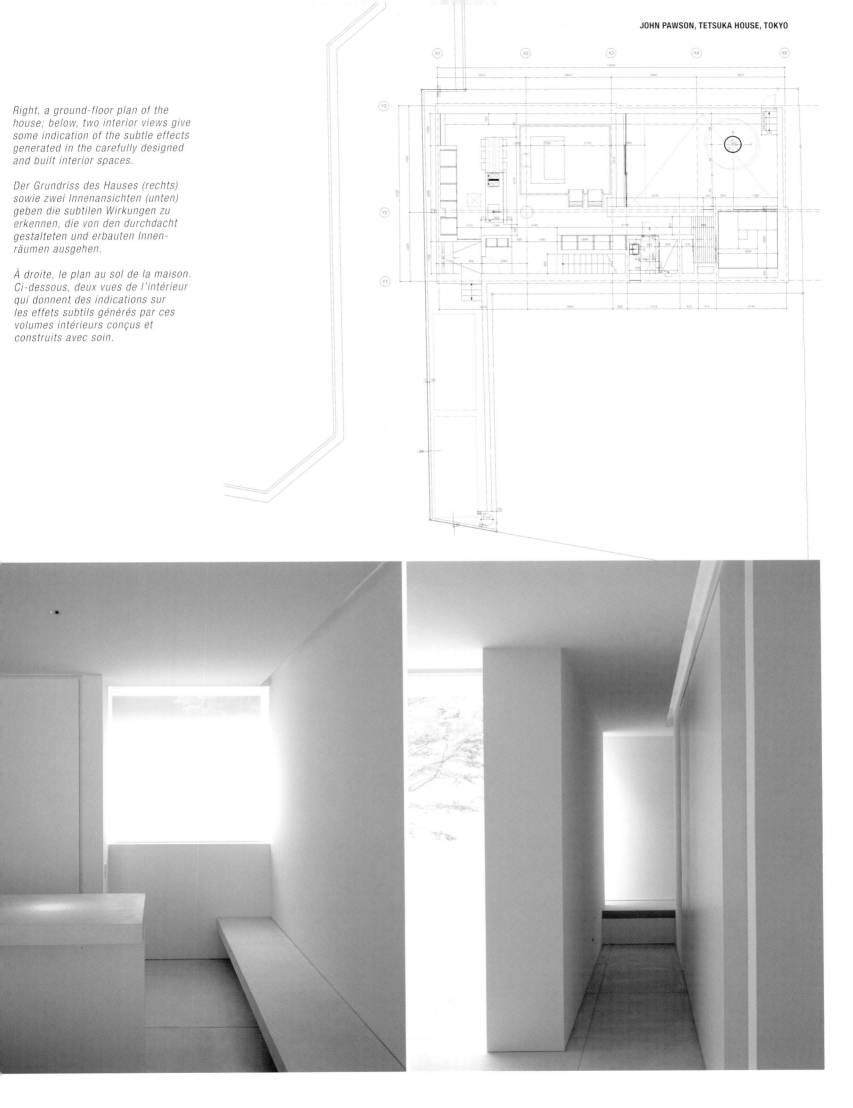

Right, a ground-floor plan of the house; below, two interior views give some indication of the subtle effects generated in the carefully designed and built interior spaces.

Der Grundriss des Hauses (rechts) sowie zwei Innenansichten (unten) geben die subtilen Wirkungen zu erkennen, die von den durchdacht gestalteten und erbauten Innenräumen ausgehen.

À droite, le plan au sol de la maison. Ci-dessous, deux vues de l'intérieur qui donnent des indications sur les effets subtils générés par ces volumes intérieurs conçus et construits avec soin.

ARSENIO PÉREZ AMARAL

Corona y P. Amaral Arquitectos
Avda. Los Pescaditos
Edif. Litoral Oficina 1 Maria Jiménez
38180 Santa Cruz de Tenerife
Spain

Tel: +34 922 598 002
Fax: +34 922 596 829
E-mail: estudio@coronaypamaral.com
Web: www.coronaypamaral.com

ARSENIO PÉREZ AMARAL was born in Santa Cruz de Tenerife in 1958. He received his degree as an architect from the ETSA in Madrid in 1982. He did post-graduate work at Cornell (1983), before becoming a partner in the firm N Tres Arquitectos (1984–2002). He was a founding partner of Corona y P. Amaral Arquitectos. He was a Guest Professor at the Escuela de Arquitectura de Las Palmas de Gran Canaria (2006–07). His recent work includes the Jet Foil Maritime Station (Santa Cruz de Tenerife, 1989); Tenerife North Airport (La Laguna, Tenerife, 2002); Central Workshop and Offices of Ground Transportation System (Santa Cruz de Tenerife, 2002); 270 Dwelling Building (Santa Cruz de Tenerife, 2003); 99 Los Molinos Building (Santa Cruz de Tenerife, 2003); and Jardín Del Sol House (Tacoronte, Tenerife, 2003–05, published here).

ARSENIO PÉREZ AMARAL wurde 1958 in Santa Cruz de Tenerife geboren. Er schloss sein Architekturstudium 1982 an der ETSA in Madrid ab. An der Cornell University setzte er seine Studien 1983 fort und wurde dann Partner im Büro N Tres Arquitectos (1984–2002). Er war Gründungspartner von Corona y P. Amaral Arquitectos. Von 2006 bis 2007 hatte er eine Gastprofessur an der Escuela de Arquitectura de Las Palmas de Gran Canaria inne. Zu seinen Bauten gehören: Jet Foil Maritime Station (Santa Cruz de Tenerife, 1989), Nordflughafen auf Teneriffa (La Laguna, Teneriffa, 2002), Zentralwerkstatt und Büros des Bodentransportsystems (Santa Cruz de Tenerife, 2002), Wohnanlage 270 (Santa Cruz de Tenerife, 2003), Wohnanlage Los Molinos 99 (Santa Cruz de Tenerife, 2003) sowie die Casa Jardín del Sol (Tacoronte, Teneriffa, 2003–05, hier vorgestellt).

ARSENIO PÉREZ AMARAL, né à Santa Cruz de Tenerife in 1958, est architecte diplômé de l'ETSA à Madrid (1982). Il fait des études supérieures à Cornell (1983) avant d'entrer comme partenaire dans l'agence N Tres Arquitectos (1984–2002). Il est associé fondateur de Corona y P. Amaral Arquitectos. Il a été professeur invité à la Escuela de Arquitectura de Las Palmas de Gran Canaria (2006–07). Parmi ses réalisations : la gare maritime d'hydroglisseurs de Santa Cruz de Tenerife (1989) ; l'aéroport nord de Tenerife, La Laguna, Tenerife (2002) ; les ateliers et bureaux du réseau de transports en commun de Santa Cruz de Tenerife (2002) ; un immeuble de 270 logements, Santa Cruz de Tenerife (2003) ; l'immeuble du 99 Los Molinos, Santa Cruz de Tenerife (2003) et la maison Jardín del Sol, Tacoronte, Tenerife (2003–05), présentée ici.

JARDÍN DEL SOL HOUSE

Tacoronte, Tenerife, Spain, 2003–05

Floor area: 317 m². Client: Arsenio Pérez Amaral
Cost: €450 000

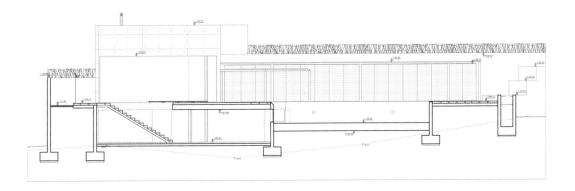

The extreme simplicity and planar
character of the architecture allows it
to blend almost seamlessly with the
horizon.

Die äußerste Schlichtheit und Flächig-
keit der Architektur lassen sie fast
nahtlos mit dem Horizont verschmelzen.

L'extrême simplicité et la construction
par plans de cette architecture lui
permettent de se fondre presque invi-
siblement avec l'horizon.

There is almost no distinction in these images between the deck, swimming pool and the sea beyond. The simplicity of the architectural design contributes to this effect.

Auf diesen Bildern ist nahezu kein Unterschied zwischen dem Schwimmbecken und dem dahinter liegenden Meer erkennbar. Die Schlichtheit der Architektur trägt zu dieser Wirkung bei.

On ne fait pratiquement pas la distinction dans ces images entre la terrasse de la piscine et la mer. La simplicité de la conception architecturale contribue à cet effet.

The architect set out to create "a monolithic concrete and glass volume over a timber platform, located at the edge of a 300-meter cliff in order to enjoy the amazing view of the cliff, a kilometer-long black-sand beach, Mount Teide, and the north coast of Tenerife Island." The bedroom and services areas are located in a one-story rectangular volume that intersects a double-height volume containing the living room, studio, and kitchen. The two volumes create the L-shaped plan around the black pond located at the edge of the platform "so that the surface of the water blends with that of the sea." "All the areas of the house thus enjoy views underlined by wood and water," says the architect. A gym with direct access from the terrace is located in the basement. A view into the pond is offered through a glass wall. Timber shutters protect the bedroom area and outside canvas shades are used in the living room. A freestanding canopy made of steel and wood shelters the central section of the terrace. The house, located on a 626-m² site, appears to be perfectly integrated into the cliff.

Der Architekt plante, „einen am Rand einer 300 m hohen Klippe gelegenen, monolithischen Baukörper aus Beton und Glas auf einer hölzernen Terrassenfläche [zu entwerfen], um die fantastischen Aussichten auf Klippe, einen Kilometer schwarzen Sandstrands, Pico de Teide und die Nordküste von Teneriffa zu genießen". Schlafzimmer und Funktionsräume befinden sich in einem eingeschossigen, rechtwinkligen Baukörper, der an einen anderen Bauteil mit doppelter Geschosshöhe stößt, in dem Wohnraum, Studio und Küche untergebracht sind. Die beiden Elemente ergeben den L-förmigen Grundriss um das schwarze Wasserbecken herum, das am Rand der Plattform liegt, „sodass die Wasseroberfläche in die des Meeres übergeht". Dem Architekten zufolge „profitieren somit sämtliche Bereiche des Hauses von durch Wald und Wasser akzentuierten Ausblicken". Ein direkt von der Terrasse aus zugänglicher Fitnessraum befindet sich im Souterrain. Eine verglaste Wand ermöglicht Ausblicke auf das Wasserbecken. Hölzerne Läden schützen den Schlafzimmerbereich, beim Wohnzimmer kommen außen angebrachte Segeltuchschirme zum Einsatz. Ein freistehendes Dach aus Stahl und Holz schützt den zentralen Abschnitt der Terrasse. Das auf einem 626 m² großen Grundstück stehende Haus wirkt, als sei es direkt in die Feldwand eingefügt.

L'architecte a réussi à créer ici un « volume monolithique en verre et béton sur une plate-forme de bois, en bordure d'une falaise de 300 mètres de haut pour profiter de la vue stupéfiante de kilomètres de plages de sable noir, le mont Teide et la côte septentrionale de l'île de Tenerife ». La chambre et les pièces de service se trouvent dans le volume rectangulaire sur un seul niveau qui vient interrompre un second volume de deux niveaux contenant le séjour, un studio et la cuisine. Ces deux éléments s'articulent en « L » autour d'une piscine noire en bordure de la plate-forme visible à travers un mur de verre « de telle façon que la surface de l'eau se fond avec celle de la mer ». « Toutes les parties de la maison bénéficient de vues mises en valeur par le bois et l'eau », précise l'architecte. Une salle de gymnastique avec accès direct à la terrasse se trouve en sous-sol. Des volets en bois protègent la zone des chambres, et des stores extérieurs en toile, le séjour. Un auvent en bois et acier abrite la partie centrale de la terrasse. La maison, implantée sur un terrain de 626 m², semble être insérée dans la falaise.

Another image shows that the house is not quite as splendidly isolated as the previous double page might lead one to believe, yet the openness of the residence remains remarkable.

Dieses Bild zeigt, dass das Haus nicht ganz so herrlich abgeschieden ist, wie die vorstehende Doppelseite glauben lässt, und doch bleibt die Offenheit des Hauses bemerkenswert.

Autre image montrant que la maison ne se trouve pas dans le splendide isolement que la double-page précédente laisse croire. Mais son ouverture reste remarquable.

The plan to the right is slightly angled to take advantage of the site. Above, the kitchen and dining area are very close to each other.

Der Grundriss ist leicht verdreht oder verschoben, um das Gelände auszunutzen. Oben liegen Küche und Essbereich nahe beeinander.

Le plan est légèrement en biseau pour mieux tirer parti du site. Ci-dessus, la cuisine et la zone des repas, très proches l'une de l'autre.

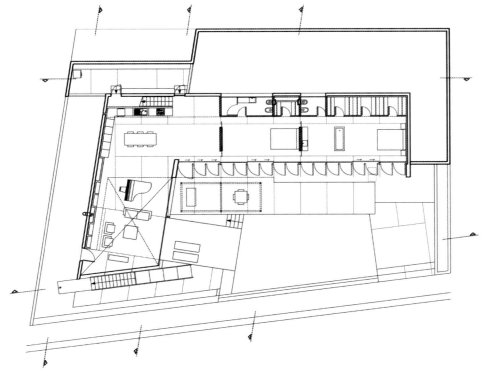

PEZO VON ELLRICHSHAUSEN ARCHITECTS

Pezo von Ellrichshausen Arquitectos
Nonguen 776, Concepcion
Chile

Tel: +56 41 221 0281
E-mail: info@pezo.cl / Web: www.pezo.cl

PEZO VON ELLRICHSHAUSEN ARCHITECTS was founded in Buenos Aires in 2001 by Mauricio Pezo and Sofía von Ellrichshausen. Mauricio Pezo was born in Chile in 1973 and completed his M.Arch degree at the Universidad Católica de Chile (Santiago, 1998). He graduated from the University of Bío-Bío (Concepción, 1999). He is a visual artist and director of the Movimiento Artista del Sur (MAS). He teaches at the School of Architecture of Bío-Bío University, Talca University, and has been Visiting Critic at AAP Cornell University in New York. Pezo was awarded the Young Chilean Architect Prize 2006. Sofía von Ellrichshausen was born in Argentina in 1976. She holds a degree in Architecture from the University of Buenos Aires (Buenos Aires, 2002). She teaches at the School of Architecture of Talca University and has been Visiting Critic at AAP Cornell University in New York. They were awarded the Commended Prize at the AR Awards for Emerging Architecture (London, 2005) and the Best Work by Young Architects Prize at the 5th Iberoamerican Architecture Biennial (Montevideo, 2006). Their built work includes XYZ Pavilions (Concepción, 2001); Rivo House (Valdivia, 2003); 120 Doors Pavilion (Concepción, 2003); Poli House (Coliumo, 2005, published here); Wolf House (Andalue, 2006–07); Parr House (Chiguayante, 2008); Fosc House (San Pedro, 2008–09); and several public art projects. Projects under construction are R15 Building in Zaragoza (Spain); Hema Studio in Buenos Aires (Argentina); and Gold Building, Cien House, and Pael House in Concepción, all in Chile unless stated otherwise.

PEZO VON ELLRICHSHAUSEN ARCHITECTS wurde 2001 von Mauricio Pezo und Sofía von Ellrichshausen in Buenos Aires gegründet. Mauricio Pezo wurde 1973 in Chile geboren, erhielt seinen M.Arch. an der Universidad Católica de Chile (Santiago, 1998) und schloss sein Studium an der Universidad del Bío-Bío (Concepción, 1999) ab. Er ist bildender Künstler und Direktor der Movimiento Artista del Sur (MAS). Er lehrt an der Fakultät für Architektur der Universidad del Bío-Bío sowie der Universidad de Talca und war Gastkritiker am College für Architektur, Kunst und Planung (AAP) der Cornell University in New York. 2006 wurde Pezo mit dem Preis für junge chilenische Architekten ausgezeichnet. Sofía von Ellrichshausen wurde 1976 in Argentinien geboren. Ihr Architekturstudium schloss sie an der Universität Buenos Aires ab (2002). Sie lehrt an der Fakultät für Architektur der Universidad de Talca und war Gastkritikerin am AAP der Cornell University in New York. Bei den AR Awards for Emerging Architecture (London, 2005) wurden ihre Arbeiten besonders hervorgehoben sowie als bestes Projekt von jungen Architekten auf der 5. Iberoamerikanischen Architekturbiennale (Montevideo, 2006) ausgezeichnet. Zu ihren realisierten Bauten zählen: XYZ-Pavillons (Concepción, 2001), Rivo House (Valdivia, 2003), 120 Doors Pavilion (Concepción, 2003), Poli House (Coliumo, 2005, hier vorgestellt), Wolf House (Andalue, 2006–07), Parr House (Chiguayante, 2008), Fosc House (San Pedro, 2008–09) sowie verschiedene öffentliche Kunstprojekte. Im Bau befinden sich derzeit R15 in Saragossa (Spanien), Hema Studio in Buenos Aires (Argentinien) sowie Gold Building, Cien House und Pael House in Concepción, alle in Chile, soweit nicht anders vermerkt.

L'agence **PEZO VON ELLRICHSHAUSEN ARCHITECTS** a été fondée à Buenos Aires en 2001 par Mauricio Pezo et Sofía von Ellrichshausen. Mauricio Pezo, né au Chili en 1973, a obtenu son M.Arch de l'Université catholique du Chili (Santiago, 1998) et est diplômé de l'université de Bío-Bío (Concepción, 1999). Artiste plasticien, il est directeur du Movimiento Artista del Sur (MAS). Il enseigne à l'École d'architecture de l'université Bío-Bío, à l'université de Talca, et a été critique invité à l'université Cornell à New York. Il a reçu le prix des jeunes architectes chiliens en 2006. Sofía von Ellrichshausen, née en Argentine en 1976, est diplômée en architecture de l'université de Buenos Aires (2002). Elle enseigne à l'École d'architecture de l'université de Talca et a été également critique invitée à l'université Cornell (NY). Ils ont reçu un prix de l'Architectural Review pour l'architecture émergente (Londres, 2005) et le prix de la meilleure œuvre de jeunes architectes à la Vᵉ Biennale d'architecture ibéro-américaine (Montevideo, 2006). Parmi leurs réalisations : les pavillons XYZ (Concepción, 2001) ; la maison Rivo (Valdivia, 2003) ; le pavillon des cent vingt portes (Concepción, 2003) ; la maison Poli (Coliumo, 2005 présentée ici) ; la maison Wolf (Andalue, 2006–07) ; la maison Parr (Chiguayante, 2008) ; la maison Fosc (San Pedro, 2008–09) ; et plusieurs projets artistiques publics. Ils ont en chantier l'immeuble R15 à Saragosse (Espagne) ; le studio Hema à Buenos Aires (Argentine) ; l'immeuble Gold, la maison Cien et la maison Pael à Concepción, le tout au Chili, sauf mention contraire.

POLI HOUSE

Coliumo Peninsula, Chile, 2003–05

Floor area: 180 m². Client: Eduardo Meissner, Rosmarie Prim (Casapoli Cultural Center)
Cost: $66 600

Located 550 kilometers south of Santiago, this house was conceived as a "multipurpose space; both as cultural center and temporary residence." Local technology, non-specialized workers, and hand-made concrete were used, as well as the wood frames employed for the concrete that were then recycled for interior insulation. The architects placed the structure as close as possible to the cliff edge on the 10 000-m² site. This location was selected "in order to capture two things: both the sensation of a natural podium surrounded by vastness and the morbid and unavoidable sight of the foot of the cliffs, where the sea explodes against the rocks." The interior floor is divided into three platforms that "adapt to the slope in a zigzagging way." A triple-height space is set on the lower platform, oriented to the northwest. The use of the structure as both a summer house and as a cultural center required the architects to reconcile domestic and "monumental" scales. The service functions (kitchen, bathrooms, closets, vertical circulation) are located at the perimeter, inside a thick wall that acts as a buffer and can be used for furniture storage. Sliding wood panels can be used to close the house entirely.

Dieses 550 km südlich von Santiago gelegene Haus war als „Mehrzweckraum [konzipiert] und sollte sowohl als Kulturzentrum wie als zeitweiliges Wohnhaus dienen". Es wurde mit heimischer Technologie, ohne Facharbeiter und mit von Hand hergestelltem Beton errichtet, außerdem wurden die für den Beton verwendeten Holzrahmen anschließend für die Dämmung des Innenraums weiterverwendet. Die Architekten platzierten den Bau so nah wie möglich an die meerseitige Abbruchkante des 10 000 m² großen Grundstücks. Man wählte den Ort, „um zwei Phänomene einzufangen: Das Empfinden eines von unermesslicher Weite umgebenen natürlichen Podiums und den morbiden und unvermeidlichen Anblick des am Fuß der Klippe gegen die Felsen donnernden Meeres". Der Innenraum verteilt sich auf drei Ebenen, die „sich zickzackförmig an den Abhang anpassen". Auf der untersten Ebene befindet sich ein nach Nordwesten ausgerichteter Raum mit dreifacher Deckenhöhe. Aufgrund der zweifachen Nutzung des Gebäudes als Sommerhaus wie auch als Kulturzentrum waren die Architekten gezwungen, häusliche und „monumentale" Größenordnungen miteinander in Einklang zu bringen. Die Funktionsräume (Küche, Bäder, Schränke, vertikale Erschließung) befinden sich am Außenrand im Inneren einer massiven Wand, die als Puffer dient und auch zum Lagern von Möbelstücken verwendet werden kann. Mittels verschiebbarer Holzplatten lässt sich das Haus komplett verschließen.

Située à 550 km au sud de Santiago du Chili, cette maison construite sur un terrain de 10 000 m² a été conçue comme un espace « polyvalent, à la fois centre culturel et résidence temporaire ». Sa construction a fait appel aux technologies maîtrisables localement, à des ouvriers non spécialisés et du béton préparé in situ dont le bois de coffrage a été recyclé pour l'isolation intérieure. Les architectes ont rapproché autant que possible la construction du bord de la falaise. Le lieu a été choisi « pour capter deux choses : la sensation d'un podium naturel entouré de l'immensité et la vue fascinante du pied des falaises où la mer explose contre les rochers ». Le volume intérieur est divisé en trois plates-formes qui « s'adaptent à la pente en zigzag ». Un espace triple-hauteur occupe la plate-forme inférieure, orientée vers le nord-ouest. La double fonction de centre culturel et de résidence d'été entraînait la conciliation des échelles domestique et « monumentale ». Les services (cuisine, salles de bains, placards, circulation verticale) ont été reportés en périmétrie dans la masse d'un mur qui joue le rôle de tampon et peut également servir au stockage de mobilier. Des panneaux de bois coulissants permettent de clore entièrement la maison.

The house sits above the Pacific, and offers a grandiose view of the setting sun.

Das Haus liegt über dem Pazifik und bietet eine grandiose Aussicht auf die untergehende Sonne.

La maison qui domine le Pacifique offre des vues magnifiques sur le soleil couchant.

The basic floor plan is a perfect square, but the architects have introduced an unusual double-shell system that means that the walls are in effect inhabited.

Der Grundriss ist im Grunde quadratisch, aber die Architekten verwenden eine ungewöhnliche doppelschalige Bauweise, das heißt, die Wandzwischenräume sind Teil der Wohnfläche.

Le plan au sol est un carré parfait, mais les architectes ont introduit un système de double-coque qui fait que les murs sont utilisés dans leur épaisseur même.

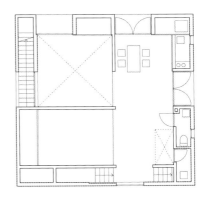

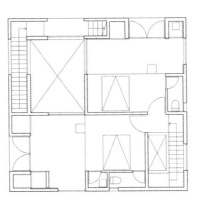

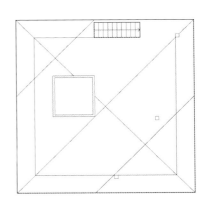

The rough finishing of the house makes it well adapted to its spectacular, but rocky, natural setting.

Die rohe Oberfläche des Hauses passt gut zu seinem grandiosen, wenngleich felsigen Standort.

La finition brute de la maison la rend bien adaptée à son cadre naturel spectaculaire et rocheux.

Windows of various sizes and set at unexpected levels animate the interior space and allow views of the ocean, while also admitting ample natural light.

Die unterschiedlich großen und in unregelmäßigen Abständen eingeschnittenen Fenster sorgen für reichlich Tageslicht, variieren den Innenraum und gestatten Ausblicke auf den Ozean.

Des fenêtres de dimensions variables, percées à des niveaux inattendus, animent l'espace intérieur et favorisent les perspectives sur l'océan, tout en laissant pénétrer une généreuse lumière naturelle.

PLASMA STUDIO

Plasma Studio
Unit 51 – Regents Studios
8 Andrews Road
London E8 4QN, UK

Tel: +44 207 812 9875 / Fax: +44 870 486 5563
E-mail: mail@plasmastudio.com / Web: www.plasmastudio.com

PLASMA STUDIO was founded by Eva Castro and Holger Kehne in London in 1999. Eva Castro studied architecture and urbanism at the Universidad Central de Venezuela and subsequently completed the Graduate Design program under Jeff Kipnis at the Architectural Association (AA) in London. She is Director of the AA Landscape Urbanism Program. Holger Kehne studied architecture at the University of Applied Sciences in Münster, Germany, and at the University of East London. He is a Unit Master for Diploma Unit 12 at the AA. Ulla Hell is an Associate Partner, and she studied at the University of Innsbruck, Austria, and the Technical University Delft and Technical University Eindhoven (The Netherlands). The office made its reputation through a number of small residential and refurbishment projects in London. The architects say: "The studio is best known for its architectural use of form and geometry. Shifts, folds and bends create surface continuities that are never arbitrary but part of the spatial and structural organization." They won the Corus/Building Design "Young Architect of the Year Award" in 2002. They participated in the Hotel Puerta America project with architects like Jean Nouvel and Zaha Hadid (Madrid, Spain, 2005), and their recent work includes the Strata Hotel (Alto Adige, 2007); Cube House (Sexten, 2005–08, published here); Tetris House, a multi-family residential compound (San Candido, 2007); and Esker House (San Candido, 2006), all in Italy. A recent project is Flowing Gardens, Xi'an World Horticultural Fair 2011 (Xi'an, China, 2009–11).

PLASMA STUDIO wurde 1999 von Eva Castro und Holger Kehne in London gegründet. Eva Castro studierte Architektur und Stadtplanung an der Universidad Central de Venezuela und schloss einen Aufbaustudiengang Entwerfen bei Jeff Kipnis an der Architectural Association (AA) in London an. Inzwischen leitet sie das Landschaftsplanungsprogramm der AA. Holger Kehne studierte Architektur an der Fachhochschule Münster/Westfalen und der University of East London. Er ist Unit Master für den Diplombereich 12 an der AA. Ulla Hell ist Partnerin und Teilhaberin des Büros und studierte an der Universität Innsbruck sowie der Technischen Universität Delft und der Technischen Universität Eindhoven (Niederlande). Einen Namen machte sich das Büro mit einer Reihe kleinerer Wohnbau- und Sanierungsprojekte in London. Die Architekten erklären: „Das Studio ist besonders für seinen architektonischen Umgang mit Formgebung und Geometrie bekannt. Materialverschiebungen, -faltungen und -biegungen schaffen Oberflächenkontinuitäten, die nie zufällig sind, sondern Teil der räumlichen und konstruktiven Organisation." 2002 erhielt das Büro den Corus/Building Design „Young Architect of the Year Award". Darüber hinaus waren sie neben Architekten wie Jean Nouvel und Zaha Hadid am Hotel Puerta America beteiligt (Madrid, Spanien, 2005). Zu ihren jüngeren Projekten zählen das Strata Hotel (Alto Adige, 2007), das Cube House (Sexten, 2005–08, hier vorgestellt), das Tetris House, ein Mehrfamilienwohnkomplex (San Candido, 2007) und das Esker House (San Candido, 2006), alle in Italien. Ein aktuelles Projekt ist Flowing Gardens, Xi'an Weltgartenschau 2011 (Xi'an, China, 2009–11).

L'agence **PLASMA STUDIO** a été fondée par Eva Castro et Holger Kehne à Londres en 1999. Eva Castro a étudié l'architecture et l'urbanisme à l'Université centrale du Venezuela, puis à l'Architectural Association (AA) à Londres (Graduate Design Program, sous la direction de Jeff Kipnis). Elle est directrice du mastère d'urbanisme paysager à l'AA. Holger Kehne a étudié l'architecture à l'Université des sciences appliquées de Münster (Allemagne) et à l'Université de l'est de Londres. Il est responsable de l'Unité de diplôme 12 à l'AA. Ulla Hell est partenaire associée. Elle a étudié à l'Université d'Innsbruck (Autriche) ainsi qu'à l'Université polytechnique de Delft et à celle d'Eindhoven (Pays-Bas). Plasma s'est fait remarquer par un certain nombre de petits projets résidentiels et de rénovation à Londres. « L'agence est surtout connue pour l'utilisation architecturale de la forme et de la géométrie. Glissements, plis et courbures créent des continuités de surface qui ne sont jamais arbitraires, et font partie de l'organisation spatiale et structurelle », expliquent les architectes. Ils ont remporté le Corus/Building Design « Prix du jeune architecte de l'année » 2002, et ont participé au projet de l'Hotel Puerta America aux côtés d'architectes comme Jean Nouvel et Zaha Hadid (Madrid, 2005). Parmi leurs réalisations récentes, toutes en Italie : la maison Esker (San Candido, 2006) ; le Strata Hotel (Haut- Adige, 2007) ; la maison Tetris, complexe résidentiel plurifamilial (San Candido, 2007) ; et la maison Cube (Sexten, 2005–08, présentée ici). Ils ont recemment complété les Flowing Gardens (Jardins en flux), Floralies internationales de Xi'an 2011 (Xi'an, Chine, 2009–11).

CUBE HOUSE

Sesto, Italy, 2005–08

Floor area: 178 m². Client: Patrick Holzer. Cost: not disclosed
Team: Eva Castro, Holger Kehne, Ulla Hell

As these three elevations show, the house gives pride of place to its balconies, as might be considered appropriate in this mountain environment. The wood cladding wraps around, leaving generous openings for the glazing.

Wie diese drei Aufrisse zeigen, kommt den Balkonen bei diesem Haus eine Schlüsselrolle zu, was inmitten der Berglandschaft durchaus angemessen scheint. Die Holzverkleidung umfängt den gesamten Bau und lässt Raum für großzügige Verglasung.

Comme le montrent ces trois éléva-tions, la maison laisse la place d'hon-neur aux balcons en retrait, ce qui est approprié dans cet environnement de montagne. L'habillage de bois contourne les vastes ouvertures vitrées.

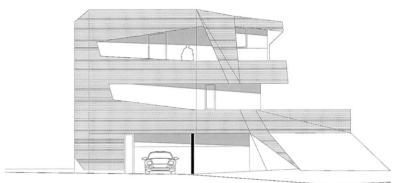

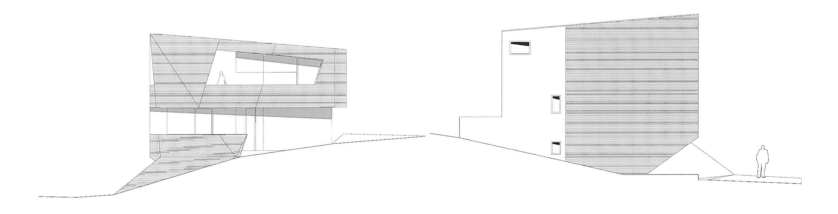

This house was designed for a steep site compressed by neighboring structures, and its angled forms, in both plan and section have a great deal to do with fitting in to the allotted space. A stairway leads up from two covered parking spots at the front of the residence to the main floor living areas, and on to the bedrooms on the second floor. Large balconies and terraces directed to the south, protected by overhanging roofs, give further effective living areas to the house. Its angled, timber-clad surfaces certainly set it apart from neighboring mountain-style architecture, but, perhaps because of its extensive use of wood, the Cube House does not appear to be shocking in its context.

Das Haus wurde für ein steiles und von Nachbarbauten beengtes Grundstück entworfen, und so hat seine winklig-geneigte Formgebung in Grund- und Aufriss viel damit zu tun, den zur Verfügung stehenden Platz zu nutzen. Eine Treppe führt von zwei überdachten Parkplätzen vor dem Haus zu den Hauptwohngeschossen hinauf und weiter zu den Schlafzimmern im zweiten Stock. Großzügige Balkone und Terrassen sind nach Süden orientiert und von überhängenden Dächern geschützt, was dem Haus zusätzliche Wohnbereiche verschafft. Mit seinen winklig-geneigten, holzverkleideten Oberflächen setzt sich das Haus eindeutig von der Bergbauernarchitektur der umgebenden Bauten ab. Trotzdem wirkt das Haus Kubus in seinem Umfeld nicht schockierend – vielleicht wegen der ausgeprägten Verwendung von Holz.

Cette maison a été conçue pour un terrain en forte pente comprimé entre des constructions voisines. Ses formes inclinées, aussi bien en plan qu'en coupe, s'ex-pliquent en grande partie par l'adaptation nécessaire à l'espace disponible. Un escalier part des deux parkings couverts implantés devant la résidence pour monter au niveau principal et jusqu'aux chambres au second niveau. De vastes balcons et terrasses orientés sud, protégés par le surplomb des toits, apportent des espaces de vie supplémentaires. Les plans inclinés habillés de bois distinguent certainement cette maison de l'architecture de montagne des constructions avoisinantes, mais, par son usage généreux du bois, elle ne semble pas choquante dans ce contexte.

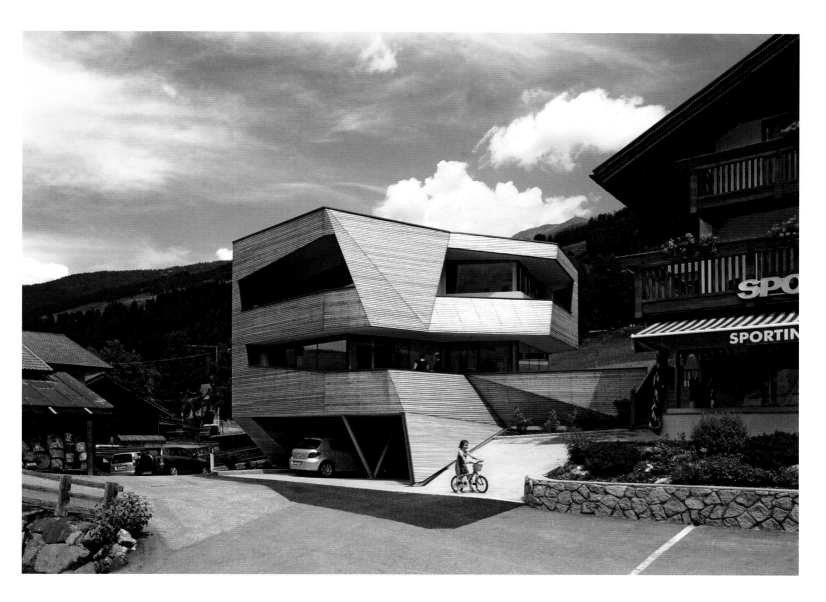

The typology of the house naturally differs from that of neighboring structures, and yet its wood cladding and terraced design show that there are connections between older buildings and this modern interpretation.

Typologisch unterscheidet sich das Haus ganz offensichtlich von seinen Nachbarbauten. Dennoch signalisieren die Holzverkleidung und die Balkone, dass es eine Verbindung zwischen den älteren Häusern und dieser moderneren Interpretation gibt.

Si le style de la maison diffère de celui de ses voisines, l'habillage de bois et la conception en plans et terrasses superposés montrent un lien entre les bâtiments anciens et cette interprétation moderne.

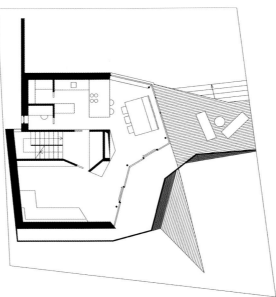

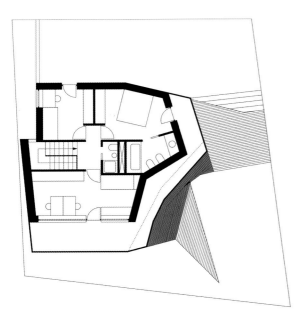

Views of the town are framed by the openings, and the house offers protected terrace space all around.

Öffnungen rahmen den Blick auf den Ort. Das Haus ist rundum mit überdachten Balkonen versehen.

Les vues du village sont cadrées par les ouvertures. La maison possède des terrasses protégées dans toutes les directions.

MICHAEL REYNOLDS

Michael Reynolds
Earthship Biotecture
P.O. Box 1041
Taos, NM 87571
USA

Tel: +1 575 751 1005
E-mail: biotecture@earthship.org
Web: www.earthship.org

MICHAEL REYNOLDS graduated with a B.Arch degree from the University of Cincinnati in 1969. He describes his own work experience as "35 years of research and development of self-sufficient housing." His concept of self-sufficiency includes the payment of little or no utilities or mortgage. He has designed and built over 300 solar structures in the United States and Canada. The *New York Times* selected him as one of its "Eco-Heroes" (April 23, 2006). He is currently working on applying his ideas to facilities for the homeless in Taos, New Mexico, and Los Angeles. A feature film about his activities, *Garbage Warrior* (www.garbagewarrior.com), has been shown in such locations as the Lincoln Center in New York (March 25, 2008) and the Museum of Modern Art (February 14, 2008). Although Reynolds is a licensed architect, his structures, long outside of the mainstream, can increasingly be considered as offering an intriguing alternative to mass-produced housing and high-energy consumption. See his Hybrid Earthship (Taos, New Mexico, 2003), published here.

MICHAEL REYNOLDS schloss sein Studium an der Universität Cincinnati 1969 mit einem B.Arch. ab. Seine Berufserfahrung beschreibt er als „35 Jahre Forschung und Entwicklung autonomer Wohnformen". Seinem Autonomiekonzept zufolge sind nur geringe oder gar keine Zahlungen für Nebenkosten und Hypotheken notwendig. In den USA und Kanada realisierte er bisher über 300 Solarbauten. Die *New York Times* ernannte ihn zu einem ihrer „Eco-Heroes" (23. April 2006). Zurzeit arbeitet er daran, seine Ideen auf Einrichtungen für Obdachlose in Taos, New Mexico, und Los Angeles zu übertragen. Ein Film über seine Aktivitäten, *Garbage Warrior* (www.garbagewarrior.com) war z. B. im Lincoln Center in New York (25. März 2008) und dem Museum of Modern Art (14. Februar 2008) zu sehen. Obwohl Reynolds Architekt ist, können seine Konstruktionen, die schon lange jenseits des Mainstreams liegen, als faszinierende Alternative zu massengefertigten Wohnbauprojekten mit hohem Energieverbrauch gelten. Das illustriert auch das hier vorgestellte Hybrid Earthship (Taos, New Mexico, 2003).

MICHAEL REYNOLDS est B. Arch de l'université de Cincinnati (1969). Il présente sa carrière professionnelle comme « 35 années de recherches et de développement sur le logement autosuffisant ». Ce concept comprend un aspect financier : le paiement de peu ou pas de charges financières d'emprunt. Il a conçu et construit plus de trois cents constructions solaires aux États-Unis et au Canada. Le *New York Times* en a fait l'un de ses « Éco-héros » (23 avril 2006). Il travaille actuellement aux applications de ses idées à des équipements pour sans-abris à Taos, Nouveau-Mexique et Los Angeles. Un documentaire sur ses activités, intitulé *Garbage Warrior* (« le guerrier des poubelles », www.garbagewarrior.com) a été présenté, dans des lieux tels que le Lincoln Center à New York, le 25 mars 2008, et le MoMA, le 14 février 2008. Bien qu'il soit architecte licencié, ses constructions, très éloignées du gros du marché, peuvent de plus en plus être considérées comme une alternative aux constructions de série à forte consommation d'énergie. A voir, pour exemple, son Hybrid Earthship (Taos, Nouveau-Mexique, 2003), présenté ici.

HYBRID EARTHSHIP

Taos, New Mexico, USA, 2003

Floor area: 158 m². Client: Earthship Biotecture. Cost: $250 000

The architect lists the materials of this house as being "tires, mud, and glass." The Earthships designed (and sold) by Reynolds are intended to obey a series of "design principles: 1) thermal/solar heating & cooling 2) solar & wind electricity 3) contained sewage treatment 4) building with natural & recycled materials 5) water harvesting 6) food production." One of his favored building materials is recycled automobile tires filled with compacted earth to form a rammed-earth brick encased in steel belted rubber. As he says: "This brick, and the resulting bearing walls it forms, is virtually indestructible." Aluminum cans and glass or plastic bottles are used for interior non-structural walls. Electricity is produced with a pre-packaged photovoltaic/wind-power system. Botanical cells and an improved version of a septic tank are used to treat water that is recycled for all purposes within the house except drinking. The Hybrid Earthship and others like it have been used by Reynolds to publicize the system he has developed to build and maintain sustainable houses. Different aesthetic options are available, but the architect clearly favors rather joyously eccentric forms that make it clear that these houses are not like other residences, even those that today place an emphasis on "green" design. The concept is carried here to a level of sustainability that cannot be attained with industrially produced architecture.

Als Baumaterialien für dieses Haus nennt der Architekt „Autoreifen, Lehm und Glas." Die von Reynolds entwickelten (und vertriebenen) Earthships entsprechen einer Reihe von „Gestaltungsprinzipien": „1) Erdwärme-/Solarheizung und -kühlung; 2) Strom aus Solar- und Windkraft; 3) Unabhängige Abwasseraufbereitung; 4) Bauen mit natürlichen und recycelten Materialien; 5) Regensammelanlagen; 6) Lebensmittelproduktion". Zu seinen Lieblingsbaumaterialien zählen recycelte Autoreifen, die mit verdichteter Erde gefüllt werden, wodurch ein Stampferdeziegel mit metallverstärktem Gummimantel entsteht. Reynolds erklärt: „Dieser Ziegel und die daraus gebauten tragenden Wände sind so gut wie unzerstörbar." Für nichttragende Innenwände werden Aluminiumdosen und Plastikflaschen genutzt. Strom wird mithilfe eines Solar- und Windkraft-Fertigbausystems erzeugt. Begrünte „Zellen" und verbesserte Klärbehälter bereiten Wasser für sämtliche Nutzungszwecke auf, ausgenommen Trinkwasser. Sein Hybrid Earthship und ähnliche Modelle nutzt Reynolds, um sein System zum Bau und zur Unterhaltung nachhaltiger Häuser bekanntzumachen. Es gibt verschiedene ästhetische Varianten, dennoch scheint der Architekt ganz offensichtlich fröhlich-exzentrische Formen zu bevorzugen, die deutlich machen, dass sich diese Häuser von anderen Wohnbauten unterscheiden, selbst von solchen, die heute besonderen Wert auf „grünes" Design legen. Sein Konzept setzt Nachhaltigkeit zu einem Grad um, der mit industriell gefertigter Architektur nicht zu erreichen ist.

Selon ses propres termes, l'architecte a utilisé pour cette maison « de la terre, des pneus et du verre ». Ces Earthships (vaisseaux terrestres) conçus (et commercialisés) par Reynolds obéissent « à plusieurs principes précis : 1) chauffage et refroidissement géothermique/solaire, 2) électricité produite par le soleil et le vent, 3) traitement intégré des rejets, 4) construction avec des matériaux naturels et recyclés, 5) récupération des eaux, 6) production d'aliments ». L'un de ses matériaux de construction favoris est le pneu d'automobile recyclé rempli de terre compactée, pour former une brique prise dans un anneau de caoutchouc à armature métallique. « Cette brique, et les murs porteurs qu'elle permet de monter, est quasiment indestructible », assure-t-il. Des boîtes d'aluminium ou des bouteilles de verre ou de plastique sont utilisées dans les cloisons internes non porteuses. L'électricité est produite par un système prémonté de cellules photovoltaïques et d'éoliennes. Des cellules végétales et une version améliorée de fosse septique traitent l'eau qui est recyclée pour tous les usages domestiques, sauf la boisson. Cette maison et d'autres du même type ont permi à Reynolds de faire connaître le système qu'il a mis au point pour construire et faire exister ces résidences durables. Différentes options esthétiques sont proposées, mais l'architecte préfère à l'évidence des formes joyeusement excentriques qui expriment clairement l'originalité de ces maisons, même par rapport à celles qui mettent aujourd'hui l'accent sur leur conception verte. Le concept de durabilité est ici porté à un niveau qui ne pourrait être atteint par une construction de type industriel.

Partially buried in its desert site, the Hybrid Earthship indeed seems to be well named, evoking an almost alien presence.

Das Hybrid Earthship ist teilweise im Wüstenboden versenkt und scheint recht passend benannt zu sein, schließlich wirkt es fast außerirdisch.

En partie enterré dans le sol du désert, ce « Vaisseau terrestre hybride » justifie son nom et évoque une présence extra-terrestre.

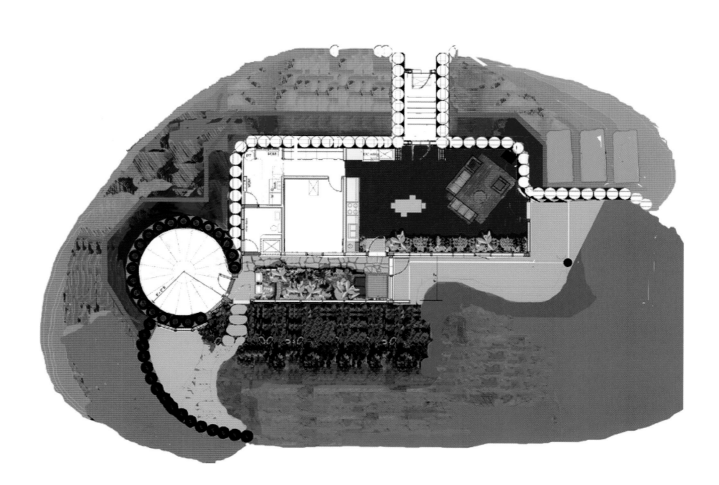

ROOM 11

5th Floor, 50 Elizabeth Street
Hobart, Tasmania 7000
Australia

Tel: +61 3 6234 2847
Fax: +61 3 6234 7253
E-mail: thomas@room11.com.au
Web: www.room11.com.au

Thomas Bailey was born in 1977. He was a cofounder of **ROOM 11** in 2003 and obtained his B.Arch degree the following year. He worked as a project architect for Morris-Nunn Associates (2005–07). Aaron Roberts was also born in 1977 in Hobart, Tasmania. He received a bachelor of environmental design (University of Tasmania 1996–98) before working with Bush Park Shugg & Moon Architects (2000) and Maria Gigney Architect (2001). He cofounded Room 11 in 2003. They completed Little Big House (Hobart, Tasmania, 2008, published here) and Allens Rivulet House 2 (Allens Rivulet, Tasmania, 2009); while their recent work includes Houses in Dodges Ferry, Lenah Valley, Sandy Bay, Sorrento, Fitzroy, and Longley as well as a Medical Center in Moonah, all in Australia, 2010. In conjunction with Scott Lloyd and Katrina Stoll, Room 11 was selected for the Australian Pavilion at the Venice Biennale (2010). Their speculative project concerns "linking Victoria and Tasmania via a hyper infrastructural spine."

Thomas Bailey wurde 1977 geboren. 2003 war er Mitgründer von **ROOM 11** und machte im darauffolgenden Jahr den B.Arch. 2005 bis 2007 arbeitete er als Projektarchitekt bei Morris-Nunn Associates. Aaron Roberts wurde ebenfalls 1977 in Hobart, Tasmanien, geboren und machte seinen Bachelor of Environmental Design (University of Tasmania, 1996–98), bevor er bei Bush Park Shugg & Moon Architects (2000) sowie Maria Gigney Architect (2001) arbeitete. 2003 war er Mitgründer von Room 11. Ausgeführte Bauten des Büros sind das Little Big House (Hobart, Tasmanien, 2008, hier veröffentlicht) und Allens Rivulet House 2 (Allens Rivulet, Tasmanien, 2009). Zu den aktuellen Arbeiten zählen Wohnhäuser in Dodges Ferry, Lenah Valley, Sandy Bay, Sorrento, Fitzroy und Longley sowie ein Ärztezentrum in Moonah, alle in Australien, 2010. Gemeinsam mit Scott Lloyd und Katrina Stoll war Room 11 mit der Planung des australischen Pavillons auf der Biennale von Venedig (2010) beauftragt. Ihr spekulatives Projekt befasste sich mit der „Verbindung von Victoria und Tasmanien durch eine hyper-infrastrukturelle Achse."

Thomas Bailey, né en 1977, cofondateur de **ROOM 11** en 2003, a obtenu son diplôme d'architecte l'année suivante. Il a été architecte de projet chez Morris-Nunn Associates (2005–07). Aaron Roberts, né en 1977 à Hobart (Tasmanie) est diplômé en design environnemental de l'université de Tasmanie (1996–98) et a travaillé pour Bush Park Shugg & Moon Architects (2000) et Maria Gigney Architect (2001). Il est cofondateur de Room 11 (2003). Ils ont réalisé Little Big House (Hobart, Tasmanie, 2008, présentée ici) et la maison Allens Rivulet 2 (Allens Rivulet, Tasmanie, 2009) et ont travaillé recemment sur des projets de maisons à Dodges Ferry, Lenah Valley, Sandy Bay, Sorrento, Fitzroy et Longley ainsi que d'un centre médical à Moonah, tous en Australie. En collaboration avec Scott Lloyd et Katrina Stoll, Room 11 a été choisi en 2010 pour le pavillon australien de la Biennale d'architecture de Venise. Leur projet portait sur une « liaison entre l'État de Victoria et la Tasmanie par un axe hyper-infrastructurel. »

LITTLE BIG HOUSE

Hobart, Tasmania, Australia, 2008

Area: 165 m². Client: Thomas Bailey, Megan Baines
Cost: $250 000

Thomas Bailey and Megan Baynes designed and built this house for themselves in Fern Tree on the eastern slope of Mount Wellington above Hobart. The location of the house takes this context into mind as well as such factors as a birch tree on the site. Set on a vacant lot between existing houses and gardens, the Little Big House is "defensive and diagrammatic" according to its architects, with a deliberately small footprint and a configuration intended to provide the owners with a maximum degree of privacy. Thomas Bailey writes: "It's just a box, a clean volume with two exceptions: a service core and an entry airlock." The designers have employed polycarbonate cladding on the eastern and western sides of the house to "render luminous shadow walls which enable the house to be concurrently light and contained." For other parts of the house, Tasmanian celery top pine from the Huon Valley, south of Hobart, was used with a "traditional vernacular 'batten-board' cladding technique common to the locale."

Thomas Bailey und Megan Baynes planten und bauten dieses Haus für sich selbst in Fern Tree über Hobart am Osthang des Mount Wellington. Der Entwurf für das Gebäude nimmt auf diesen Standort ebenso Rücksicht wie etwa auf eine auf dem Grundstück vorhandene Birke. Das auf einen freien Bauplatz zwischen bestehenden Häusern und Gärten gesetzte Little Big House ist, laut Aussage der Architekten, „defensiv und schematisch", mit bewusst klein gehaltenem Grundriss und einer Raumplanung, die den Bewohnern ein Maximum an Rückzugsmöglichkeiten bietet. Thomas Bailey schreibt: „Es ist nur eine Kiste, ein geschlossenes Volumen mit zwei Ausnahmen: einem Versorgungskern und einem Windfang am Eingang." Für die Ost- und die Westseiten des Gebäudes wählten die Architekten eine Verkleidung aus Polykarbonat, um „helle und schattenspendende Wände zu erzeugen, die das Haus licht und abgeschlossen zugleich machen". Für andere Bereiche wurde tasmanische Celery-Top-Kiefer aus dem Huon Valley südlich von Hobart für die „traditionelle, regional übliche Bretterverkleidung" verwendet.

Thomas Bailey et Megan Baynes ont conçu cette maison pour leur propre usage à Fern Tree sur la pente orientale du Mont Wellington au-dessus d'Hobart. L'implantation du projet prend en compte ce contexte de même que certains facteurs comme la présence d'un bouleau sur le terrain. Édifiée sur une parcelle vide entre des maisons et des jardins existants, Little Big House est « défensive et schématique » pour reprendre le descriptif des architectes. Son emprise au sol est délibérément réduite et sa configuration veut offrir à ses occupants le maximum d'intimité. Pour Thomas Bailey : « C'est juste une boîte, un volume net à deux exceptions près, le noyau de services et le sas d'entrée. » Les architectes ont utilisé un bardage en polycarbonate sur les faces est et ouest pour « rendre lumineuse l'ombre des murs qui permettent à la maison de paraître à la fois légère et compacte. » Les autres parties sont parées de pin de Tasmanie issu de la vallée d'Huon au sud d'Hobart et posé selon un principe vernaculaire de bardage à clins, technique traditionnelle répandue dans la région. »

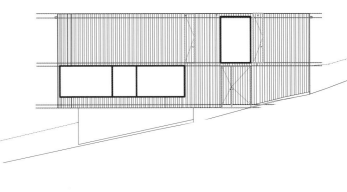

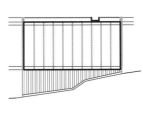

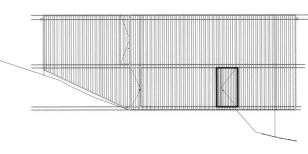

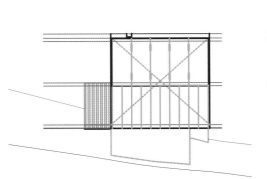

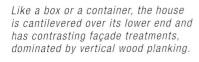

Like a box or a container, the house is cantilevered over its lower end and has contrasting façade treatments, dominated by vertical wood planking.

Dieses Haus in Form einer Kiste oder eines Containers kragt über seine untere Seite aus und zeigt unterschiedliche Fassadenbehandlungen, die von der vertikalen Holzverkleidung bestimmt werden.

En forme de boîte ou de container, la partie inférieure de la maison est en léger porte-à-faux. Ses façades sont composées d'éléments contrastants, même si le bardage vertical en bois reste dominant.

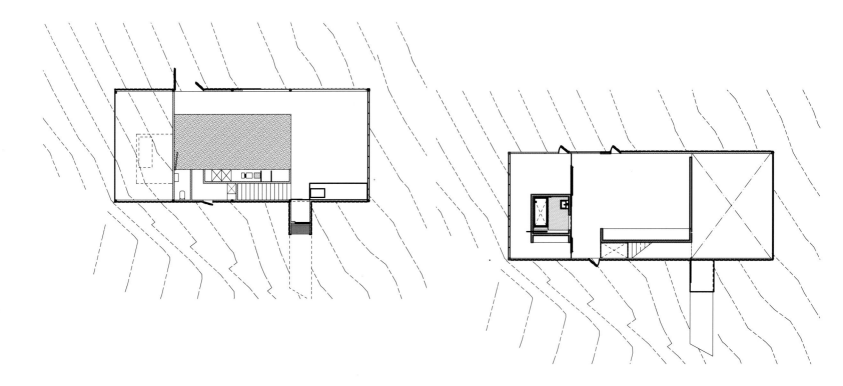

The plan is a simple rectangle. Interior volumes are quite strict, in keeping with the outside shapes of the house.

Der Grundriss ist ein einfaches Rechteck. Auch die Innenräume sind streng gestaltet, um der Außenform des Hauses zu entsprechen.

Le plan est un simple rectangle. Les volumes intérieurs sont assez stricts, en accord avec le style extérieur de la maison.

A long, glazed strip brings light into the living and dining areas (above). The side view (right) appears to show the house in a perilous equilibrium over the rocky site.

Ein langes Fensterband lässt Tageslicht in den Wohn- und Essbereich (oben) einfallen. Die Seitenansicht (rechts) zeigt das Haus in scheinbar prekärem Gleichgewicht über dem felsigen Gelände.

Un bandeau de fenêtres éclaire le séjour et la salle à manger (ci-dessus). Vue de côté, la maison semble se tenir dans un équilibre instable sur son site escarpé.

RURAL STUDIO

Rural Studio
College of Architecture, Design and Construction / Auburn University School of Architecture
P.O. Box 278 / Newbern, AL 36765 / USA
Tel: +1 334 624 4483 / Fax: +1 334 624 6015
E-mail: rstudio@auburn.edu / Web: www.ruralstudio.org

Samuel Mockbee, born in 1945, founded Mockbee/Coker Architects, based in Canton, Mississippi, and in Memphis, Tennessee, with Coleman Coker in 1978. The firm completed a number of structures, including the Barton House and the Cook House, both located in Mississippi. They enjoy considerable reknown in the region, established through their contemporary interpretations of local architecture. Samuel Mockbee taught at Yale, at the University of Oklahoma, and was a Professor of Architecture at Auburn University beginning in 1991. He created the **RURAL STUDIO** with Dennis K. Ruth in 1993 to improve living conditions in rural Alabama and to include hands-on experience in architectural pedagogy, while "extending the study of architecture into a socially responsible context." Three programs, lasting from a semester to a year, are organized for students at Auburn. Mockbee died in 2001, but it was immediately decided that the work of the Rural Studio would continue. The studio is today under the direction of Professor Andrew Freear, who was born in Yorkshire, England. He graduated from the Polytechnic of Central London and the Architectural Association in London. He taught at the University of Illinois before joining Auburn University. Completed community projects include the Akron Senior Center in Hale County (2001–02); the Lee County AIDS Alabama House (2002–03); and the Perry Lakes Pedestrian Bridge (2003–04). Other completed houses include: Lucy House in Mason's Bend and Shiles House, both completed in Hale County in 2001–02; and the Music Man House (Hale County, 2002–03). More recent work includes Christine's House (Mason's Bend, 2005–06, published here); and the St. Luke's Church Renovation in Old Cahawba (2006–08), all in Alabama, USA.

Samuel Mockbee, geboren 1945, gründete 1978 gemeinsam mit Coleman Coker sein Büro Mockbee/Coker Architects mit Sitz in Canton, Mississippi, und Memphis, Tennessee. Das Büro realisierte zahlreiche Bauten, darunter das Haus Barton sowie das Haus Cook, beide in Mississippi. Durch ihre zeitgenössische Interpretation ortstypischer Architektur erwarb sich das Büro einen beachtlichen Ruf in der Region. Samuel Mockbee lehrte in Yale sowie an der Universität Oklahoma und war seit 1991 Professor für Architektur an der Universität Auburn in Alabama. 1993 gründete er mit Dennis K. Ruth das Büro **RURAL STUDIO**, um die Lebensbedingungen in ländlichen Gegenden Alabamas zu verbessern. Zugleich ging es ihm darum, praktische Erfahrungen in Architekturpädagogik zu vermitteln und „das Architekturstudium in den sozial verantwortlichen Bereich zu erweitern". Studenten an der Universität Auburn werden drei Programme mit einer Dauer von einem Semester bis zu einem Jahr angeboten. Mockbee starb 2001, doch man beschloss sofort, die Arbeit von Rural Studio fortzusetzen. Heute wird das Studio von Professor Andrew Freear geleitet, der in Yorkshire geboren wurde. Er studierte an der Polytechnic of Central London und der Architectural Association in London. Bevor er nach Auburn kam, lehrte er an der Universität von Illinois. Zu den realisierten Gemeinschaftsprojekten zählen u. a. das Akron Senior Center in Hale County (2001–02), das Lee County AIDS Alabama House (2002–03) sowie die Perry-Lakes-Fußgängerbrücke (2003–04). Andere Hausbauten sind das Lucy House in Mason's Bend und das Shiles House (beide 2001–02 in Hale County fertiggestellt) sowie das Music Man House (Hale County, 2002–03). Zu den aktuelleren Projekten zählen Christine's House (Mason's Bend, 2005–06, hier vorgestellt) sowie die Sanierung der Kirche St. Luke's in Old Cahawba (2006–08), alle in Alabama.

Samuel Mockbee, né en 1945, a fondé Mockbee/Coker Architects avec Coleman Coker en 1978. L'agence basée à Canton, Mississippi, et Memphis, Tennessee, a réalisé un certain nombre de projets dont la maison Barton et la maison Cook, toutes deux dans le Mississippi. Elle bénéficie d'une importante réputation dans la région grâce à ses interprétations contemporaines de l'architecture locale. Samuel Mockbee a enseigné à Yale, à l'université de l'Oklahoma et a été professeur d'architecture à l'université Auburn à partir de 1991. Il a créé **RURAL STUDIO** avec Dennis K. Ruth, en 1993, pour améliorer les conditions de vie dans l'Alabama rural et mettre en pratique une expérience directe du chantier dans sa pédagogie, tout en « étendant l'étude de l'architecture dans un contexte social responsable ». Trois programmes, d'une durée d'un semestre à un an, sont organisés à Auburn pour les étudiants. Mockbee est mort en 2001, mais il a été immédiatement décidé que Rural Studio devait continuer. Il est aujourd'hui placé sous la direction du professeur Andrew Freear, né dans le Yorkshire en Grande-Bretagne. Il est diplômé de la London Polytechnic et de l'Architectural Association de Londres. Il a enseigné à l'université de l'Illinois, avant de rejoindre celle d'Auburn. Parmi les projets communautaires achevés figurent le Centre Akron Senior dans le comté de Hale County (2001–02) ; l'AIDS Alabama House dans le comté de Lee (2002–03) et la passerelle piétonnière du lac Perry (2003–04). Parmi leurs maisons réalisées : la maison Lucy à Mason's Bend et la maison Shiles (comté de Hale, 2001–02) ; la maison Music Man (comté de Hale, 2002–03) ; la maison de Christine (Mason's Bend, 2005–06, présentée ici, et la rénovation de l'église St. Luc à Old Cahawba (2006–08), le tout en Alabama.

CHRISTINE'S HOUSE

Mason's Bend, Alabama, USA, 2005–06

Floor area: 83 m². Client: Christine Green. Cost: not disclosed
Project Architects: Amy Green Bullington, Stephen Long. Project Instructor and Rural Studio Director: Andrew Freear
Structural Engineer: Joe Farruggia. Environmental Engineer: Paul Stroller

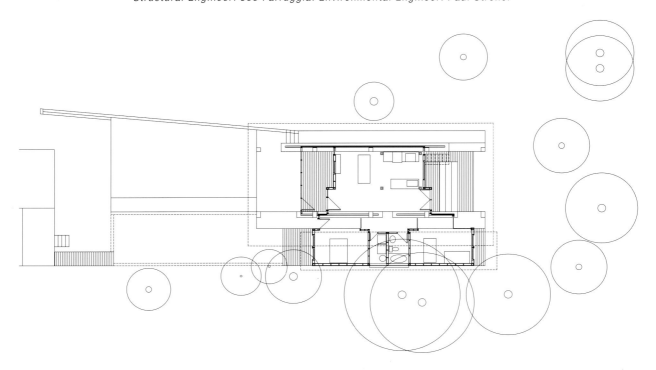

Like other Rural Studio work, Christine's House was an Auburn University architectural thesis. Both the young architects involved in this house, Amy Green Bullington and Stephen Long, received their B.Arch degrees from Auburn in 2005. They took advantage of the area's abundant red clay—mixing 70% earth, 25% pulped newspaper and 5% Portland cement, poured into cardboard boxes of various sizes—to make bricks for two main walls of the house. As Amy Bullington explains: "This hybrid adobe mix, a simple modification to traditional brick making, requires few special skills and little equipment, and its high insulation value (R33 for a 30.5 cm wall) is attractive in terms of long-term client cost." A wind tower inspired by Middle Eastern designs was placed over the kitchen of the house to encourage airflow. The students carefully studied the social patterns of Mason's Bend, where a number of other Rural Studio projects have been built, so that this new addition would fit into its surroundings. Aside from the economical construction design, a clear interest in sustainability has informed this project.

Wie andere Projekte von Rural Studio war auch Christine's House eine Abschlussarbeit in Architektur an der Universität Auburn. Die zwei an der Planung des Hauses beteiligten jungen Architekten, Amy Green Bullington und Stephen Long, erlangten ihre B.-Arch.-Abschlüsse 2005. Sie nutzten die in der Gegend verbreitete rote Tonerde, um aus einer Mischung aus 70 % Erde, 25 % Pappmaschee aus Zeitungen und 5 % Portlandzement, die sie in Pappkartons unterschiedlicher Größe gossen, Ziegel für die beiden Hauptwände des Hauses herzustellen. Amy Bullington erklärt: „Dieser hybride Lehmziegelmix ist eine einfache Modifikation der traditionellen Ziegelfertigung und erfordert kaum besondere Fertigkeiten oder technische Ausrüstung, sein hoher Dämmfaktor (R33 bei einer 30,5 cm starken Wand) macht ihn für den Auftraggeber attraktiv im Hinblick auf Langzeitkosten." Ein von der nahöstlichen Tradition inspirierter Windturm wurde über der Küche installiert und fördert die Belüftung. Die Studenten hatten sich intensiv mit dem Sozialgefüge in Mason's Bend auseinandergesetzt, wo Rural Studio bereits zahlreiche andere Projekte realisiert hat, sodass sich der neueste Bau sinnvoll einfügt. Abgesehen von der sparsamen Bauweise ist das Projekt auch von einem Interesse an Nachhaltigkeit geprägt.

Comme d'autres travaux de Rural Studio, la « maison de Christine » est en réalité l'aboutissement d'une thèse d'architecture préparée à l'université Auburn. Les deux jeunes architectes impliqués dans ce projet, Amy Green Bullington et Stephen Long, ont reçu leur diplôme de B. Arch d'Auburn en 2005. Ils ont profité de la présence abondante d'argile rouge dans la région pour fabriquer des briques de diverses dimensions en mélangeant 70 % d'argile, 25 % de pulpe de papier et 5 % de ciment Portland. Elles constituent les deux murs principaux. Comme l'explique Amy Bullington : « Ce mélange hybride d'adobes, simple modification du processus traditionnel de fabrication des briques, demande peu de compétence ou d'équipement, et son pouvoir élevé d'isolation (taux d'isolation très élevé de R33 pour un mur de 30,5 cm d'épaisseur) est séduisant sur le plan du coût à long terme pour le client. » Une tour à vent, inspirée d'une typologie moyen-orientale, a été installée au-dessus de la cuisine pour faciliter la ventilation naturelle. Les étudiants ont soigneusement étudié les rapports sociaux de Mason's Bend, où un certain nombre de projets de Rural Studio ont été réalisés, pour que cette nouvelle construction s'intègre de façon appropriée. En dehors des aspects économiques de sa construction, ce projet est clairement placé sous le signe de la durabilité.

The emphasis on natural, locally obtained materials and simple methods of aeration make the house, a very basic structure, ecologically sound.

Die Konzentration auf natürliche, lokal verfügbare Materialien und einfache Belüftungsmethoden machen das Haus, eine sehr einfache Konstruktion, zu einem ökologisch verträglichen Bau.

L'accent mis sur les matériaux naturels locaux et des méthodes d'aération simples fait de cette construction très basique un exemple de solution écologique.

LAURENT SAVIOZ

Laurent Savioz Architecte
Ch. St-Hubert 2
1950 Sion
Switzerland

Tel: +41 27 322 54 91
Fax: +41 27 322 68 83
E-mail: contact@loar.ch
Web: www.loar.ch

LAURENT SAVIOZ was born in 1976 and received his degree in Architecture from the Haute École Spécialisée (HES) of Fribourg (1998). He worked in the office of Bonnard & Woeffray in Monthey, Switzerland (1999–2003), before co-founding Savioz Meyer Fabrizzi in Sion with François Meyer and Claude Fabrizzi in 2004. He carried forward the Roduit House (Chamoson, 2004–05, published here) on his own. Projects he has worked on with Savioz Meyer Fabrizzi include the Hôtel de la Poste (Sierre, 2006–07), while they are currently working on a footbridge over the Rhone at Finges (Sierre, 2006–); the construction supervision of a new building at the mountain Cabane de Moiry (Grimentz, 2006–); the Iseli House (Venthône, 2007–); and a primary school (Vollèges, 2007–), all in Switzerland.

LAURENT SAVIOZ wurde 1976 geboren und schloss sein Architekturstudium 1998 an der Haute École Spécialisée (HES) in Fribourg ab. Er arbeitete für Bonnard & Woeffray in Monthey, Schweiz (1999–2003), bevor er 2004 mit François Meyer und Claude Fabrizzi das Büro Savioz Meyer Fabrizzi gründete. Das Haus Roduit (Chamoson, 2004–05, hier vorgestellt) realisierte er allein. Zu den gemeinsamen Projekten von Savioz Meyer Fabrizzi zählt das Hôtel de la Poste (Sierre, 2006–07), zu den neueren Projekten zählen eine Fußgängerbrücke über die Rhône bei Finges (Sierre, 2006–), die Bauleitung bei einem Neubau am Berg Cabane de Moiry (Grimentz, 2006–), das Haus Iseli (Venthône, 2007–) und eine Grundschule (Vollèges, 2007–), alle in der Schweiz.

LAURENT SAVIOZ, né en 1976, est diplômé d'architecture de la Haute École Spécialisée (HES) de Fribourg (1998). Il a travaillé dans l'agence Bonnard & Woeffray à Monthey, Suisse (1999–2003), avant de cofonder Savioz Meyer Fabrizzi à Sion avec François Meyer et Claude Fabrizzi, en 2004. Il a conçu lui-même la maison Roduit (Chamoson, 2004–05, présentée ici). Parmi ses projets pour Savioz Meyer Fabrizzi, tous en Suisse : l'Hôtel de la Poste (Sierre, 2006–07) ; une passerelle sur le Rhône à Finges (Sierre, 2006–) ; la supervision de la construction d'un nouveau bâtiment de montagne à la Cabane de Moiry (Grimentz, 2006–) ; la maison Iseli (Venthône, 2007–) et une école primaire (Vollèges, 2007–).

RODUIT HOUSE
Chamoson, Switzerland, 2004–05

Floor area: 258 m². Clients: Josyane and Michel Roduit
Cost: not disclosed

Chamoson is located in the mountains above the Rhône Valley in the Canton of the Valais. Set against a soaring cliff face, the town includes a number of old structures such as the 1814 stone and wood structure that Josyane and Michel Roduit asked the young architect Laurent Savioz to renovate in 2003. Owners of a much more traditional wooden vacation house directly adjacent to the older building, the Roduits allowed Savioz a good deal of freedom—which he used to replace the wooden upper section with thick concrete walls, retaining the original natural stone walls at the base. The renovated house contains a living room, kitchen, office, bedroom, and on the lower level a wine cellar, painting studio, and small exhibition gallery for the owner's paintings. Given the rather conservative nature of the township, it was somewhat surprising that they allowed this very modern conversion, insisting nonetheless that openings in the house correspond to the locations of the original windows. Laurent Savioz designed the kitchen for the house as well, and the owners have respected the rather harsh interior concrete surfaces, that seem to be as much inspired by the typical "Swiss box" contemporary architecture as they are by certain modern Japanese dwellings. What sets the Roduit House apart is that it retains its old, natural stone base and original form.

Chamoson liegt in den Bergen über dem Rhônetal im Kanton Wallis. In dem vor einer beeindruckenden Steilwand gelegenen Städtchen stehen auch einige Altbauten wie das Haus aus Stein und Holz von 1814, das Josyane and Michel Roduit 2003 von dem jungen Architekten Laurent Savioz umbauen ließen. Die Roduits, auch Eigentümer eines wesentlich traditionelleren Ferienhauses aus Holz unmittelbar neben dem älteren Gebäude, ließen Savioz viel Freiheit – die er nutzte, um den oberen Bereich des Hauses aus Holz durch massive Betonmauern zu ersetzen, dabei jedoch die Natursteinmauern des Untergeschosses erhielt. Das umgebaute Haus umfasst Wohnzimmer, Küche, Büro, Schlafzimmer sowie im unteren Geschoss einen Weinkeller, ein Maleratelier und eine kleine Galerie für die Bilder des Eigentümers. Angesichts des eher konservativen Umfelds im Ort ist es erstaunlich, dass man diesem sehr modernen Umbau zustimmte. Allerdings beharrte man darauf, dass die Öffnungen des Hauses mit den ursprünglichen Fensteröffnungen übereinzustimmen hätten. Laurent Savioz entwarf auch die Küche des Hauses, und die Auftraggeber akzeptierten die eher strengen Betonoberflächen im Interieur, die ebenso sehr von der typischen zeitgenössischen „Swiss-Box"-Architektur inspiriert zu sein scheinen, wie von manchen modernen Wohnbauten in Japan. Was das Haus Roduit zu etwas Besonderem macht, ist die Erhaltung des alten Natursteinsockels und der ursprünglichen Hausform.

Chamoson est une petite ville du canton du Valais, située au-dessus de la vallée du Rhône. Implantée au pied d'une falaise, elle possède un certain nombre de constructions anciennes comme cette maison de pierre et de bois datant de 1814, que Josyane et Michel Roduit ont demandé au jeune architecte Laurent Savioz de rénover en 2003. Propriétaires d'une maison de vacances en bois de facture beaucoup plus traditionnelle directement adjacente à l'ancienne construction, les Roduit ont accordé une grande liberté à Savioz, qu'il a mise à profit pour remplacer la partie supérieure en bois par d'épais murs de béton, tout en conservant les murs de pierre de la base. La maison rénovée contient un séjour, une cuisine, un bureau, une salle de bains et, à l'étage inférieur, une cave à vin, un atelier de peinture et une petite galerie d'exposition pour les peintures du propriétaire. Étant donnée la nature assez conservatrice de la ville, on peut être surpris que le permis de construire ait été accordé à une conversion aussi moderne, avec cependant l'obligation pour les ouvertures de se trouver à la même place que les anciennes. Laurent Savioz a également conçu la cuisine, et les propriétaires ont respecté les surfaces de béton assez brutes de l'intérieur, qui semblent être aussi bien inspirées par le concept de la « boîte suisse », typique de l'architecture contemporaine, que par certaines réalisations japonaises. Ce qui caractérise la maison Roduit réside dans le choix d'avoir retenu sa base en vieilles pierres naturelles, et conservé sa forme originale.

Although the house is based on existing stone walls, the use of concrete to replace the original timber upper section gives it a strong, contemporary presence.

Zwar ruht das Haus auf seinen alten Steinmauern, doch durch das Ersetzen des oberen hölzernen Fassadenabschnitts durch Beton gewinnt es eine bewusst zeitgenössische Präsenz.

Bien que la maison ait été construite à partir de murs existants, le recours au béton pour remplacer la partie supérieure en bois lui assure une forte présence contemporaine.

The house sits beneath the sheer cliff faces that rise above Chamoson, connecting its stone base to the site in an almost literal way.

Das Haus liegt unterhalb der Felswände über Chamoson, die einen geradezu buchstäblichen Bezug zwischen dem steinernen Sockel des Hauses und der Umgebung herstellen.

La maison se dresse sous une paroi de pierre qui s'élève au-dessus de la commune de Chamoson ; la connexion au site semble presque littérale.

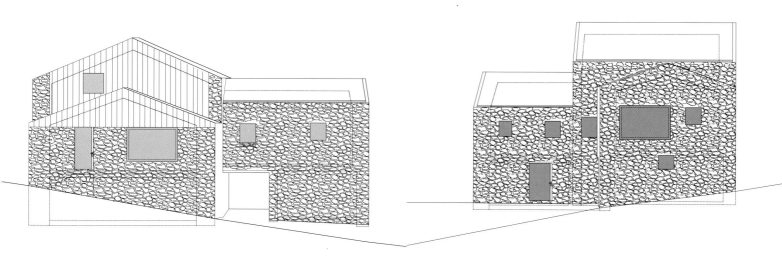

The interior of the house is largely made of concrete, with an austerity frequently seen in contemporary "Swiss box" architecture.

Beton dominiert das Interieur des Hauses, eine Strenge, die bei zeitgenössischer „Swiss-Box"-Architektur oft zu beobachten ist.

L'intérieur de la maison est en grande partie en béton. Ce type d'austérité est fréquent dans l'architecture contemporaine de la « boîte suisse ».

The orange color in the kitchen was selected by the client. Other tones in the house are decidedly muted. Below, right, the master bedroom with an overhead window that looks out to the cliffs above.

Das Orange in der Küche wurde vom Bauherrn ausgewählt. Die übrigen Farben im Haus sind entschieden gedämpfter. Rechts unten das Haupt-schlafzimmer mit einem Dachfenster mit Blick auf die aufragenden Felsen.

La couleur orange de la cuisine a été choisie par le client. Les autres couleurs présentes dans la maison sont nettement plus assourdies. Ci-dessous, à droite, la chambre princi-pale avec un vasistas donnant sur les falaises.

SEARCH & CMA

SeARCH
Hamerstraat 3
1021 JT Amsterdam
The Netherlands

Tel: +31 20 788 99 00
Fax: +31 20 788 99 11
E-mail: info@search.nl
Web: www.search.nl

CMA / Christian Müller Architects
Delftseplein 36
3013 AA Rotterdam
The Netherlands

Tel: +31 10 213 67 63
E-mail: mail@christian-muller.com
www.christian-muller.com

SEARCH is an architecture office, established in Amsterdam in 2002 by Bjarne Mastenbroek and Ad Bogerman. Bjarne Mastenbroek was born in 1964, attended the TU Delft Faculty of Architecture (1982–89) and then worked in the Van Gameren Mastenbroek project team that was part of architectengroep in Amsterdam from 1993. SeARCH currently employs 20 people. Christian Müller was born in 1963 in Switzerland, and graduated from the ETH in Zurich in 1989. He is the Principal of Christian Müller Architects (**CMA**, Rotterdam) and is currently collaborating with SeARCH, Kraaijvanger, Urbis, and GGAU on a number of projects. SeARCH has worked on the Dutch Embassy in Addis Ababa (1998–); Triade, the conversion and extension of a cultural education center (Den Helder, 1997–2001); Bredero College, extension to a trade school (Amsterdam Noord, 1998–2001); and buildings in Lelystad and Alemere. They also completed the Posbank Tea Pavilion (National Park Veluwe Zoom, Rheden, 1998–2002); the TwentseWelle museum in Enschede (2003–08); a watchtower in Putten (2004–09); and Villa Vals (Vals, Switzerland, 2005–09, published here), which is the work of SeARCH (Bjarne Mastenbroek) and Christian Müller Architects (Christian Müller), all in the Netherlands unless stated otherwise. Recent projects are a new synagogue (2005–10) in Amsterdam; a conference and activity center in Hillerød (Denmark (2007–11); large-scale mixed-use projects in Leuven (Belgium, 2003–12); and several projects in Bahrain.

Das Architekturbüro **SEARCH** wurde 2002 von Bjarne Mastenbroek und Ad Bogerman in Amsterdam gegründet. Bjarne Mastenbroek wurde 1964 geboren, studierte an der Fakultät für Architektur der TU Delft (1982–89) und arbeitete anschließend im Projektteam Van Gameren Mastenbroek, das ab 1993 Teil der architectengroep in Amsterdam war. Derzeit beschäftigt SeARCH 20 Mitarbeiter. Christian Müller wurde 1963 in der Schweiz geboren und schloss sein Studium 1989 an der ETH Zürich ab. Er leitet Christian Müller Architects (**CMA**, Rotterdam) und arbeitet zurzeit an verschiedenen Projekten mit SeARCH, Kraaijvanger, Urbis und GGAU zusammen. SeARCH arbeitete an der niederländischen Botschaft in Addis Abeba (ab 1998), und hat Triade, den Umbau und die Erweiterung eines Kulturbildungszentrums (Den Helder, 1997–2001), die Erweiterung einer Handelsschule am Bredero College (Amsterdam Noord, 1998–2001) sowie Bauten in Lelystad und Alemere geplant. Realisieren konnten sie außerdem den Posbank Teepavillon (Nationalpark Veluwe Zoom, Rheden, 1998–2002), das Museum TwentseWelle in Enschede (2003–08), die Villa Vals (Vals, Schweiz, 2005–09, hier vorgestellt) – eine Kooperation von SeARCH (Bjarne Mastenbroek) und Christian Müller Architects (Christian Müller) – sowie einen Wachturm in Putten (2004–09), alle in den Niederlanden sofern nicht anders angegeben. Aktuelle Projekte sind eine neue Synagoge in Amsterdam (2005–10), ein Konferenz- und Fitnesszentrum in Hillerød (Dänemark, 2007–11), ein Großprojekt mit gemischter Nutzung in Löwen (Belgien, 2003–12) und verschiedene Projekte in Bahrain.

SEARCH est une agence créée à Amsterdam en 2002 par Bjarne Mastenbroek et Ad Bogerman. Bjarne Mastenbroek, né en 1964, a étudié à la Faculté d'architecture de la TU de Delft (1982–89), puis dans l'équipe de projet de Van Gameren Mastenbroek faisant partie de l'architectengroep d'Amsterdam à partir de 1993. SeARCH emploie actuellement vingt personnes. Christian Müller, né en 1963 en Suisse, est diplômé de l'ETH de Zurich (1989). Il dirige Christian Müller Architects (**CMA**, Rotterdam) et collabore actuellement avec SeARCH, Kraaijvanger, Urbis et GGAU sur un certain nombre de projets. SeARCH a réalisé l'ambassade néerlandaise à Addis Abeba (1998–) ; Triade, conversion et extension d'un centre éducatif culturel (Den Helder, 1997–2001) ; le Bredero College, extension d'une école de commerce (Amsterdam Noord, 1998–2001) ; et des immeubles à Lelystad et Alemere. Ils ont également réalisé le pavillon de thé de la Posbank (Parc national Veluwe Zoom, Rheden, 1998–2002) ; le musée TwentseWelle à Enschede (2003–08) ; une tour de guet à Putten (2004–09) ; et la villa Vals (Vals, Suisse, 2005–09, présentée ici), œuvre de SeARCH (Bjarne Mastenbroek) et de Christian Müller Architects (Christian Müller), le tout aux Pays-Bas, sauf mention contraire. Parmi leurs projets actuels, on compte une nouvelle synagogue (2005–10) à Amsterdam ; un centre de conférences et d'activités à Hillerød (Danemark, 2007–11) ; des projets d'immeubles mixtes de grandes dimensions à Louvain (Belgique, 2003–12) ; et plusieurs projets au Bahreïn.

VILLA VALS
Vals, Switzerland, 2005–09

Area: 285 m². Client: not disclosed
Cost: not disclosed

In the rather enclosed and remote valley of Vals, known mainly for the Thermal Baths by Peter Zumthor located there, the new house is set into the hillside, not far from the green stone structure by the Swiss master.

Im abgelegenen Tal von Vals, bekannt in erster Linie für die von Peter Zumthor gestaltete Therme, liegt das Haus eingebettet in den Hang, nicht weit vom grünlichen Steinbau des Schweizer Meisters.

Dans cette vallée plutôt isolée et encaissée, la maison s'insère dans le flanc d'une montagne, non loin de l'établissement thermal en pierre verte réalisé par le maître suisse Peter Zumthor, qui a fait la célébrité de Vals.

Until the completion of this house, the mountain village of Vals was best known for its mineral water and the Thermal Baths (1996) designed there by Peter Zumthor. Villa Vals is located close to the site of Zumthor's building, but it is largely below grade. "Shouldn't it be possible to conceal a house in an Alpine slope while still exploiting the wonderful views and allowing light to enter the building?", ask the architects. A central patio with a steep angle emphasizes and enlarges the views from the house, without challenging those of Zumthor's Baths. Local authorities approved the design of this house despite their reputation for conservative rulings. The placement of a typical old barn near the entrance to the house and the fact that access is through a tunnel seems to have swayed the authorities. The architects explain: "Switzerland's planning laws in this region dictate that it is only possible to grant a definitive planning permission after a timber model of the building's volume has first been constructed on site. This can then be accurately appraised by the local community and objected to if considered unsuitable. For this proposal, logic prevailed and this part of the process was deemed to be unnecessary."

Bis zur Fertigstellung dieses Hauses war das Bergdorf Vals am ehesten für sein Mineralwasser und die von Peter Zumthor entworfene Therme Vals (1996) bekannt. Die Villa Vals liegt nicht weit von Zumthors Bau, jedoch weitgehend unter der Geländeoberfläche. „Sollte es nicht möglich sein," fragen die Architekten, „ein Haus in einem Alpenhang zu verbergen und dabei trotzdem die wunderbare Aussicht zu nutzen und Licht in den Bau zu lassen?" Ein zentraler Innenhof mit steiler Neigung unterstreicht den Blick, den das Haus bietet, und lässt ihn noch spektakulärer wirken, ohne den Ausblick von Zumthors Therme zu beeinträchtigen. Die örtlichen Behörden genehmigten den Bau trotz ihres Rufs, äußerst konservativ zu sein. Dass in der Nähe des Eingangs eine traditionelle alte Scheune steht und man den Bau durch einen Tunnel betritt, scheint die Behörden positiv gestimmt zu haben. Die Architekten erklären: „Die schweizerischen Bauvorschriften dieser Region sehen vor, dass eine verbindliche Baugenehmigung nur erteilt werden kann, wenn zuvor ein Holzmodell des Baukörpers vor Ort errichtet wurde. Dies erlaubt es den Anwohnern, das Gebäude genau zu beurteilen und Einspruch zu erheben, falls es unpassend erscheint. Bei diesem Entwurf jedoch war es ein Gebot der Logik, dass dieser Teil des Procederes für unnötig befunden wurde."

Jusqu'à l'achèvement de cette maison, le village de montagne de Vals était surtout connu pour son eau et ses thermes conçus par Peter Zumthor (1996). La villa Vals se trouve non loin de ce bâtiment mais est en grande partie enterrée. « Ne serait-il pas possible de dissimuler une maison dans une pente d'alpage, tout en bénéficiant de vues magnifiques et en permettant au soleil d'éclairer cette construction ? », se sont demandés les architectes. Un patio central découpé dans la pente exploite la vue splendide, sans gêner celle de l'établissement de bains de Zumthor. Les autorités locales ont approuvé ce projet malgré leur réputation de conservatisme. L'implantation d'une vieille grange typique près de l'entrée de la maison et son accès par un tunnel les ont sans doute rassurées. « La réglementation de la construction suisse dans cette région dit que l'on ne peut obtenir de permis de construire définitif qu'après l'édification d'une maquette en bois du volume du bâtiment sur le site, ce qui permet à la communauté de juger du projet et de faire ses observations. Pour notre proposition, la logique a prévalu et cette partie du processus d'autorisation a été jugée inutile. »

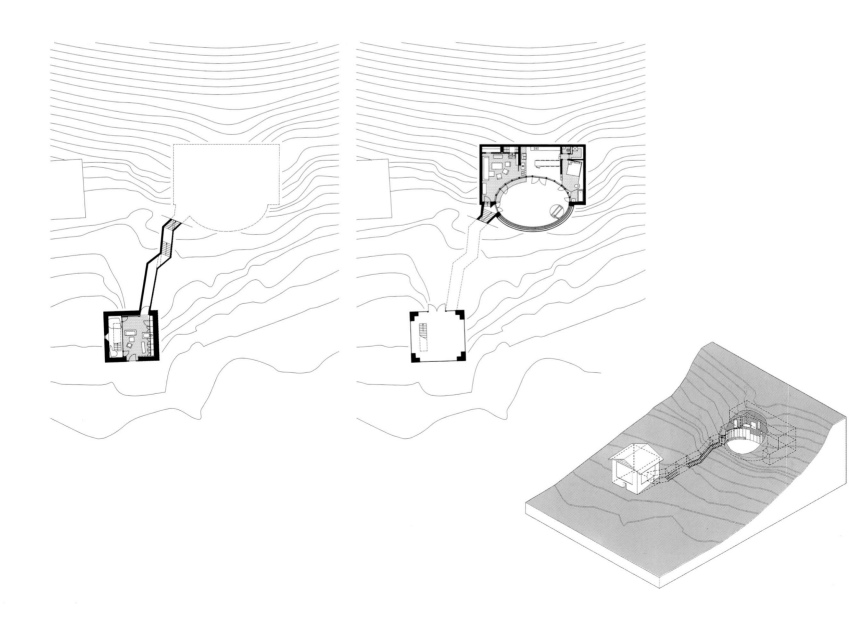

The oval form of the house, visible in the plans to the left, is echoed in the curious emergent part of the largely buried structure.

Die ovale Form des Hauses, zu sehen an den Grundrissen links, wird formal im eigentümlich aufragenden Teil des überwiegend versenkten Baus aufgegriffen.

La forme ovale de la maison visible sur les plans de gauche, se retrouve dans l'étrange partie émergeante de la structure, autrement enterrée pour la plupart.

The concrete surfaces of the house are rough like the mountain terrain into which it is embedded.

Die Betonoberflächen des Hauses sind ebenso rau wie das Felsterrain, in das das Domizil eingebettet wurde.

À l'intérieur, les murs de la maison sont restés en béton brut, rappelant le terrain montagnard dans lequel elle s'inscrit.

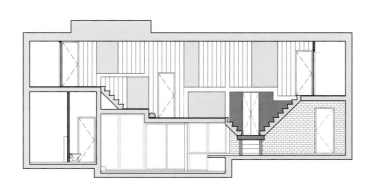

Concrete alternates with stone and furniture that may be more "cozy" than the architects would have imagined.

Beton im Wechselspiel mit Stein und einem Mobiliar, das möglicherweise „gemütlicher" ist, als es sich die Architekten vorgestellt haben.

Le béton alterne avec des parties en pierre mais aussi des meubles de style peut-être plus cosy que les architectes ne l'auraient souhaité.

As the drawing to the right demonstrates, the house is largely underground, with its concrete surfaces in some sense echoing the stone of the mountain itself.

Wie die Zeichnung rechts veranschaulicht, liegt das Haus überwiegend unter der Geländeoberfläche. In gewisser Weise antworten die Betonflächen auf den Fels des Berges.

Comme le montre l'élévation de sa « façade » à droite, la maison est en grande partie enterrée. Le béton omniprésent fait écho au sol caillouteux de la montagne.

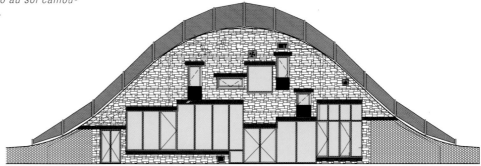

SELGASCANO

SELGASCANO
Guecho 27
28023 Madrid
Spain

Tel: +34 91 30 76 481
E-mail: selgas1@selgascano.com
Web: www.selgascano.net

JOSÉ SELGAS was born in Madrid in 1965. He got his architecture degree at the ETSAM in 1992 and then worked with Francesco Venecia in Naples, Italy (1994–95). **LUCÍA CANO** was also born in Madrid in 1965, and received her degree from the ETSAM in 1992. She worked with Julio Cano Lasso from 1997 to 2003. Selgas and Cano created their present firm in 2003. They have won a number of First Prize awards in competitions, including: Ideas Competition for Social Housing (Madrid, 1993); the competition for the Badajoz Center (1999–2006); for the Cartagena Conference and Auditorium (2001–08); and for a similar facility in Plasencia (2005–09), all in Spain. They also participated in the "On-Site: New Architecture in Spain" exhibition at the Museum of Modern Art (New York, 2006). After the Silicon House (La Florida, Madrid, 2006, published here), the architects are presently completing the construction of 20 garden villas in Vallecas, Madrid, Spain.

JOSÉ SELGAS wurde 1965 in Madrid geboren. Sein Architekturstudium schloss er 1992 an der ETSAM ab; anschließend arbeitete er für Francesco Venecia in Neapel (1994–95). **LUCÍA CANO** wurde ebenfalls 1965 in Madrid geboren und machte ihren Abschluss 1992 an der ETSAM. Von 1997 bis 2003 arbeitete sie für Julio Cano Lasso. Ihr gegenwärtiges Büro gründeten Selgas und Cano 2003. Sie haben bereits mehrfach erste Preise bei Wettbewerben gewonnen, darunter bei einem Ideenwettbewerb für ein Sozialbauprojekt (Madrid, 1993), einem Wettbewerb für das Badajoz Center (1999–2006) sowie für das Konferenzzentrum und Auditorium in Cartagena (2001–08) und eine ähnliche Einrichtung in Plasencia (2005–09), alle in Spanien. Darüber hinaus waren sie auch in der Ausstellung „On-Site: New Architecture in Spain" am Museum of Modern Art vertreten (New York, 2006). Seit der Fertigstellung der Casa de Silicona (La Florida, Madrid, 2006, hier vorgestellt) arbeiten die Architekten zurzeit an 20 Gartenvillen in Vallecas, Madrid, Spanien.

JOSÉ SELGAS, né à Madrid en 1965, est diplômé en architecture de l'ETSAM (1992). Il a ensuite travaillé pour Francesco Venecia à Naples, Italie (1994–95). **LUCÍA CANO**, également née à Madrid en 1965, est diplômée de l'ETSAM (1992). Elle a travaillé avec Julio Cano Lasso de 1997 à 2003. Selgas et Cano ont créé leur agence en 2003. Ils ont remporté un certain nombre de premiers prix lors de concours en Espagne dont un concours d'idée pour des logements sociaux (Madrid, 1993) ; celui du centre de Badajoz (1999–2006) ; celui pour le centre de conférences et auditorium de Cartagène (2001–08) et un autre projet similaire à Plasencia (2005–09). Ils ont également participé à « On-Site : New Architecture in Spain », exposition organisée au Museum of Modern Art (New York, 2006). Après la maison Silicone (La Florida, Madrid, 2006, présentée ici), ils achèvent actuellement la construction de 20 villas-jardin à Vallecas, Madrid, Espagne.

SILICON HOUSE

La Florida, Madrid, Spain, 2006

Floor area: 160 m². Client: SELGASCANO
Cost: not disclosed

The architects started by plotting the location of trees on their site, and built this house around them, basing the design on two main platforms. Since the owners have planted even more trees, José Selgas says that, with time, he imagines that the house will become almost invisible. "The only thing we can say about the interior space is that it goes unnoticed," say the architects; "this is a project that is only related to the exterior." Colored orange and dark blue with paints designed for oil rigs, the rather freely formed platforms circle partially around a large exterior terrace that also allows for trees to emerge. The platforms are essentially divided between night and day. The partially buried living room, with its large collection of books, looks out on the natural setting through a continuous band of Plexiglas windows, while light also comes from above through Plexiglas bubbles in the roof. Plastic or rubber is present almost everywhere—with recycled tires being used as roofing material, and Verner Panton objects within. There is a curious opposition between a house made largely of synthetic materials and the extreme respect for nature displayed in the location and openness of the house.

Die Architekten kartierten zunächst den Standort der Bäume auf ihrem Grundstück und bauten das Haus, das im Wesentlichen auf zwei Plattformen ruht, schließlich um sie herum. Da die Bauherren inzwischen noch weitere Bäume gepflanzt haben, geht José Selgas davon aus, dass das Haus mit der Zeit geradezu verschwinden wird. „Das einzige was wir über den Innenraum sagen können, ist, dass man ihn übersieht", sagen die Architekten. „Dieses Projekt sucht seine Bezüge ausschließlich im Außenraum." Die frei geformten Plattformen sind orange und dunkelblau gestrichen worden, Farben, die sonst bei Bohrinseln verwendet werden. Sie schmiegen sich zum Teil um eine große Außenterrasse, aus der ebenfalls Bäume herauszuwachsen scheinen. Die Plattformen teilen sich mehr oder weniger in Tag und Nacht. Vom teilweise in den Boden versenkten Wohnraum mit seiner umfangreichen Büchersammlung erlaubt ein durchgängiges Band von Plexiglasfenstern Ausblicke in die Umgebung, Licht fällt zudem durch Plexiglasbullaugen in der Decke ein. Plastik und Gummi sind nahezu allgegenwärtig – recycelte Autoreifen dienen als Dachmaterial, im Innern des Hauses finden sich Verner-Panton-Möbel. Es ist ein eigentümlicher Gegensatz zwischen dem überwiegend aus synthetischen Materialien gebauten Haus und dem außerordentlichen Respekt vor der Natur, der sich in der Anlage und Offenheit des Hauses spiegelt.

Les architectes ont commencé par noter l'implantation des arbres sur le terrain et construit la maison tout autour sur deux plates-formes principales. Comme les propriétaires ont continué à planter de nouveaux arbres, José Selgas pense qu'avec le temps leur maison sera presque invisible. « La seule chose que nous pouvons dire de l'espace intérieur est qu'il se déploie sans se faire remarquer, précise l'architecte, c'est un projet en relation unique avec l'extérieur. » Colorées en orange et bleu sombre à l'aide de peintures utilisées pour les exploitations pétrolières, les plates-formes, de contours assez libres, entourent partiellement une vaste terrasse extérieure transpercée de quelques arbres. Elles sont divisées en zone de jour et zone de nuit. Le séjour, en partie enterré, qui se caractérise par une importante collection de livres, donne sur la nature par des fenêtres en bandeau, en Plexiglas. La lumière provient également de petites bulles en Plexiglas qui traversent le toit. Le plastique ou le caoutchouc sont des matériaux omniprésents. Des pneus recyclés ont servi à recouvrir la toiture et l'on trouve des créations de Verner Panton à l'intérieur. L'opposition est curieuse entre cette maison réalisée en grande partie en matériaux synthétiques et l'extrême respect de la nature manifesté dans son implantation et son ouverture.

The bright color or plastics used in the house are in intentional contrast to the natural setting, but the house is willfully integrated into its site.

Die kräftigen Farben und Kunststoffe am Haus sind ein gewollter Kontrast zur umgebenden Natur. Dennoch ist das Haus bewusst in das Grundstück integriert.

La couleur vive et les plastiques utilisés sont en contraste volontaire avec le cadre naturel, mais la maison s'intègre heureusement à son site.

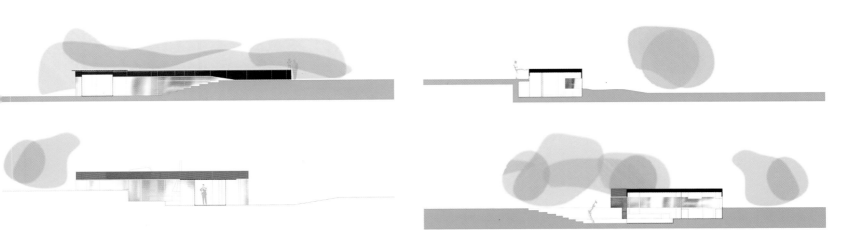

The house is an unexpected combination of clean modern lines and a brightly colored roof slab with spherical windows that looks like it might have come directly out of the 1960s.

Das Haus ist eine überraschende Kombination aus moderner Linienführung und einer leuchtendfarbigen Dachplatte mit sphärischen Oberlichtern, die wirken, als seien sie direkt den 1960er-Jahren entsprungen.

La maison est une combinaison inattendue de lignes nettes et modernes et d'une toiture plate à verrières sphériques d'un style inspiré des années 1960.

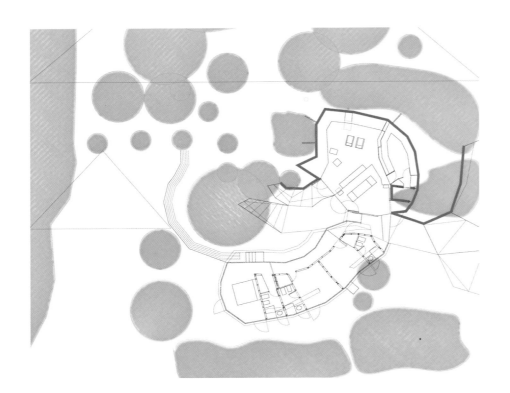

A site plan shows how the house was integrated into existing groups of vegetation. The kitchen (below) has a broad strip window looking out to the garden.

Ein Lageplan illustriert, wie das Haus in die bestehende Begrünung integriert wurde. Die Küche (unten) hat ein breites Fensterband mit Ausblick in den Garten.

Le plan du terrain montre l'intégration de la maison dans la végétation existante. La cuisine, ci-dessous, possède une importante fenêtre en bandeau qui donne sur le jardin.

Furniture, often in plastic, animates
the interior and continues the theme
of intentional playfulness.

*Das Mobiliar, oft aus Kunststoff,
belebt das Interieur und setzt das
spielerische Gesamtthema fort.*

*Souvent en plastique, le mobilier
anime l'intérieur et reprend le thème
ludique du projet.*

SHIM-SUTCLIFFE

Shim-Sutcliffe Architects Inc.
441 Queen Street East
Toronto
Ontario M5A 1T5
Canada

Tel: +1 416 368 3892
Fax: +1 416 368 9468
E-mail: info@shimsut.com
Web: www.shim-sutcliffe.com

Brigitte Shim was born in Kingston, Jamaica, in 1958. She received her B.Arch and her Bachelor of Environmental Studies degrees from the University of Waterloo in Ontario. She worked in the office of Arthur Erickson (1981), and Baird/Sampson in Toronto, before creating her own firm, Brigitte Shim Architect (1988–94). She is a principal and co-founder of **SHIM-SUTCLIFFE**, created in Toronto in 1994. She is presently an Associate Professor at the University of Toronto's Faculty of Architecture and Design. Howard Sutcliffe was born in Yorkshire, England, in 1958. He also received his B.Arch and his Bachelor of Environmental Studies degrees from the University of Waterloo in Ontario. He worked in the offices of Barton Myers (1984–86) and Merrick Architecture until 1993, creating Shim-Sutcliffe with Brigitte Shim the following year. They have recently completed the Ravine Guest House (Don Mills, Ontario, 2003–04, published here); the house on Hurricane Lake (Haliburton, Ontario, 2004–05); the Craven Road Studio (Toronto, 2006); and the Massey College in the University of Toronto (2002–06), all in Canada. Their current work includes the Bet Ha'am Synagogue (Portland, Maine, USA); and the Integral House (Toronto, Canada).

Brigitte Shim wurde 1958 in Kingston, Jamaica, geboren. Sie absolvierte ihren B.Arch. sowie ihren Bachelor of Environmental Studies an der University of Waterloo in Ontario. Sie arbeitete für Arthur Erickson (1981) und Baird/Sampson in Toronto, bevor sie ihr Büro Brigitte Shim Architect (1988–94) gründete. Sie ist Seniorpartnerin und Mitbegründerin von **SHIM-SUTCLIFFE**, gegründet 1994 in Toronto. Derzeit ist sie außerordentliche Professorin an der Fakultät für Architektur und Design an der Universität Toronto. Howard Sutcliffe wurde 1958 in Yorkshire, England, geboren. Auch er absolvierte seinen B.Arch. und seinen Bachelor of Environmental Studies an der University of Waterloo in Ontario. Bis 1993 arbeitete er für Barton Myers (1984–86) sowie Merrick Architecture und gründete mit Brigitte Shim im darauf folgenden Jahr Shim-Sutcliffe. Zu den neueren Projekten gehören das Ravine Guest House (Don Mills, Ontario, 2003–04, hier vorgestellt), das Haus am Hurricane Lake (Haliburton, Ontario, 2004–05), das Craven Road Studio (Toronto, 2006) sowie das Massey College an der Universität Toronto (2002–06), alle in Kanada. Aktuelle Projekte sind u. a. die Synagoge Bet Ha'am (Portland, Maine, USA) sowie das Integral House (Toronto, Kanada).

Brigitte Shim, née à Kingston, Jamaïque, en 1958, a obtenu un diplôme d'architecture et un diplôme d'études environnementales à l'université de Waterloo en Ontario. Elle a travaillé dans l'agence d'Arthur Erickson (1981) et chez Baird/Sampson à Toronto, avant de créer sa propre structure, Brigitte Shim Architect (1988–94). Elle est directrice et cofondatrice de **SHIM-SUTCLIFFE**, agence fondée à Toronto en 1994. Actuellement, elle est professeure associée à la faculté d'architecture et de design de l'université de Toronto. Howard Sutcliffe, né dans le Yorkshire, Grande-Bretagne, en 1958, a fait les mêmes études que Brigitte Shim en Ontario. Il a travaillé dans les agences de Barton Myers (1984–86) et de Merrick Architecture jusqu'en 1993, fondant Shim-Sutcliffe avec Brigitte Shim l'année suivante. Ils ont récemment achevé la Ravine Guest House (Don Mills, Ontario, 2003–04, présentée ici) ; une maison sur le lac Hurricane (Haliburton, Ontario, 2004–05) ; le Craven Road Studio (Toronto, 2006) et le Massey College à l'université de Toronto (2002–06). Actuellement, ils travaillent sur la synagogue Bet Ha'am (Portland, Maine, États-Unis) et sur la maison intégrale (Toronto, Canada).

RAVINE GUEST HOUSE

Don Mills, Ontario, Canada, 2003–04

Floor area: 42 m². Client: not disclosed. Cost: not disclosed
Team: Brigitte Shim, Howard Sutcliffe, Tony Azevedo, Min Wang

This guesthouse is located in the 1.2-hectare grounds of a Toronto property near a ravine. According to the architects, "It is conceived of as a glowing lantern in the forest, typologically related to greenhouses and traditional garden outbuildings." There is a bedroom, sitting room, bathroom, and kitchen in the Ravine Guest House, but the architects insist on ambiguity between indoor and outdoor spaces, despite the rigorous winter climate of Toronto. A large central "indoor-outdoor" fireplace confirms this effort. Folding wood and glass doors allow the living space and bedroom to open to the exterior in warm weather. A wooden footbridge, reflecting pool, and wooden terrace complete the 111 m² of exterior space that are part of the project.

Das Gästehaus liegt auf einem 1,2 ha großen Grundstück in Toronto unweit einer Schlucht. Den Architekten zufolge wurde es „als leuchtende Laterne im Wald entworfen, typologisch angelehnt an Gewächshäuser und traditionelle Gartenhäuser". Das Ravine Guest House umfasst Schlafzimmer, Wohnzimmer, Bad und Küche. Die Architekten beharren auf der Mehrdeutigkeit von Innen- und Außenraum, ungeachtet der strengen Winter in Toronto. Ein großer zentraler „Innen-/Außen"-Kamin unterstreicht dieses Anliegen. Falttüren aus Glas und Holz erlauben, Wohnraum und Schlafzimmer bei warmem Wetter vollständig nach außen zu öffnen. Eine Holzbrücke, ein Teich und eine Terrasse aus Holz vervollständigen die 111 m² großen Außenanlagen des Projekts.

Cette maison d'hôtes est implantée sur un terrain de 1,2 hectare près de Toronto, à proximité d'un ravin. « Elle est pensée comme une lanterne éclairée en forêt, et peut se relier typologiquement aux serres et aux cabanes de jardin traditionnelles », expliquent les architectes. Elle comprend une chambre, un salon, une salle de bains et une cuisine. Ses auteurs insistent sur l'ambiguïté de la relation entre les espaces intérieurs et extérieurs, malgré la rigueur des hivers de Toronto. La grande cheminée « intérieure/extérieure » renforce cet aspect. Des portes pliantes en bois et verre permettent d'ouvrir par beau temps l'espace de séjour et la chambre sur la nature. Une passerelle en bois, un bassin et une terrasse également en bois complètent les 111 m² d'espaces extérieurs qui font partie intégrante du projet.

Certainly not a typical holiday cabin, the small guest house orchestrates opaque, translucent and transparent surfaces to create a shelter that is in communion with the natural surroundings.

Das kleine Gästehaus, sicherlich kein typisches Ferienhaus, orchestriert opake, transluzente und transparente Flächen zu einem schützenden Ort, der sich harmonisch in sein natürliches Umfeld fügt.

Résidence de vacances atypique, la petite maison des invités orchestre savamment les plans opaques, translucides ou transparents pour créer un abri en communion avec l'environnement naturel.

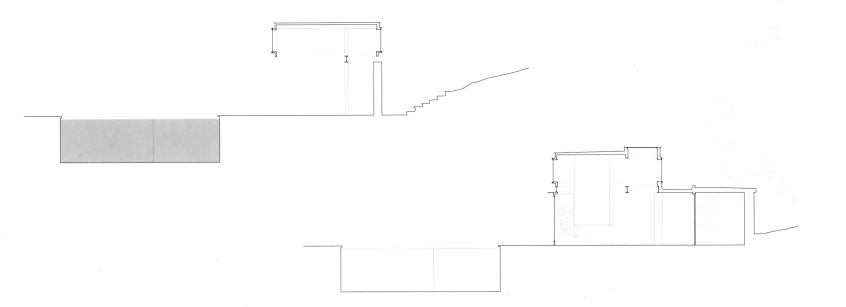

SIMAS AND GRINSPUM

Simas and Grinspum
Rua Fidalga 163, Casa 2
05432–070 São Paulo, SP
Brazil

Tel: +55 11 8299 3099
E-mail: marisimas@gmail.com

GABRIEL GRINSPUM was born in 1978 in São Paulo, Brazil, and attended the FAU-USP (Faculdade de Arquitetura e Urbanismo de São Paulo da Universidade de São Paulo, 1998–03). He has been working at Brazil Architecture since 1998, where he is currently developing a project for the new headquarters of the Shalom Community. He has had his own office since 2004, carrying forward the remodeling of apartments and houses; an Education Center linked to the Rainha da Paz School and a Community Center for the Christian Congregation, both located in Morro Grande (São Paulo); Pier House (Paraty, Rio de Janeiro, 2009, published here); and a Family House (Marumbi, São Paulo, 2010), all in Brazil. He works in partnership with **MARIANA SIMAS,** who is a collaborator of Marcio Kogan (Studio MK27).

GABRIEL GRINSPUM wurde 1978 in São Paulo, Brasilien, geboren und studierte von 1998 bis 2003 an der FAU-USP (Faculdade de Arquitetura e Urbanismo de São Paulo da Universidade de São Paulo). Er arbeitet seit 1998 bei Brazil Architecture, wo er gegenwärtig ein Projekt für das neue Hauptquartier der Gemeinschaft Shalom entwickelt. Sein eigenes Büro besteht seit 2004 und saniert Wohnbauten und Einfamilienhäuser, plant ein Ausbildungszentrum im Verbund mit der Schule Rainha da Paz, ein Gemeindezentrum für die christliche Ordensgemeinschaft, beide in Morro Grande (São Paulo), das Pier House (Paraty, Rio de Janeiro, 2009, hier veröffentlicht) sowie ein Wohnhaus (Marumbi, São Paulo, 2010), alle in Brasilien. Er arbeitet in Partnerschaft mit **MARIANA SIMAS,** einer Mitarbeiterin von Marcio Kogan (Studio MK27).

GABRIEL GRINSPUM, né en 1978 à São Paulo, a étudié à la FAU-USP (faculté d'architecture et d'urbanisme de Sao Paulo, à l'université de São Paulo, 1998–03). Il travaille à Brazil Architecture depuis 1998, où il met actuellement au point un projet pour le nouveau siège de la communauté Shalom. Il a ouvert sa propre agence en 2004, avec laquelle il a réalisé la rénovation d'appartements et de maisons : un centre éducatif lié à l'école « Rainha da Paz » et un centre communautaire pour une congrégation chrétienne, tous deux à Morro Grande (São Paulo) ; la maison de la jetée (Pier House, Paraty, Rio de Janeiro, 2009, présentée ici) et une maison pour une famille (Marumbi, São Paulo, 2010). Il travaille avec **MARIANA SIMAS,** collaboratrice de Marcio Kogan (Studio MK27).

PIER HOUSE
Paraty, Rio de Janeiro, Brazil, 2009

Area: 60 m²
Client: not disclosed. Cost: $100 000

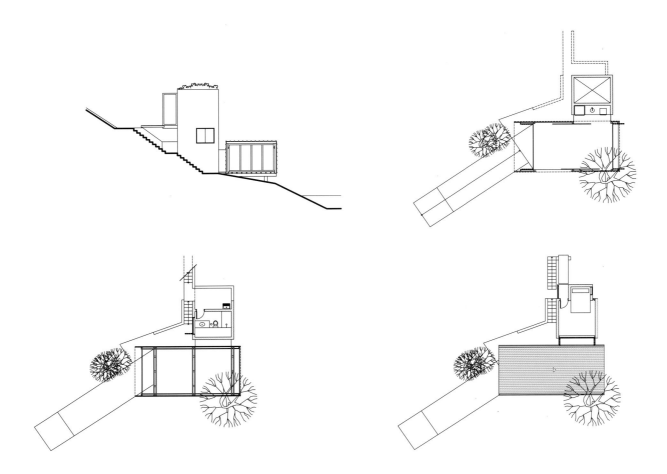

The Pier House assumes the typology of a boat house, with living space incorporated. As the drawings show, it is set on a slope.

Das Pier House folgt der Typologie eines Bootshauses mit darin enthaltenem Wohnraum. Wie die Zeichnungen zeigen, steht es auf einem Abhang.

La maison de la jetée reprend la typologie d'un hangar à bateaux à espace de vie intégré. Comme le montre le dessin, elle est implantée dans une pente.

This structure "was built to house a sailboat during the week and its owners during the weekends." One part of the house is made up of a solid, whitewashed box erected with construction methods inherited from colonial times, while the other part is made of prefabricated wood elements and metal tiles. The house had to be built near the water to allow the boat to be easily moved, a decision that also allowed the preservation of rainforest vegetation on the site. The architects explain that the "site is in the Saco do Mamanguá, a tropical fjord accessible only by boat without power, the very archetype of a lost paradise. In this context, the house brings together the idea of the 'noble savage' with the modern 'eulogy of the machine'."

Dieses Gebäude „wurde errichtet, um ein Segelboot während der Woche und seine Besitzer an den Wochenenden unterzubringen". Ein Teil des Hauses ist eine massive, weiß verputzte Kiste, die mit Baumethoden errichtet wurde, die aus der Kolonialzeit stammen. Der andere Teil wurde aus vorgefertigten Holzelementen und Metallplatten erbaut. Der Bau sollte dicht am Wasser stehen, um das Boot leichter manövrieren zu können – eine Entscheidung, die es auch ermöglichte, die Regenwaldvegetation auf dem Gelände zu erhalten. Die Architekten erklären: „Der Bauplatz liegt am Saco do Mamanguá, einem tropischen Fjord, der nur mit Booten ohne Motor anzufahren ist – einem wahren Urbild des verlorenen Paradieses. In diesem Kontext vereinigt das Haus die Vorstellung vom ‚edlen Wilden' mit der modernen ‚Verehrung der Maschine'."

Cette construction a été réalisée pour « abriter un voilier pendant la semaine et ses propriétaires pendant le week-end ». Une partie de la maison est une structure en forme de boîte fermée, passée à la chaux, édifiée à l'aide de techniques de construction héritées de la période coloniale ; l'autre partie est en éléments de bois préfabriqués et dalles de métal. La maison devait évidemment se trouver à proximité de l'eau pour recevoir le bateau, décision qui permettait également de préserver la végétation de type forêt pluviale qui règne sur le site. Les architectes expliquent que « le site se trouve dans le Saco do Mamanguá, un fjord tropical accessible uniquement en bateau sans moteur, l'archétype d'un paradis perdu. Dans ce contexte, la maison réunit les concepts du 'noble sauvage' et de 'l'eulogie de la machine moderne' ».

Surrounded by dense vegetation, the house can easily be opened on the sides to create covered living spaces that are close to the natural setting.

Die Wände des von üppiger Vegetation umgebenen Hauses können geöffnet werden, sodass ein überdachter Aufenthaltsraum inmitten der Natur entsteht.

Entourée d'une végétation dense, la maison peut facilement s'ouvrir sur les côtés pour créer un espace de vie couvert proche de la nature.

A wooden boat ramp leads up to the house, as seen in these images. On the right page, sun flows into the small kitchen and dining area, with the shutters open to the forest.

Wie diese Bilder zeigen, führt eine hölzerne Bootsrampe hinauf zum Haus. Rechte Seite: Die Sonne scheint in die kleine Wohnküche; die Läden sind zum Wald geöffnet.

Une rampe à bateaux en bois conduit à la maison, comme le montrent ces images. En bas à droite, le soleil inonde la petite cuisine et le coin des repas. Les volets ouvrent sur la forêt.

ÁLVARO LEITE SIZA VIEIRA

Álvaro Leite Siza Vieira
Rua do Aleixo 53 – Cave A
4150 – 043 Porto
Portugal

Tel: +351 22 610 8575
Fax: +351 22 610 8574
E-mail: alvarinhosiza@sapo.pt

ÁLVARO LEITE SIZA VIEIRA was born in Porto, in 1962. He worked with his father, Álvaro Siza Vieira, on the first projects for the Chiado area of Lisbon (1987), and completed the Vanzeller House in Afife (1992), before graduating from the Faculty of Architecture of the University of Porto (FAUP) in 1994. His own work includes the Estado Novo Discotheque (Matosinhos, 1996); Garrett House (Foz do Douro, Porto, 1998); Francisco Ramos Pinto House (Francelos, 2000); and Leite Faria House (Porto, 2001), all in Portugal. His recent work includes the Rua de Fez Houses (Porto); Tóló House (Freguesia de Cerva, 2005, published here); and an urban project for Fontaínhas Lane and Park (Porto, 2006).

ÁLVARO LEITE SIZA VIEIRA wurde 1962 in Porto geboren. Er arbeitete mit seinem Vater Álvaro Siza Viera an den ersten Projekten für das Chiado-Viertel in Lissabon (1987) und stellte das Haus Vanzeller in Afife (1992) fertig, ehe er an der Architekturfakultät der Universität Porto (FAUP) 1994 sein Studium abschloss. Zu seinen eigenen Bauten gehören: Diskothek Estado Novo (Matosinhos, 1996), Haus Garrett (Foz do Douro, Porto, 1998), Haus Francisco Ramos Pinto (Francelos, 2000) und Haus Leite Faria (Porto, 2001), alle in Portugal. Neuere Werke sind die Häuser Rua de Fez (Porto), Haus Tóló (Freguesia de Cerva, 2005, hier vorgestellt) sowie ein urbanes Projekt für Fontaínhas-Straße und -Park (Porto, 2006).

ÁLVARO LEITE SIZA VIEIRA, né à Porto in 1962, a travaillé avec son père, Álvaro Siza Vieira, sur les premiers projets pour le quartier du Chiado à Lisbonne (1987) et complétait la maison Vanzeller à Afife (1992), avant même d'être diplômé de la Faculté d'architecture de l'Université de Porto (FAUP) en 1994. Ses propres réalisations comprennent la discothèque Estado Novo, Matosinhos (1996) ; la maison Garrett, Foz do Douro, Porto (1998) ; la maison Francisco Ramos Pinto, Francelo (2000) et la maison Leite Faria, Porto (2001), toutes au Portugal. Actuellement, il a réalisé les maisons Rua de Fez, Porto ; la maison Tóló, Freguesia de Cerva (2005) publiée ici et le projet d'urbanisme de l'avenue et du parc Fontaínhas à Porto (2006).

TÓLÓ HOUSE

Lugar das Carvalhinhas – Alvite, Freguesia de Cerva, Portugal, 2000–05

*Floor area: 180 m². Client: Luís Marinho Leite Barbosa da Silva
Cost: not disclosed*

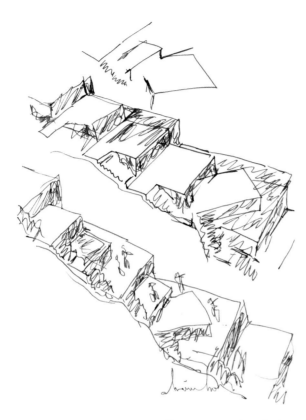

Set on a steeply inclined, 1000-m² site, this is a three-bedroom holiday house, including a living room, dining room, kitchen, and a small outdoor pool. Given the topography of the site, the architect decided to create a long, narrow plan facing south for optimum solar exposure. The entrance is at the northern, or higher, end of the lot, and the house is fragmented into a series of small interconnected volumes. The roof serves as a support for gardens, and an attempt was made to preserve all existing trees on the site. An outdoor path links the top and bottom of the house, but as the architect says, "The house itself is a path." A relatively low budget suggested that part of the house should be buried, for reasons of thermal conservation and security. "The choice of exposed concrete," explains the architect, "creates an idea like that of massive stones appearing naturally on the site. In this way, expressiveness is extracted from a continuous structure of reinforced concrete, the most efficient on the lot with these characteristics, and making optimum use of the modest economic resources available." PVC canvas was used to seal the foundations because of a high water-table on the site. Non-load-bearing walls were built with cement blocks filled with sand, plastered, and painted white inside. Interior floors and doors are made of wood; exterior doors and windows of metal with double-glazing, for reasons of thermal and acoustic insulation.

Dieses Ferienhaus mit drei Schlafzimmern, Wohn- und Essraum, Küche und kleinem Außenpool liegt auf einem steil abfallenden, 1000 m² großen Gelände. Angesichts der Topografie entschied sich der Architekt für einen langen, schmalen Grundriss, der wegen der Sonne nach Süden ausgerichtet ist. Der Eingang befindet sich am nördlichen, höheren Ende des Grundstücks und das Haus ist in eine Abfolge kleinerer, miteinander verbundener Baukörper gegliedert, deren Dachflächen für Gartenanlagen genutzt werden. Beim Bau des Hauses wurde größtmögliche Rücksicht auf vorhandene Bäume genommen. Ein im Freien verlaufender Weg verbindet die beiden Enden des Hauses, aber wie der Architekt sagt, „ist das Haus selbst ein Weg". Aufgrund eines eher begrenzten Budgets wurden Teile des Hauses unter die Erde verlegt, um Wärmedämmung und Sicherheit zu gewährleisten. Nach Meinung des Architekten „entsteht durch das Material Sichtbeton der Eindruck natürlich auf dem Gelände vorhandener Steinblöcke. Aus dem fortlaufenden Baukörper aus Stahlbeton entsteht Expressivität und die bescheidenen ökonomischen Mittel werden optimal genutzt". Wegen des hohen Grundwasserspiegels auf dem Gelände wurden die Fundamente sorgfältig mit PVC-beschichteten Planen abgedichtet. Nichttragende Wände wurden aus sandgefüllten Betonblöcken errichtet, verputzt und innen weiß gestrichen. Fußböden und Türen im Inneren wurden aus Holz gefertigt, Außentüren und Fenster aus Metall mit Doppelverglasung zur besseren Wärme- und Geräuschdämmung.

Implantée sur un terrain très incliné de 1 000 m², cette maison de vacances contient quatre chambres, un séjour, une salle à manger, une cuisine et une petite piscine extérieure. Etant donné la topographie, l'architecte a opté pour un plan allongé et étroit face au sud afin d'obtenir une exposition solaire maximale. L'entrée se fait par le nord, à l'extrémité haute de la parcelle, et la maison se fragmente en une succession de petits volumes interconnectés. Le toit sert de soutien aux jardins, et la plupart des arbres existants ont été conservés. Un passage extérieur relie le haut et le bas de la maison, mais, comme l'architecte le dit lui-même « cette maison est en soi un cheminement ». Pour des raisons de protection thermique, de sécurité et de budget, une partie a été enterrée. « Le choix du béton apparent, précise l'architecte, évoque d'une certaine façon les blocs de pierre massifs présents sur le site. Ainsi l'expressivité vient-elle de cette structure continue en béton armé, forme la plus efficace pour un terrain présentant ces caractéristiques et pour tirer un parti maximum du modeste budget alloué. » Une toile en PVC a permis d'étanchéifier les fondations, une nécessité du fait de la proximité de la nappe phréatique. Les murs non porteurs ont été construits en parpaings de ciment remplis de sable, plâtrés et peints sur leur face intérieure. Les sols et les portes intérieurs sont en bois, les portes et les fenêtres extérieures en métal à double vitrage, pour une meilleure isolation thermique et acoustique.

Álvaro Leite Siza's house is inscribed into the hillside, in a gesture that may recall the natural integration of houses, such as those by Eduardo Souto de Moura, for example, while remaining original nonetheless.

Álvaro Leite Sizas Haus schmiegt sich auf eine Art an den Hang, die an in die Landschaft integrierte Häuser wie die von Eduardo Souto de Moura erinnert, und bleibt doch gänzlich originell.

La maison d'Álvaro Leite Siza s'inscrit dans le flanc d'une colline, en un geste qui peut évoquer des réalisations comme celles d'Eduardo Souto de Moura par exemple, tout en conservant néanmoins son originalité.

Simple wooden furniture echoes the use of wood planks for the steps here.

Schlichte Holzmöbel greifen die hölzernen Treppenstufen auf.

Un mobilier de bois simple vient faire écho aux planches utilisées pour les escaliers.

The numerous windows looking out onto the leafy surroundings and the constant presence of openings and stairways imposed by the sloped terrain allow light into the space.

Die zahlreichen Fenster mit Blick auf die grüne Umgebung und die vom abschüssigen Terrain bedingten allgegenwärtigen Öffnungen und Treppen lassen Licht in die Räume.

Les nombreuses fenêtres qui donnent sur la verdure environnante, et la présence constante d'ouvertures et d'escaliers imposées par la pente du terrain facilitent la pénétration de la lumière.

The very site creates a variety of the forms in the architecture, while careful attention is paid to the visual communication of the light and passageways.

Das Baugelände selbst bedingt die vielfältigen Formen der Architektur; große Aufmerksamkeit wird der von Licht oder Durchgängen ermöglichten visuellen Kommunikation gewidmet.

Le terrain lui-même génère les différentes formes architecturales. L'attention a été portée à la communication visuelle née de l'éclairage et de la lumière naturelle.

Narrow stairs pass through brightly lit spaces in the house whose basic form is that of a cascade of pavilions connected by steps.

In dem Haus, das aus einer Folge von durch Treppen verbundenen Pavillons besteht, erschließen schmale Treppen hell erleuchtete Räume.

D'étroits escaliers traversent les volumes lumineux de la maison, qui est constituée d'une cascade de pavillons connectés par des marches.

ÁLVARO SIZA

Álvaro Siza Arquitecto, Lda
Rua do Aleixo 53 2
4150–043 Porto
Portugal

Tel: +351 22 616 72 70
Fax: +351 22 616 72 79
E-mail: siza@mail.telepac.pt

Born in Matosinhos, Portugal, in 1933, **ÁLVARO SIZA** studied at the University of Porto School of Architecture (1949–55). He created his own practice in 1954, and worked with Fernando Tavora from 1955 to 1958. He has been a Professor of Construction at the University of Porto since 1976. He received the European Community's Mies van der Rohe Prize in 1988 and the Pritzker Prize in 1992. He has built a large number of small-scale projects in Portugal, and has worked on the restructuring of the Chiado (Lisbon, 1989–); the Meteorology Center (Barcelona, Spain, 1989–92); the Vitra Furniture Factory (Weil am Rhein, Germany, 1991–94); the Porto School of Architecture (Porto University, 1986–95); the University of Aveiro Library (Aveiro, 1988–95); the Portuguese Pavilion for the 1998 Lisbon World's Fair; and the Serralves Foundation (Porto, 1998). More recent projects include the 2005 Serpentine Pavilion (with Eduardo Souto de Moura, Kensington Gardens, London, UK); the Adega Mayor Winery, Argamassas Estate (Campo Maior, 2005–06); Viana do Castelo Public Library (Viana do Castelo, 2001–07); the Multipurpose Pavilion (Gondomar, 2005–07); the House in Mallorca (Mallorca, Spain, 2004–08, published here); the Museum for the Iberê Camargo Foundation (Porto Alegre, Brazil, 2008); and the extension to the Hombroich Museum (in collaboration with Rudolf Finsterwalder, Neuss-Hombroich, Germany, 2008),all in Portugal unless stated otherwise.

Der 1933 in Matosinhos, Portugal, geborene **ÁLVARO SIZA** studierte Architektur an der Universität von Porto (1949–55). 1954 gründete er sein eigenes Büro, in dem er von 1955 bis 1958 mit Fernando Tavora zusammenarbeitete. Seit 1976 ist er Professor für Baukonstruktion an der Universität Porto. Ihm wurden 1988 der Mies-van-der-Rohe-Preis von der Europäischen Kommission und 1992 der Pritzker Prize verliehen. Siza hat in Portugal eine große Zahl kleinerer Projekte verwirklicht, darüber hinaus der Wiederaufbau des Stadtbezirks Chiado (Lissabon, Portugal, 1989–); das Meteorologische Zentrum im Olympiadorf (Barcelona, Spanien, 1989–92); die Möbelfabrik Vitra (Weil am Rhein, Deutschland, 1991–94); das Architekturgebäude der Universität Porto (Porto, 1986–95); die Bibliothek der Universität Aveiro (Aveiro, Portugal, 1988–95); den Portugiesischen Pavillon für die Weltausstellung in Lissabon 1998 sowie das Gebäude der Stiftung Serralves (Porto, 1998). Zu seinen neueren Projekten zählen der Serpentine Pavilion von 2005 (mit Eduardo Souto de Moura, Kensington Gardens, London); die Weinkellerei Adega Mayor, Argamassas (Campo Maior, Portugal, 2005–06); die Stadtbücherei Viana do Castelo (Viana do Castelo, Portugal, 2001–07); der Mehrzweck-Pavillon (Gondomar, Portugal, 2005–07); ein Haus auf Mallorca (Mallorca, Spanien, 2004–08, hier vorgestellt); das Museum der Stiftung Iberê Camargo (Porto Alegre, Brasilien, 2008) und die Erweiterung des Museums Insel Hombroich (in Zusammenarbeit mit Rudolf Finsterwalder, Neuss-Hombroich, 2008).

Né à Matosinhos (Portugal) en 1933, **ÁLVARO SIZA** a étudié à l'École d'architecture de l'Université de Porto (1949–55). Il a créé son agence en 1954 et travaillé avec Fernando Tavora de 1955 à 1958. Il est professeur de construction à l'Université de Porto depuis 1976. Il a reçu le Prix Mies van der Rohe de la Communauté européenne en 1988 et le Prix Pritzker en 1992. Il a réalisé un grand nombre de projets de petites dimensions au Portugal et est intervenu sur la restructuration du quartier du Chiado (Lisbonne, 1989). Il a construit le Centre de météorologie (Barcelone, 1989–92); l'usine de meubles Vitra (Weil-am-Rhein, Allemagne, 1991–94); l'École d'architecture de Porto (Université de Porto, 1986–95); la bibliothèque de l'Université d'Aveiro (Aveiro, Portugal, 1988–95); le Pavillon portugais pour l'Exposition universelle de Lisbonne de 1998 et la Fondation Serralves (Porto, 1998). Plus récemment, il a réalisé le Pavillon de la Serpentine 2005 (Kensington Gardens, Londres) en collaboration avec Eduardo Souto de Moura ; le chais Aldega Mayor (domaine d'Argamassas, Campo Maior, 2005–06) ; la Bibliothèque publique de Viana do Castelo (Viana do Castelo, Portugal, 2001–07) ; un Pavillon polyvalent (Gondomar, Portugal, 2005–07) ; la maison à Majorque (Mallorca, Espagne, 2004–08, présentée ici) ; le musée de la Fondation Iberê Camargo (Porto Alegre, Brésil, 2008) et l'extension du musée d'Hombroich (en collaboration avec Rudolf Finsterwalder, Neuss-Hombroich, Allemagne, 2008).

HOUSE IN MALLORCA
Mallorca, Spain, 2004–08

Area: 707 m². Client: not disclosed
Cost: not disclosed

This is a summer house located on the island of Mallorca. The site is steeply inclined towards the Mediterranean, with the topmost entry point 26 meters above sea level. The architect writes that the structure was inspired by the rugged landscape and "planned in a fragmented volumetric composition to unfold as one descends towards the water level." The three major volumes of the building are connected by a platform set at 22 meters above sea level. The east block contains the main entrance, main and guest bedrooms, and a stairway. The west block is the central volume, and connects to the eastern and western elements at 18.6 meters above the water. Three bedrooms arranged around a light well are located here, as well as a living room with a patio at the bottom of the well. The north block containing two bedrooms and a shared living room is reserved for the caretaker.

Hierbei handelt es sich um ein Sommerhaus auf der Insel Mallorca. Das Gelände fällt steil zur Mittelmeerküste ab, und der Zugang liegt auf dem höchsten Punkt, 26 m über Meeresspiegel. Der Architekt gibt an, dass der Entwurf des Gebäudes von der unberührten Landschaft bestimmt und „als aufgebrochene volumetrische Komposition geplant" worden sei, „die sich erst erschließt, wenn man sich abwärts zum Ufer begibt". Die drei großen Volumen des Gebäudes sind durch eine Plattform verbunden, die 22 m über Meeresspiegel liegt. Der östliche Trakt enthält den Haupteingang, die Schlafräume der Bewohner und für Gäste sowie das Treppenhaus. Der westliche Trakt bildet das zentrale Volumen, welches das Ost- und das Westelement auf einer Höhe von 18,6 m über Meeresspiegel miteinander verbindet. Hier sind drei weitere Schlafräume um einen Lichtschacht sowie unten ein Wohnraum mit Patio angeordnet. Der nördliche Trakt enthält zwei Schlafräume sowie einen gemeinsam nutzbaren Wohnraum für den Hausmeister.

Cette maison d'été est située sur l'île de Majorque. Le terrain est en pente forte vers la Méditerranée, son entrée se situant à 26 mètres au-dessus du niveau de la mer. L'architecte explique que ce projet lui a été inspiré par le paysage rocheux et a été « organisé en une composition volumétrique fragmentée qui se déploie en descendant vers la mer. » Les trois principaux volumes sont reliés par une plate-forme à 22 mètres au-dessus du niveau de l'eau. Le bloc Est contient l'entrée principale, la chambre principale, les chambres d'amis et un escalier. Le bloc central, Ouest, se trouve à 18,6 mètres d'altitude. Il comprend trois chambres disposées autour d'un puits de lumière, le séjour et un patio en partie inférieure. Le bloc Nord contient deux chambres et un séjour, réservés au gardien.

Siza makes use of strict geometry but plays with the setting and the views he usually frames with the willful placement of windows. Here the house is seen to arc itself along the water's edge, providing views of the Mediterranean.

Siza verwendet eine strenge Geometrie, spielt aber mit der Umgebung und den Ausblicken, die er meist gezielt durch die Position der Fenster einrahmt. Hier sieht man, wie die Linie des Hauses der Uferfront folgt und den Blick zum Mittelmeer freigibt.

Bien que Siza fasse appel à une géométrie stricte, il joue avec l'environnement et les perspectives qu'il cadre soigneusement par des fenêtres. La maison semble suivre la ligne de la côte pour offrir ses perspectives sur la Méditerranée.

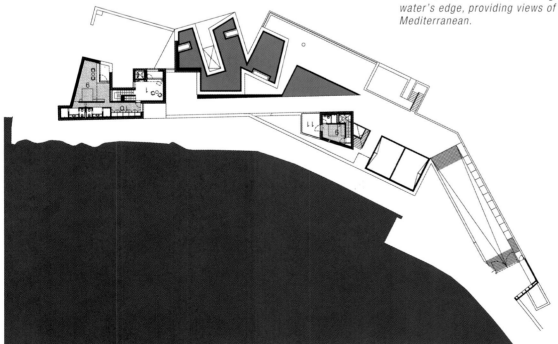

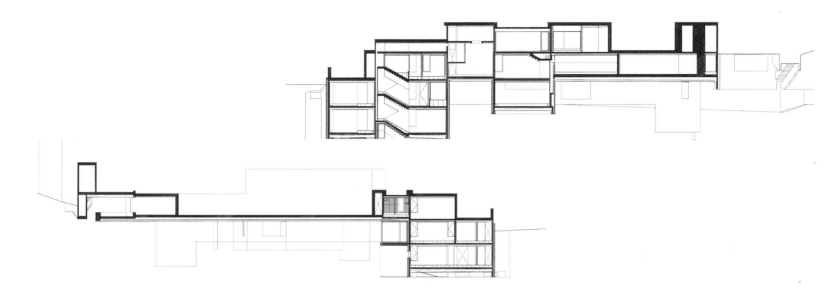

At once rigorous in its architectural development and yet richly articulated, the house offers a sculptural appearance at night.

Das in seiner architektonischen Ausrichtung strenge und dennoch vielfach gegliederte Haus bietet nachts ein plastisches Erscheinungsbild.

À la fois rigoureuse dans son phrasé architectural et richement articulée, la maison prend la nuit une apparence sculpturale.

With simple furniture and skilful contrasts created between light and dark, or opacity and translucency, Siza continues to be one of the great masters of contemporary architecture.

Mit einfacher Möblierung und durch den geschickt eingesetzten Kontrast von Hell und Dunkel oder Geschlossenheit und Transparenz erweist sich Siza nach wie vor als großer Meister der zeitgenössischen Architektur.

Par un mobilier simple et d'habiles contrastes entre ombre et lumière, opacité et transparence, Siza s'affirme une fois encore comme l'un des grands maîtres de l'architecture contemporaine.

ROSS STEVENS

Ross Stevens
Lot 5
Pounui Ridge
RD3 Western Lake Rd
Featherston, 5773
New Zealand

Tel: +64 6 307 7678
E-mail: ross.e.stevens@gmail.com

ROSS STEVENS was born in 1966 in Wairo, New Zealand. He received an Industrial Design diploma from Wellington Polytechnic in 1986. He holds a Master's degree in Industrial Design from Victoria University, Wellington. He was an industrial designer at Fisher and Paykel in Wellington (1987–91). He has been an Industrial Design Consultant for B&W Loudspeakers (UK, 1992–95); Thomson Consumer Electronics and Philippe Starck (1992–95); and an exhibition designer for Te Papa MONZ (New Zealand, 1994–96). He is Design Director for Plinius Audible Technology (New Zealand). The Container House published here is his only built work.

ROSS STEVENS wurde 1966 in Wairo, Neuseeland, geboren. 1986 erwarb er am Wellington Polytechnikum ein Diplom in Industriedesign. An der Victoria University in Wellington hat er seinem Abschluss als Master in Industriedesign gemacht. Von 1987 bis 1991 war er bei Fisher und Paykel in Wellington als Industrie-designer angestellt. Von 1992 bis 1995 war er bei der Firma B & W Loudspeakers in England, bei Thomson Consumer Electronics und Philippe Starck als beratender Industriedesigner tätig, sowie von 1994 bis 1996 als Ausstellungsdesigner für Te Papa MONZ (Neuseeland). Bei Plinius Audible Technology (Neuseeland) ist er als leitender Designer beschäftigt. Das hier publizierte Containerhaus ist sein einziges gebautes Werk.

ROSS STEVENS, né en 1966 à Wairo, Nouvelle-Zélande, est diplômé en design industriel de l'École polytechnique de Wellington (1986), et est titulaire d'un mastère dans la même discipline à la Victoria University, Wellington. Il a travaillé comme designer pour Fisher and Paykel à Wellington (1987–91), comme designer consultant pour B&W Loudspeakers (Grande-Bretagne, 1992–95) ; puis pour Thomson Consumer Electronics et Philippe Starck (1992–95), et a conçu des expositions pour Te Papa MONZ, Nouvelle-Zélande (1994–96). Il est directeur du design pour Plinius Audible Technology, Nouvelle-Zélande. La maison Container, présentée ici, est son unique réalisation architecturale.

CONTAINER HOUSE

Owhiro Bay, Wellington, New Zealand, 2000–07

Floor area: 90 m² interior; 45 m² covered deck; 60 m² garage. Client: Ross Stevens
Cost: $170 000 (not including personal labor)

This house is made up of 3 x 30-m² insulated refrigeration containers. It has a large covered deck made of 3 x 15-m² shipping platforms. These units were placed on three industrial tower crane sections. As Ross Stevens explains, "I am an industrial designer, so the idea of making architecture out of standard industrial components allowed me to work in a way more similar to industrial design while on the scale of architecture." The site of the Container House is an irregular hole in a rock, which required the 50-millimeter-thick steel deck (industrial waste) to be cut with a gap of no more than 100 millimeters from the rock. In this way, Stevens avoided the legal requirement to erect a fence around the house. He explains, "Personally I have no one belief of good design, so I enjoy clashing different styles: for example modular with site specific, high-tech with decorative, or new and immaculate with old and decaying."

Dieses Haus besteht aus drei jeweils 30 m² großen, isolierten Kühlbehältern. Es verfügt über eine große, überdachte Fläche aus drei je 15 m² großen Schiffsrampen. Diese Einheiten wurden auf drei Teile von serienmäßigen Industrieturmkränen platziert. Dazu Ross Stevens: „Ich bin Industriedesigner, sodass mir die Idee, mit genormten Industriekomponenten Architektur herzustellen, ermöglichte, in einer dem Industriedesign ähnlichen Weise und doch in der Größenordnung von Architektur zu arbeiten." Der Standplatz des Containerhauses befindet sich in einem unregelmäßigen Einschnitt in eine Felswand, die es erforderlich machte, die 50 mm starke Bodenplatte aus Stahl (Industrieabfall) mit höchstens 100 mm Abstand zur Felswand zu schneiden. Auf diese Weise umging Stevens den gesetzlich vorgeschriebenen Zaun um das Haus. „Ich persönlich habe keine feste Vorstellung von gutem Design, also macht es mir Spaß, unterschiedliche Stile aufeinanderprallen zu lassen: z. B. standardisiert mit ortsspezifisch, hightech mit dekorativ, oder neu und makellos mit alt und zerfallend."

Cette maison est constituée de trois containers réfrigérants de 30 m². Elle possède une vaste terrasse couverte comprenant trois plates-formes d'expédition de 15 m². Ces éléments ont été fixés sur trois sections de grues industrielles. Selon Stevens : « Je suis designer industriel, et l'idée de faire de l'architecture à partir de composants industriels standard m'a permis de travailler de façon assez similaire à celle du design industriel, mais à l'échelle architecturale. » Le site de cette maison Conteneur est un trou de forme irrégulière pratiqué dans la roche qui a demandé de découper la plate-forme en acier de 50 mm d'épaisseur de telle sorte que l'interstice laissé entre elle et le rocher ne dépasse pas 100 mm. De cette façon, Stevens a pu contourner l'obligation de dresser une barrière autour de sa maison. « Personnellement, je ne crois pas à un » bon « design, et j'aime les heurts entre différents styles, par exemple, le modulaire et le spécifique, le high-tech avec le décoratif, ou le nouveau et l'immaculé avec le vieux et le délabré. »

The basic idea of the Container House is quite simple—an industrial volume used for purposes other than those it was originally intended for.

Das Containerhaus folgt einem einfachen Grundgedanken – ein Industriebehältnis wird für andere als die ursprünglich vorgesehenen Zwecke genutzt.

La maison Container suit une idée de base simple : utiliser des matériaux industriels pour d'autres fonctions que celles pour lesquelles ils ont été conçus.

The insertion of the house into the rocky site required a great deal of precision, particularly in the cut-out form of the rear terrace.

Das Einfügen des Hauses in die Felswand erforderte ein Höchstmaß an Präzision, insbesondere die Ausschnitte auf der rückseitigen Terrasse.

L'insertion de la maison dans ce site rocheux exigeait une grande précision, en particulier dans la découpe de la terrasse arrière.

There is something of the practical spirit of Charles and Ray Eames in the Container House, and the engineering background of Ross Stevens, who is an industrial designer rather than an architect.

Im Containerhaus ist etwas vom praktischen Geist von Charles und Ray Eames spürbar und von Ross Stevens' Hintergrund als Industriedesigner und nicht Architekt.

On retrouve quelque chose de l'esprit pratique de Charles et Ray Eames dans cette maison comme dans la formation de Ross Stevens, qui est designer industriel et non pas architecte.

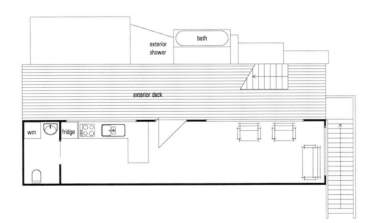

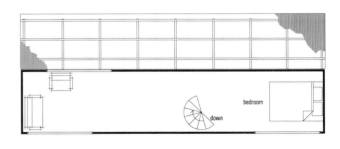

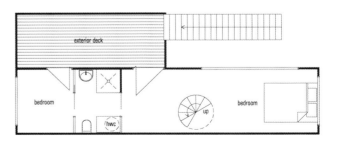

The idea of a technical or, more precisely, machine-like metal environment is understandably appealing to an industrial designer. His house and office space thus become a reflection of his profession.

Die Vorstellung einer technisch oder präziser maschinell gefertigten Umgebung aus Metall sagt einem Industriedesigner verständlicherweise zu. Derart werden sein Haus und Büro zum Spiegelbild seiner Profession.

L'idée d'un environnement technique, ou plus précisément métallique, est sans doute séduisant pour un designer industriel. Sa maison et son bureau reflètent ainsi sa profession.

PHILIPPE STUEBI

Philippe Stuebi Architekten GmbH
Hardstr. 219
8005 Zurich
Switzerland

Tel: +41 44 440 7777
Fax: +41 44 440 7779
E-mail: ps@philippestuebi.ch
Web: www.philippestuebi.ch

PHILIPPE STUEBI was born in Lausanne, Switzerland, in 1963, and received his degree in Architecture from the Swiss Federal Institute of Technology (ETH) in Zurich in 1993, where he studied under Hans Kollhoff. He set up his own office, Philippe Stuebi Architekten, in Zurich in 1996, with the goal of creating "networked architecture," linking issues like art, ecology, and economics, designing every project down to the smallest interior details. Philippe Stuebi was a co-founder and associate of the Kunstclub HeiQell in Zurich (1988–93), a gallery for contemporary art. His built work includes the Restaurant/Bar Josef und Maria (Zurich, 1998); the Maison Draeger (Corsika, 2000); the Villa Polana (Uitikon, 2000); Beaufort 12, Expo '02 Pavilion (Neuchâtel, 2002); the Würzgraben Housing Estate for the building authority of Zurich (2003); the Levy-Fröhlich House (Zollikon, 2005); and the O House on Lake Lucerne (2005–07, published here). He is currently working on a chapel in Unterbäch; a beachhouse at Zurich Obersee; and a beachhouse on the island Silba in Croatia.

PHILIPPE STUEBI wurde 1963 in Lausanne, Schweiz, geboren und schloss sein Architekturstudium 1993 an der Eidgenössischen Technischen Hochschule (ETH) in Zürich ab, wo er bei Hans Kollhoff studiert hatte. Sein Zürcher Büro Philippe Stuebi Architekten gründete er 1996 mit dem Ziel, eine „vernetzte Architektur" zu schaffen, bei der Fragen wie Kunst, Ökologie und Ökonomie miteinander verbunden werden sollten und jedes Projekt bis ins kleinste Detail der Innenausstattung vom Architekten selbst betreut würde. Philippe Stuebi war Mitbegründer und Teilhaber des Kunstclubs HeiQell in Zürich (1988–93), einer Galerie für zeitgenössische Kunst. Zu seinen gebauten Projekten zählen u. a. Restaurant/Bar Josef und Maria (Zürich, 1998), Maison Draeger (Korsika, 2000), Villa Polana (Uitikon, 2000), Beaufort 12, Pavillon für die Expo '02 (Neuchâtel, 2002), Wohnsiedlung Würzgraben für das Amt für Hochbauten Zürich (2003), die Villa Levy-Fröhlich (Zollikon, 2005) sowie das Haus O am Vierwaldstättersee (2005–07, hier vorgestellt). Aktuelle Projekte sind u. a. eine Kapelle in Unterbäch, ein Haus am Ufer des Zürichsees und ein Strandhaus auf der kroatischen Insel Silba.

PHILIPPE STUEBI, né à Lausanne, Suisse, en 1963, est diplômé d'architecture de l'Institut fédéral suisse de technologie (ETH) à Zurich à 1993, où il a étudié sous la direction de Hans Kollhoff. Il a créé sa propre agence, Philippe Stuebi Architekten, à Zurich en 1996, afin de créer une « architecture en réseau » traitant d'enjeux comme l'art, l'écologie et l'économie, et concevant chaque projet jusqu'aux plus petits détails d'aménagement intérieur. Il a été cofondateur du Kunstclub HeiQell à Zurich (1988–93), une galerie d'art contemporain. Parmi ses réalisations : le Restaurant/Bar Josef und Maria (Zurich, 1998) ; la maison Draeger (Corse, 2000) ; la villa Polana (Uitikon, 2000) ; Beaufort 12, Pavillon pour Expo '02 (Neuchâtel, 2002) ; les immeubles de logement de Würzgraben pour l'organisme de construction de Zurich (2003) ; la maison Levy-Fröhlich (Zollikon, 2005) et la maison O sur le lac des Quatre-Cantons (2005–07, présentée ici). Il travaille actuellement sur les projets d'une chapelle à Unterbäch; une maison sur le lac de Zurich et une autre sur l'île de Silba en Croatie.

O HOUSE

Lake Lucerne, Switzerland, 2005–07

Floor area: 700 m². Client: not disclosed. Cost: not disclosed
Team: Philippe Stuebi with Eberhard Tröger

An unexpected and powerful pattern of large regular circular openings marks a façade of the house (below).
.

Ein überraschendes und ausdrucksstarkes Muster aus regelmäßigen Kreisöffnungen dominiert die Fassade des Hauses (unten).

Un motif puissant et surprenant d'ouvertures circulaires marque la façade de la maison (ci-dessous).

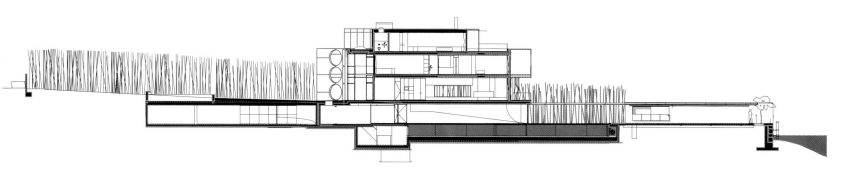

A broad window and simple interior finishes place the emphasis on the remarkable view of the lake seen in the image above of the living room.

Das breite Fenster und die schlichte Inneneinrichtung lenken die Aufmerksamkeit auf den eindrucksvollen Ausblick, den man vom Wohnzimmer auf den See hat.

Une énorme baie et la simplicité de l'aménagement intérieur magnifient la vue remarquable sur le lac que l'on a depuis le séjour.

The front and lake sides of this large house are characterized by "sculptural elements" imagined by the architect—large round openings facing Mount Pilatus and "protruding, glistening loggia made of round glass bricks" on the side facing the lake, the Rigi and the Bürgenstock. A regular pattern three large circles high gives a decidedly sculptural appearance to the entry side of the house, echoed in smaller circles shielding the balconies, but opening out onto the spectacular lake view. The side façades are rendered in a rougher way. Despite its ample size, the house is furnished in a spare, modern way, with such touches as a glass balustrade on the main stairway confirming the modernity expressed in the façades and overall layout of the house. The basement includes a 25-meter, partially covered swimming pool and a generous fitness area. A walkway leads past the pool to a concrete boat jetty that extends into the water, allowing direct access from the lake. The somewhat angular plan of the house fits it well into its site and maximizes the lake views.

Vorder- und Seeseite der großen Villa werden von „skulpturalen Elementen" dominiert – auf der zum Pilatus gewandten Vorderseite von großen runden, vom Architekten entworfenen Maueraussparungen sowie zur Seeseite mit Rigi und Bürgenstock von einer „auskragenden, funkelnden Loggia aus runden Glasbausteinen". Ein regelmäßiges Muster, drei große Kreise übereinander, lässt die Eingangsseite des Hauses besonders plastisch wirken, was von kleineren Kreismotiven aufgegriffen wird, die die Balkone abschirmen. Zum See jedoch öffnet sich das Haus der spektakulären Aussicht. Die seitlichen Fassaden sind rauer gestaltet. Trotz seiner großzügigen Dimensionen ist das Haus sparsam und modern möbliert. Elemente wie ein Glasgeländer an der Haupttreppe knüpfen an die moderne Anmutung der Fassaden und der gesamten Anlage des Hauses an und unterstreichen sie. Auf der unteren Gebäudeebene liegen ein teilüberdachter Pool mit 25-Meter-Bahnen sowie ein großzügiger Fitnessbereich. Ein Pfad führt am Pool entlang zu einem Bootssteg aus Beton, der über das Wasser ragt und vom See direkten Zugang zum Haus erlaubt. Der eher geradlinige Grundriss des Hauses fügt sich optimal in das Grundstück ein und maximiert den Ausblick auf den See.

La façade d'accès de cette vaste demeure et celle qui donne sur le lac sont caractérisées par des « éléments sculpturaux » imaginés par l'architecte : de grandes ouvertures circulaires face au Mont Pilate et « une loggia, projection scintillante faite de briques de verre rondes » face au lac, au Rigi et au Bürgenstock. L'alignement régulier des grandes formes circulaires confère une apparence très sculpturale à la façade d'entrée, et ce motif se retrouve dans les petits cercles de verre qui protègent les balcons ouvrant sur de spectaculaires vues sur le lac. Les façades latérales sont moins sophistiquées. D'importantes dimensions, la maison est meublée avec parcimonie dans un style moderne avec quelques touches originales comme une balustrade de verre le long de l'escalier principal qui confirme la modernité des façades, comme le plan d'ensemble de la maison. Le sous-sol comprend une piscine de 25 mètres en partie couverte et de généreuses installations de remise en forme. Un passage le long de la piscine conduit à une jetée qui permet un accès direct au lac. Le plan, assez anguleux, est bien adapté au terrain et optimise les vues sur le plan d'eau.

Left page, a view toward the boat jetty. Above, the pattern of large circular openings is here echoed by screens and ceiling finishes that also employ circles.

Linke Seite, Blick zum Bootsanleger. Oben, das große Lochmuster wird hier in Wandschirmen und Deckenplatten aufgegriffen, die ebenfalls kreisrunde Muster aufweisen.

Page de gauche, vue vers la jetée. Ci-dessus, le motif des ouvertures circulaires de la façade repris par les écrans et le décor des plafonds.

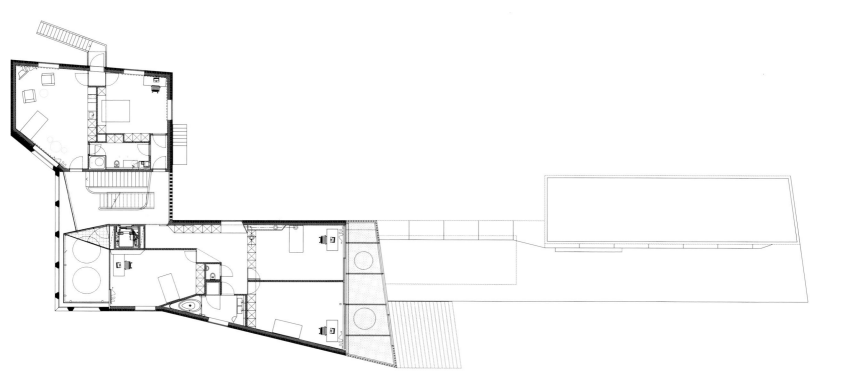

Below, a bedroom with a partial
perforated screen looks out on the
lake. Right, the glass balustrade and
successive chandeliers of the main
stairway.

*Ein Schlafzimmer (unten) mit teil-
weise perforiertem Wandschirm und
Aussicht auf den See. Rechts die
Glasgeländer und Lüster an der
Haupttreppe.*

*Ci-dessous, une chambre dont le mur
ajouré du balcon cadre une vue sur le
lac. À droite, un garde-corps en verre
et une succession de lustres dans la
cage de l'escalier principal.*

PETER STUTCHBURY

Stutchbury & Pape Pty Ltd.
4/364 Barrenjoey Road
Newport Beach NSW 2106
Australia

Tel: +61 299 79 50 30 / Fax +61 299 79 53 67
E-mail: info@peterstutchbury.com.au / Web: www.peterstutchbury.com.au

A graduate of the University of Newcastle, Australia, in 1978, as a child **PETER STUTCHBURY** lived "on the land" and with aborigines on the banks of the Darling River, and with tribes in the highlands of New Guinea. He works on houses "that nurture their occupants and celebrate a palpable spirit of place." The firm has been given 26 awards by the Royal Australian Institute of Architects (RAIA) since 1999. In 2003, Peter Stutchbury was the first architect ever to win both the top National Architecture Awards from the RAIA for residential and non-residential projects with the Robin Boyd Award for houses for the Bay House at Watson's Bay, Sydney, and the Sir Zelman Cowan Award for Public Buildings for Birabahn, the Aboriginal Cultural Center at the University of Newcastle. Architect of the Sydney 2000 Olympics Archery Pavilion, he has also built several structures on the University of Newcastle campus, including the Design Building and the Nursing Building (with EJE Architecture); the Aboriginal Center (with Richard Leplastrier and Sue Harper); and the Life Sciences Building (with Suters Architects). His built work includes: the Israel House (Paradise Beach, NSW, 1982–92); the Treetop House (Clareville, NSW, 1991); the McMaster Residence (Hawk's Nest, NSW, 1995–98); the Kangaroo Valleys Pavilion (Kangaroo Valley, NSW, 1996–98); the Reeves House (Clareville Beach, NSW, 1997–99); and the Wedge House (Whale Beach, NSW, 2001). More recent works are the Beach House (Newport Beach, NSW, 2002–06); the Outcrop House (Northern Beaches, Sydney, NSW, 2006–07); the Avalon House (Avalon, NSW, 2007); and the Flying Museum (Cessnock, NSW, 2004–08), all in Australia.

PETER STUTCHBURY schloss sein Studium an der University of Newcastle, Australien, 1978 ab. Als Kind lebte er „auf dem Land", mit den Aborigines am Ufer des Darling River und mit verschiedenen Stämmen im Hochland von Neuguinea. Er realisiert Häuser, die „ihre Bewohner hegen und nähren und den spürbaren Geist des Ortes würdigen". Seit 1999 hat das Büro 26 Preise des Royal Australian Institute of Architects (RAIA) erhalten. 2003 war Peter Stutchbury der erste Architekt, der jemals die beiden höchsten nationalen Architekturpreise des RAIA für Wohn- bzw. öffentliche Bauten erhielt: Ausgezeichnet wurden das Bay House in der Watson's Bay, Sydney, mit dem Robin Boyd Award für Wohnbauten sowie das Birabahn Aboriginal Cultural Center an der Universität Newcastle mit dem Sir Zelman Cowan Award für öffentliche Bauten. Stutchbury war der Architekt des Bogenschützenpavillons für die Olympischen Spiele in Sydney (2000) und entwarf außerdem verschiedene Bauten auf dem Campus der Universität Newcastle, darunter die Schulen für Design und für Krankenpflege (mit EJE Architecture), das Aboriginal Center (mit Richard Leplastrier und Sue Harper) sowie das Institut für Biowissenschaften (mit Suters Architects). Zu seinen realisierten Bauten zählen das Israel House (Paradise Beach, NSW, 1982–92), das Treetop House (Clareville, NSW, 1991), die McMaster Residence (Hawk's Nest, NSW, 1995–98), der Kangaroo Valleys Pavilion (Kangaroo Valley, NSW, 1996–98), das Reeves House (Clareville Beach, NSW, 1997–99) sowie das Wedge House (Whale Beach, NSW, 2001). Jüngere Projekte sind u. a. das Beach House (Newport Beach, NSW, 2002–06), das Outcrop House (Northern Beaches, Sydney, NSW, 2006–07), das Avalon House (Avalon, NSW, 2007) sowie das Flying Museum (Cessnock, NSW, 2004–08), alle in Australien.

Diplômé de l'université de Newcastle, Australie, en 1978, **PETER STUTCHBURY** avait vécu enfant « à l'intérieur des terres » avec des Aborigènes sur les rives de la Darling River et dans les tribus des plateaux de Nouvelle-Guinée. Il travaille sur des projets de maisons « qui enrichissent leurs occupants et célèbrent un esprit palpable du lieu ». L'agence a reçu pas moins de 26 prix du Royal Australian Institute of Architects (RAIA) depuis 1999. En 2003, Peter Stutchbury a été le premier architecte à remporter à la fois les National Architecture Awards du RAIA pour des projets résidentiels et non résidentiels ; le Robin Boyd Award pour les maisons (Bay House à Watson's Bay, Sydney) ; et le Sir Zelman Cowan Award pour les bâtiments publics pour le Birabahn, le centre culturel aborigène de l'université de Newcastle. Architecte du pavillon de tir à l'arc pour les jeux Olympiques de Sydney en 2000, il également construit plusieurs bâtiments sur le campus de l'université de Newcastle, dont celui des études de design et d'infirmerie (avec EJE Architecture) ; l'Aboriginal Center (avec Richard Leplastrier et Sue Harper) et le bâtiment des sciences de la vie (avec Suters Architects). Il a également réalisé : la maison Israel (Paradise Beach, NSW, 1982–92) ; la maison Treetop (Clareville, NSW, 1991) ; la résidence McMaster (Hawk's Nest, NSW, 1995–98) ; le Pavillon Kangaroo Valleys (Kangaroo Valley, NSW, 1996–98) ; la maison Reeves (Clareville Beach, NSW, 1997–99) et la maison Wedge (Whale Beach, NSW, 2001). Plus récemment, il a construit la Beach House (Newport Beach, NSW, 2002–06) ; la maison Outcrop (Northern Beaches, Sydney, NSW, 2006–07) ; la maison Avalon (Avalon, NSW, 2007) et le Flying Museum (Cessnock, NSW, 2004–08), tous en Australie.

SPRINGWATER

Seaforth, Sydney, New South Wales, Australia, 1999–2002

Floor area: 514 m² (including terraces). Client: not disclosed. Cost: not disclosed

Built on a 1478-m² site on Sydney Harbor "foreshore", the Springwater House has a floor area of 514 m² (including terraces, decks and lap pool). Stutchbury says that the house is "conceived as a reliable camp, the frame is concrete on stone." Galvanized steel frames are bolted onto the structure, and "long building fingers down the site toward the harbor allow the land a conscious freedom." Set on three levels, with ceiling heights adjusted according to their position on site, "the building is skinned simply allowing the user to operate walls, adjusting to views and cooling breezes as required." The architect says that "the house sits as only a veil within the landscape" allowing constant views of the landscape, or alternatively a certain amount of shelter as required by the inhabitants. Built for a relatively low cost, in part because of "systematic and repetitive structure/formwork and similar door/window systems," Springwater is entered "deliberately down, toward the view, onto an open courtyard ... North."

Das Springwater-Haus wurde auf einem 1478 m² großen Grundstück im Küstenvorland des Hafens von Sydney gebaut. Die Terrassen, Decks und den Bahnenpool eingerechnet beträgt die Grundfläche des Hauses 514 m². Stutchbury sagt: „Das Haus ist als ein ‚verlässlicher Ruheplatz' entworfen. Die Konstruktion ist aus Beton, der Untergrund aus Stein." An das Haus sind verzinkte Stahlkonstruktionen angeschraubt, und lange ‚Gebäudefinger' in Richtung Hang und Hafen lassen dem Grundstück bewusst seine Freiheit". Das Haus hat drei Ebenen. Die Deckenhöhen richten sich nach der Position der Ebenen auf dem Grundstück. Das Gebäude „ist einfach gebaut, damit die Nutzer auf einfache Weise Wände verschieben können, je nach dem, welche Aussicht sie wünschen oder wo sie eine kühlende Brise benötigen". Der Architekt kommentiert: „Das Haus liegt wie ein Schleier auf der Landschaft" und bietet den Bewohnern, je nach ihren Bedürfnissen, Blicke in die Natur oder aber auch ein bestimmtes Maß an Schutz. Die Baukosten waren relativ niedrig, z. T. aufgrund „einer systematischen und sich wiederholenden Konstruktion bzw. Schalung und ähnlicher Tür- und Fenstersysteme". Springwater wird absichtlich in Richtung des Hangs, also nach „unten, betreten, zum Ausblick hin, auf einen offenen Hof ... nach Norden.»

Édifiée sur un terrain de 1478 m² sur le port même de Sydney, la maison Springwater a une superficie de 514 m² (y compris ses terrasses, ses plates-formes et le bassin). Pour Stutchbury, cette maison est « conçue comme un camp dans lequel on se sentirait en sécurité... l'ossature en béton est posée sur la pierre ». Les cadres d'acier galvanisé sont boulonnés sur l'ossature et « les ailes qui s'avancent comme des doigts vers le port créent un sentiment de liberté ». Comptant deux étages, avec des hauteurs sous plafond variant en fonction de la position sur le terrain, « la maison a été habillée d'une peau simple qui permet à l'occupant de modifier les murs, à volonté pour les adapter au panorama et aux brises rafraîchissantes... elle est comme un voile dans le paysage » et le propriétaire peut soit profiter de la vue, soit recréer une certaine protection, en fonction de ses désirs. Construite pour un budget relativement réduit grâce, notamment, à des « coffrages d'ossature systématisés et répétitifs et à des systèmes de portes et fenêtres similaires », la maison s'ouvre au visiteur « délibérément par le bas, vers la vue, sur une cour ouverte ... vers le nord ».

Springwater is a spectacular juxtaposition of strong architectural elements with an equally powerful natural setting.

Springwater ist eine spektakuläre Gegenüberstellung von kraftvollen architektonischen Elementen und einer ebenso kraftvollen Naturkulisse.

Springwater est une juxtaposition spectaculaire d'éléments architecturaux puissants dans un cadre naturel tout aussi fort.

The twisting form of tree trunks does not seem to be contradictory to the sharply defined verticals and horizontals of the house. Gaps and openings allow the natural setting to be admired while creating a dynamism in the architecture itself.

Die verschlungenen Formen der Baumstämme wirken den klar definierten Vertikalen und Horizontalen des Hauses nicht entgegen. Lücken und Öffnungen erlauben es, die natürliche Umgebung zu genießen und lassen die Architektur dynamisch wirken.

Les silhouettes tordues des troncs d'arbres ne contrarient nullement les verticales et les horizontales très nettes de la maison. Les ouvertures et les failles permettent d'admirer la nature tout en dynamisant l'architecture.

SYSTEMARCHITECTS

SYSTEMarchitects
9 Desbrosses Street No. 512A
New York, NY 10013
USA

Tel: +1 212 239 8001
Fax: +1 800 796 4152
E-mail: system@systemarchitects.net
Web: www.systemarchitects.net

SYSTEMARCHITECTS was created by Jeremy Edmiston and Douglas Gauthier in New York in 1998. Jeremy Edmiston received his B.Arch from the University of Technology, Sydney (1989), and his M.Arch from Columbia University (1992). A 1992 research project on environmental architecture earned him a Harkness Fellowship and Fulbright Scholarship. He has served as Visiting Professor in the Schools of Architecture at Columbia University, Syracuse, Roger Williams University, and City College. Douglas Gauthier holds degrees from Columbia University and the University of Notre Dame. He was a 1994 Fulbright Architectural Scholar to the Czech and Slovak Republics for research entitled "Parallel Modernism: Building Practices in the Former East Bloc." He has taught and lectured at Columbia, Parsons, Syracuse, Barnard, Yale, and Princeton. Their work includes participation in the P. S. 1 / MoMA 2003 Warm-Up Young Architect Series (Queens, New York, 2003); the New Housing New York competition (Third Prize, 2004); as well as completion of the kit home BURST*003 (North Haven, Australia, 2005, published here).

SYSTEMARCHITECTS wurde 1998 von Jeremy Edmiston und Douglas Gauthier in New York ins Leben gerufen. Jeremy Edmiston erwarb seinen B.Arch. 1989 an der University of Technology in Sydney und 1992 seinen M.Arch. an der Columbia University in New York. Ein Forschungsprojekt zu umweltgerechter Architektur brachte ihm 1992 eine Harkness Fellowship und ein Fulbright-Stipendium ein. Er war als Gastprofessor an den Architekturfakultäten der Columbia University, Syracuse, der Roger Williams University und am City College tätig. Douglas Gauthier besitzt Abschlüsse der Columbia University und der University of Notre Dame. Für Forschungen zum Thema „Parallele Moderne: Architekturpraxis im früheren Ostblock" hielt er sich 1994 als Fulbrightprofessor in Tschechien und Slowakien auf. Er hielt Vorlesungen und Vorträge in Columbia, Parsons, Syracuse, Barnard, Yale und Princeton. Gemeinsam beteiligten sich Edmiston und Gauthier 2003 an der P. S. 1/MoMA 2003 Warm-Up Young Architect Series (Queens, New York, 2003), am Wettbewerb für neuen Wohnungsbau in New York (3. Preis, 2004) und stellten das hier publizierte Bausatzhaus BURST*003 fertig (North Haven, Australien, 2005).

SYSTEMARCHITECTS a été créé par Jeremy Edmiston et Douglas Gauthier à New York en 1998. Jeremy Edmiston est B. Arch. de l'Université de technologie de Sydney (1989), et M. Arch. de Columbia University (1992). Son projet de recherche de 1992 sur l'architecture environnementale lui a valu une bourse Harkness et une bourse Fulbright. Il a été professeur invité des écoles d'architecture de Columbia University, Syracuse, Roger Williams University, et City College. Douglas Gauthier est diplômé de Columbia University et de l'Université Notre-Dame. En 1994, il a été « Fulbright Architectural Scholar » en République tchèque et slovaque pour sa recherche intitulée « Modernisme parallèle : Pratiques constructives dans l'ancien bloc de l'Est ». Il a enseigné et donné des conférences à Columbia, Parsons, Syracuse, Barnard, Yale et Princeton. Parmi leurs travaux : participation à la P. S. 1/MoMA 2003 Warm-Up Young Architect Series, Queens, New York ; au concours New Housing New York (troisième prix, 2004) ; et à la maison en kit BURST*003, North Haven, Australie (2005), présentée ici.

BURST*003

North Haven, New South Wales, Australia, 2005

Floor area: 93 m² of interior space with 46 m² of exterior deck and bleachers. Clients: Andrew Katay and Catriona Grant
Cost: $250 000. Project Team: Sarkis Arakelyan, Amber Lynn Bard, Ayat Fadaifard, Sara Goldsmith,
Henry Grosman, Kobi Jakov, Joseph Jelinek, Ginny Hyo-jin Kang, Gen Kato, Yarek Karawczyk, Ioanna Karagiannakou, Tony Su
Site Architects: Robin Edmiston & Associates. Site/Project Architect: Chris Knapp

Built for a young family with three children on a 725-m² lot three hours from Sydney, BURST*003 is a prototype kit home. The plywood rib structure of the three-bedroom house was cut from 25-millimeter plywood by a computer-controlled laser. The architects explain that "each piece is pre-cut and numbered, delivered to the site, and assembled. Using digital processes, the geometry is complex and the form responsive to the relationship between natural forces on the site and the program. This relationship produces a low energy house that uses construction material and labor in a highly efficient manner." Local building regulations required that the residence be lifted 1.8 meters off the ground because it is located close to the shore. The architects conclude, "In the BURST* project, architecture successfully spatializes the outdoors. Through a series of deliberate overlaps, gaps, and slits within the building's skin, one's eye obliquely captures the surrounding landscape to interiorize the exterior. The human figure moves within, over, and under the folded skin, ambiguously occupying inside and outside. BURST*003 was built in 2005 and is being developed into a responsive parametric housing system that is earthquake, hurricane, and flood resistant." The house received the 2006 RAIA Wilkinson Award.

Das auf einem 725 m² großen Grundstück drei Stunden von Sydney entfernt stehende BURST*003 ist der Prototyp eines Bausatzhauses für eine junge Familie mit drei Kindern. Die Rippenkonstruktion des Hauses mit drei Schlafräumen wurde von einem computergesteuerten Laser aus 25 mm starkem Sperrholz geschnitten. Die Architekten erläutern: „Jedes Teil wird vorgeschnitten und nummeriert an den Bauplatz geliefert und dort montiert. Dank der Nutzung digitaler Prozesse ist die Geometrie komplex und die Form reagiert auf die Beziehung zwischen natürlichen Kräften vor Ort und dem Programm. Diese Beziehung ergibt ein Niedrigenergiehaus, das Baumaterial und Arbeitskraft höchst effizient nutzt." Lokalen Bauvorschriften entsprechend muss das Wohnhaus 1,8 m über den Boden angehoben werden, weil es nahe am Ufer liegt. „Mit dem BURST*-Projekt gelingt es der Architektur, den Außenraum zu ‚verräumlichen'. Durch eine Reihe von absichtlichen Überschneidungen, Lücken und Schlitzen in der Außenhaut nimmt das Auge die umgebende Landschaft indirekt wahr und verinnerlicht die Außenwelt. Die menschliche Figur bewegt sich in, über und unter der gefalteten Haut und nimmt dabei das Innen und Außen vieldeutig in Anspruch. BURST*003 wurde 2005 gebaut und wird zurzeit zu einem elastischen parametrischen Wohnsystem entwickelt, das Erdbeben, Hurrikans und Überflutungen standhalten kann." Das Haus erhielt 2006 den RAIA Wilkinson Award.

La maison BURST*003, construite pour une famille de trois enfants sur une parcelle de 725 m², située à trois heures de Sydney, est un prototype à construire soi-même. Sa structure, en nervures de contreplaqué, a été découpée au laser à commande numérique dans du contreplaqué de 25 mm d'épaisseur : « Chaque pièce est prédécoupée et numérotée, livrée sur site et assemblée. La géométrie complexe fait appel à des processus numériques et la forme répond à une relation entre les forces naturelles présentes sur le terrain et le programme. Cette relation donne naissance à une maison à faible consommation énergétique, qui utilise les matériaux de construction et la main d'œuvre nécessaires de façon extrêmement efficace. » La réglementation locale de la construction voulait que la maison soit surélevée de 1,8 mètres par rapport au sol, à cause de la côte très proche. Pour les architectes : « L'architecture » spatialise « avec succès l'extérieur. Grâce à une série de superpositions, de manques et de fentes aménagés dans la peau du bâti, le regard est capté obliquement par le paysage environnant pour intérioriser l'extérieur. L'habitant se déplace dans, sur et sous cette peau pliée, en occupant, non sans ambiguïté, l'intérieur et l'extérieur. BURST*003 a été construite en 2005 et sert de base à un système de logements paramétrés, résistant aux tremblements de terre, aux ouragans et aux marées. » La maison a reçu le RAIA Wilkinson Award 2006.

Lifted up off the ground because of the potential danger of flooding, the house is made in good part of computer-cut plywood. Despite its unusual appearance, BURST*003 is a kit house that can be assembled quickly.

Wegen möglicher Überflutung angehoben, besteht BURST*003 zum Großteil aus vom Computer zugeschnittenem Sperrholz. Trotz des ungewöhnlichen Aussehens handelt es sich um ein Baukastenhaus, das sich schnell montieren lässt.

Suspendue au-dessus du sol pour limiter les dangers d'inondation, la maison est en grande partie composée de contreplaqué découpé par ordinateur. Malgré son aspect inhabituel, c'est une maison en kit qui peut s'assembler rapidement.

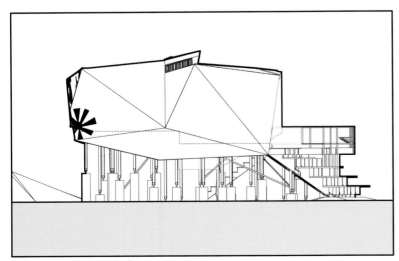

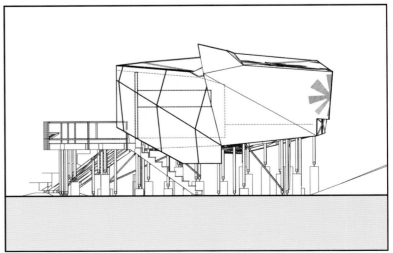

Kit houses generally lack originality or unusual spaces. In this instance, computer technology has been used to render both the design and the production of the residence simpler, allowing for greater spatial experimentation.

Baukastenhäusern fehlt es in der Regel an Originalität oder besonderen Räumen. In diesem Fall wurde die Computertechnik genutzt, um Design und Produktion des Wohnhauses einfacher zu gestalten und so räumliches Experimentieren zu ermöglichen.

Les maisons à monter manquent généralement d'originalité. Ici, la technologie numérique a servi à simplifier la conception et la production de ce projet et à profiter d'une plus grande liberté d'expérimentation spatiale.

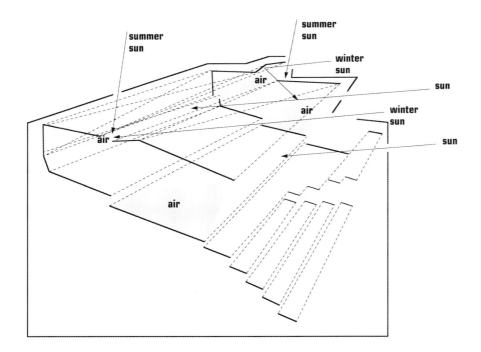

The assembly pattern of the plywood panels is related to the original computer-driven design and production process, making unusual forms much easier to deal with than in the past.

Die Montageweise der Sperrholzplatten steht in Verbindung zum ursprünglichen, computergesteuerten Entwurf, wodurch die Herstellung ungewöhnlicher Formen sehr viel einfacher ist als früher.

Le processus d'assemblage des panneaux de contreplaqué vient de la conception et de la production assistées par ordinateur, qui rendent les formes inhabituelles beaucoup plus faciles à gérer que par le passé.

BURST*003 has something of the atmosphere of a beach house, and is both cheerful and dynamic in ways that were previously unattainable for kit houses.

Wenngleich es etwas von der Atmosphäre eines Strandhauses hat, wirkt BURST*003 auf eine Weise fröhlich und dynamisch, die man von früheren Baukastenhäusern nicht kennt.

Bien qu'elle soit une sorte de maison de plage, BURST*003 est chaleureuse et dynamique d'une manière jusquelà inconnue pour une maison en kit.

P 604

Tenchi Hous

MASAHARU TAKASAKI

Takasaki Architects
1–42–22 Kamoike
Kagoshimashi
Japan

Tel: +81 99 284 0081
Fax: +81 99 284 0082
E-mail: ta@takasaki-architects.co.jp
Web: www.takasaki-architects.co.jp

MASAHARU TAKASAKI was born in Kagoshima in 1953. He studied at the Technical University of Graz, Austria, under Peter Cook, and at the University of Stuttgart, Germany. He created the Takasaki Monobito Institute in 1982, and his firm Takasaki Architects in 1990. He is an Honorary Fellow of the Royal Institute of British Architects, a Professor at the Kyoto University of Art and Design, and a Professor at Innsbruck University. His built work includes the Kuju National Park Restaurant (Kumamoto, Oita, 1994); Kihoku Astronomical Museum (Kihoku, Kagoshima, 1996); Shomyo Kindergarten (Mizobe, Kagoshima, 1996); Nanohanakan, Kagoshima Community Center for Seniors (Nanohanakan, Kagoshima, 1996–98); and Tenchi House, Mono Cosmology (Nagoya, 2009, published here), all in Japan.

MASAHARU TAKASAKI wurde 1953 in Kagoshima geboren. Er studierte an der Technischen Universität Graz bei Peter Cook und an der Universität Stuttgart. 1982 gründete er das Takasaki Monobito Institute, 1990 dann sein Büro Takasaki Architects. Er ist Ehrenmitglied des Royal Institute of British Architects, Professor an der Kyoto University of Art and Design, sowie Professor an der Universität Innsbruck. Zu seinen realisierten Bauten zählen das Restaurant im Nationalpark Kuju (Kumamoto, Oita, 1994), das Kihoku Astronomie-Museum (Kihoku, Kagoshima, 1996), der Shomyo Kindergarten (Mizobe, Kagoshima, 1996), ein Seniorenzentrum in Nanohanakan (Kagoshima, 1996–98) sowie das Tenchi House, Mono Cosmology (Nagoya, 2009, hier vorgestellt), alle in Japan.

MASAHARU TAKASAKI, né à Kagoshima en 1953, a étudié à l'Université polytechnique de Graz en Autriche, auprès de Peter Cook, et à l'Université de Stuttgart. Il a fondé l'Institut Takasaki Monobito en 1982 et son agence Takasaki Architects en 1990. Il est membre honoraire du Royal Institute of British Architects, professeur à l'Université d'art et de design de Kyoto et professeur à l'Université d'Innsbruck. Parmi ses réalisations, toutes au Japon, on peut citer le restaurant du Parc national de Kuju (Kumamoto, Oita, 1994) ; le Musée d'astronomie de Kihoku (Kihoku, Kagoshima, 1996) ; le jardin d'enfant de Shomyo (Mizobe, Kagoshima, 1996) ; le centre communautaire pour personnes âgées de Kagoshima (Nanohanakan, Kagoshima, 1996–98) et la maison Tenchi, Mono Cosmology (Nagoya, 2009, présentée ici).

TENCHI HOUSE

Nagoya, Aichi, Japan, 2009

Area: 151 m². Client: Keiko Ito
Cost: not disclosed

The entrance to this unusual house is located at its center. A front gate is formed to resemble the word "mind" in Japanese. Masaharu Takasaki states: "This entrance has the shape of a sculptural circle that suggests 'architecture becomes human.' It is a symbol leading to the time of art space." He states that the house is an "unfinished entity" that "absorbs the energy of the natural universe through metamorphosis reflecting seasonal changes." Suggesting that his architecture "embraces chaos," Takasaki also states that the Tenchi House is "an artificial organic space serving as a mind art house." The house is a surprising mixture of apparently organic forms with shapes that seem more mechanical than human. Materials also underline this dichotomy. The house occupies its site almost fully, standing out sharply from the more conventional buildings around it.

Der Eingang zu diesem ungewöhnlichen Haus liegt in seiner Mitte. Ein Gartentor wurde so gestaltet, dass es an das japanische Zeichen für „Geist" erinnert. Masaharu Takasaki erklärt: „Der Eingang hat die Form eines skulpturalen Kreises, der zu sagen scheint: ‚Architektur wird menschlich'. Er ist ein Symbol, der in die Zeit eines Kunstraums führt." Er bezeichnet ds Haus als „unfertiges Gebilde", das „die Energie des natürlichen Universums durch Metamorphose in sich aufnimmt und die Veränderungen der Jahreszeiten spiegelt." Takasaki deutet an, seine Architektur „bejahe das Chaos", und meint zugleich, das Tenchi House sei „ein künstlich-organischer Raum, der als Geist-Kunst-Haus dient". Das Haus ist eine überraschende Kombination aus augenscheinlich organischen Formen und solchen, die eher mechanisch als menschlich wirken. Auch die Baumaterialien unterstreichen diese Dichotomie. Das Haus nutzt das Grundstück fast vollständig aus und kontrastiert scharf mit den eher konventionellen Bauten in der Nachbarschaft.

L'entrée de cette étonnante maison se trouve en son centre. Le portail d'entrée évoque l'idéogramme qui signifie « esprit » en japonais. Pour l'architecte : « Cette entrée a la forme d'un cercle sculptural qui suggère que "l'architecture devient humaine". C'est un symbole conduisant au temps de l'espace conçu comme art. » Il explique que sa maison est une « entité non finie » qui « absorbe l'énergie de l'univers naturel par une métamorphose reflétant le changement des saisons ». Suggérant que son architecture « étreint le chaos », Takasaki pense également que sa maison Tenchi est « un espace organique artificiel, une maison de l'art et de l'esprit ». C'est un surprenant mélange de formes apparemment organiques et d'autres qui semblent plus mécaniques qu'humaines. Les matériaux mettent également en évidence cette dichotomie. La maison occupe la quasi-totalité de son terrain, et se détache avec violence de son environnement construit de manière plus conventionnelle.

Although the architect has been designing unusually shaped structures for many years, it would seem that his extravagance may once again be fashionable.

Obwohl der Architekt bereits seit Jahren formal ungewöhnliche Bauten entwirft, scheint es jetzt, als würde diese Extravaganz wieder in Mode kommen.

L'architecte conçoit des structures assez étonnantes depuis des années et ce type d'extravagance semble revenir à la mode.

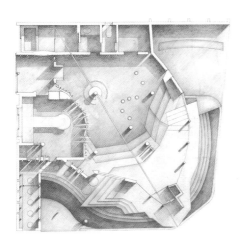
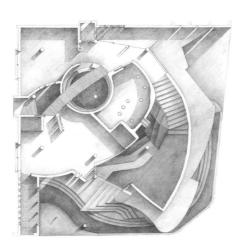
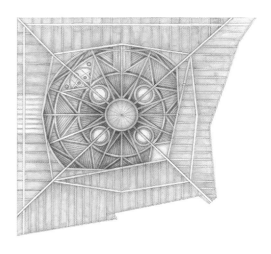

The interior is just as complex as the outside of the house, echoing and developing the designer's cosmological view of architecture.

Die Innenräume des Hauses sind ebenso komplex wie der Außenbau und zugleich ein Spiegel und eine Weiterentwicklung des kosmologischen Architekturverständnisses des Architekten.

Exprimant la vision cosmologique de l'architecture que défend son auteur, l'intérieur est aussi complexe que l'extérieur.

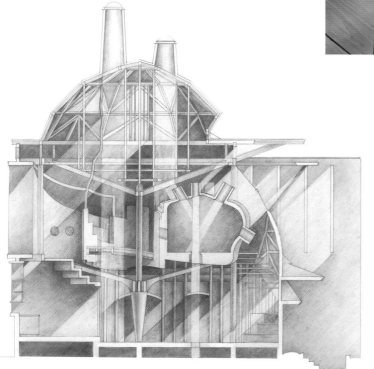

Remarkable detailed drawings, which also seem as though they are from another era, show the complexity of the design, also visible in the image above.

Auch die erstaunlichen, detaillierten Zeichnungen wirken, als stammten sie aus einer anderen Zeit und illustrieren die Komplexität des Designs, die sich auch in der Aufnahme oben zeigt.

Des dessins remarquablement détaillés, qui semblent dater d'une autre époque, montrent la complexité du projet, également perceptible dans la photographie ci-dessus.

JYRKI TASA

Jyrki Tasa
Architectural Office
Nurmela-Raimoranta-Tasa Ltd.
Kalevankatu 31
00100 Helsinki
Finland

Tel: +358 96 86 67 80
Fax: +358 96 85 75 88
E-mail: tasa@n-r-t.fi
Web: http://n-r-t.fi/

Born in Turku, Finland, in 1944, **JYRKI TASA** graduated from the Helsinki University of Technology in 1972. He set up an architectural office with Matti Nurmela and Kari Raimoranta in Helsinki the same year. He has been a Professor at the Helsinki University of Technology and a Professor of Contemporary Architecture at the University of Oulu. He won the Finnish State Prize in Architecture and Planning in 1987. His most significant work includes the Malmi Post Office (Helsinki, 1986); the Kuhmo Library (1988); the BE Pop Shopping Center (Pori, 1989); the Paavo Nurmi Stadium (Turku, 1997); the Into House (Espoo, 1998); the Moby Dick House (Espoo, 2002–03, published here); the Hollola Library (2004); and the Katajanokka Residential District (Helsinki, 2006–07). More recently Jyrki Tasa worked on the Seafarer's Beach Complex (Lauttasaari, Helsinki, 2003–); and the Pasilan housing complex (Helsinki, 2007–), all in Finland.

Der 1944 in Turku, Finnland, geborene **JYRKI TASA** beendete 1972 sein Studium an der Technischen Universität Helsinki. Im selben Jahr gründete er mit Matti Nurmela und Kari Raimoranta in Helsinki ein Architekturbüro. Er ist Professor an der Technischen Universität Helsinki und lehrt moderne Architektur an der Universität von Oulu. Tasa wurde 1987 der Finnische Staatspreis für Architektur und Planung verliehen. Zu seinen wichtigsten Bauten zählen das Postamt von Malmi (Helsinki, 1986); die Bibliothek in Kuhmo (1988); das Stadion Paavo Nurmi in Turku (1997); das Haus Into in Espoo (1998); das Shopping Center BE Pop in Pori (1998) und das Haus Moby Dick (Espoo, hier vorgestellt). Ein neueres Projekt ist die Wohnbebauung Katajanokka (Helsinki, 2006–07). In jüngerer Zeit arbeitete Jyrki Tasa am Seafarer's Beach Complex (Lauttasaari, Helsinki, 2003–) und an der Wohnanlage Pasilan (Helsinki, 2007–). Alle diese Bauten stehen in Finnland.

Né à Turku (Finlande) en 1944, **JYRKI TASA** est diplômé de l'Université de technologie d'Helsinki (1972). Il a fondé une agence d'architecture en association avec Matti Nurmela et Kari Raimoranta à Helsinki la même année. Il a été professeur à l'Université de technologie d'Helsinki et professeur d'architecture contemporaine à l'Université d'Oulu. Il a remporté le Prix d'architecture et d'urbanisme national de Finlande en 1987. Parmi ses œuvres les plus importantes (toutes en Finlande) : la bibliothèque de Kuhmo ; le stade Paavo Nurmi à Turku (1997) ; la maison Into à Espoo (1998) ; le centre commercial BE Pop à Pori (1998) et la maison Moby Dick présentée ici. Plus récemment, il a réalisé le quartier résidentiel de Katajanokka (Helsinki, 2006–07) et travaille actuellement sur le complexe balnéaire Seafarer (Lauttasaari, Helsinki, 2003 – en cours) et le projet de logements de Pasilan (Helsinki, 2007 – en cours).

HOUSE MOBY DICK

Espoo, Finland, 2002–03

Client: a four person family (private).
Total floor area: 570 m². Costs: not disclosed

Few houses appear as different as this one when seen from one side (below) or the other (right). Elevations show better how this surprising transition is accomplished.

Wenige Häuser wirken so unterschiedlich, wenn man sie von verschiedenen Seiten (unten und rechts) betrachtet. Die Aufrisse machen die Ausführung der Übergänge deutlich.

Peu de maisons présentent autant de différences d'une façade (ci-dessous) à l'autre (à droite). Les élévations expliquent cette surprenante transition.

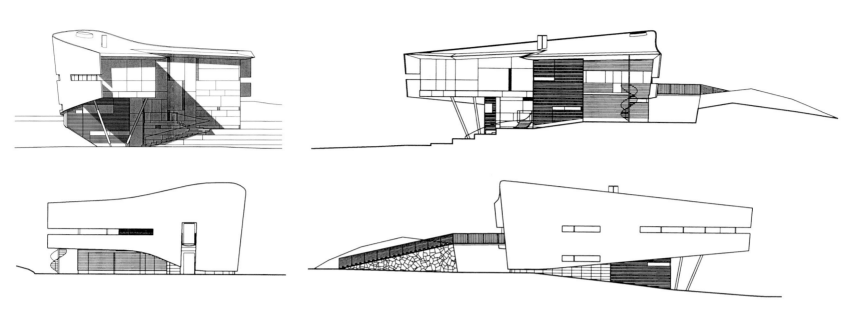

Built for a four-person family, this 570-m^2 "biomorphic" house is approached via a stone stairway and a steel bridge leading to the first floor above ground level. At the entrance level, there are a living room, library, master bedroom, and two balconies. The ground floor contains the children's spaces, a guestroom, and a garage, while a sauna, fireplace, and gym are in the basement of the house. A two-story-high winter garden, three translucent glass and steel bridges and a staircase forming the spatial core of the house all participate in the open movement of the residence. The stairway offers views into every area of the house. The curving exterior of the structure, evoked by its name "Moby Dick," contrasts with the rectangular interior walls. Made with concrete-filled steel pillars, concrete-steel composite slabs and a steel and wood roof, the house is mostly clad with plywood or pine. The house is equipped with a heat pump and floor heating system.

Der Zugang zu dem für eine vierköpfige Familie gebauten „biomorphen" Haus erfolgt über eine Steintreppe und eine Stahlbrücke, die zum ersten Stock führen. Auf dieser Ebene liegen ein Wohnraum, die Bibliothek, das Elternschlafzimmer und zwei Balkone. Das Erdgeschoss enthält die Räume der Kinder, ein Gästezimmer und eine Garage, während Sauna, Kamin und Fitnessraum im Souterrain untergebracht sind. Ein Wintergarten mit doppelter Raumhöhe, drei durchscheinende Brücken aus Glas und Stahl und ein Treppenaufgang bilden den räumlichen Kern des Gebäudes und tragen in ihrer Gesamtheit zu seiner offenen, rhythmischen Gestaltung bei. Die geschwungenen Fassaden, von denen das Haus den Namen Moby Dick hat, kontrastieren mit den rechtwinkligen Innenwänden. Die Konstruktion besteht aus Stahlsäulen mit Betonfüllung, Betonstahlplatten und einem Dach aus Stahl und Holz. Die Außenverkleidung ist hauptsächlich aus Sperrholz oder Kiefernholz gefertigt.

On accède à cette maison biomorphique de 570 m^2, construite pour une famille de quatre personnes, par une allée pavée et une passerelle d'acier qui conduit directement au premier étage, niveau au-dessus du rez-de-chaussée. Celui-ci comprend le séjour, une bibliothèque, la chambre principale et deux balcons. Le rez-de-chaussée regroupe les espaces pour les enfants, une chambre d'amis et un garage, tandis que le sous-sol comprend un sauna, une cheminée et une salle de gymnastique. Le jardin intérieur sur deux niveaux, trois murs de verre translucide, des passerelles et un escalier en acier constituent le noyau de cette maison et assurent une circulation ouverte. La façade incurvée, qui justifie le nom de « Moby Dick » contraste avec les murs intérieurs orthogonaux. L'ensemble a fait appel à des piliers d'acier remplis de béton, des dalles de béton armé, un toit en bois et acier. La façade est habillée pour l'essentiel de contreplaqué ou de pin.

Contrary to what the closed entrance façade might imply, the house is bright, open and light in its articulation.

Im Gegensatz zu dem, was man von der geschlossenen Eingangsfassade erwarten könnte, ist das Haus hell, offen und von lockerer Eleganz.

Contrairement à ce que la façade d'entrée, plus fermée, laisse penser, la maison est très ouverte et d'articulation légère.

Daylight floods the interior space where wood and glazing form the major surfaces. Plans below show the rather unusual disposition of the structure.

Das Tageslicht durchflutet den Innenraum, in dem Holz und Glas vorherrschen. Die Grundrisse unten zeigen die ungewöhnliche Anordnung des Gebäudes.

La lumière naturelle inonde l'intérieur, traité essentiellement en bois et en verre. Les plans ci-dessous montrent le plan assez curieux de l'ensemble.

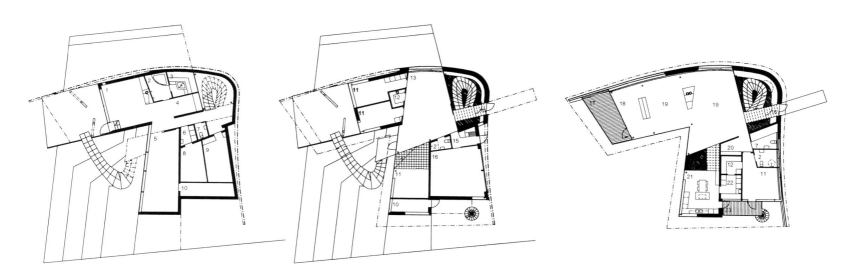

An unusual irregular spiral staircase connects the interior levels of the house, and the architect uses a full palette of materials to surprise and delight the inhabitant or visitor.

Eine auffallend unregelmäßige Wendeltreppe verbindet die Geschossebenen des Hauses. Die volle Palette von Materialien überrascht Bewohner wie Besucher.

Un escalier irrégulier et inhabituel relie les niveaux intérieurs. L'architecte a fait appel à une palette variée de matériaux pour surprendre et ravir l'occupant ou le visiteur.

CHRIS TATE

Chris Tate Architecture
PO Box 52051
Kingsland, Auckland
New Zealand

Tel: +64 9 630 2514
Fax: +64 9 630 2515
E-mail: chris@christate.co.nz
Web: www.christate.co.nz

CHRIS TATE was born in 1971 in Auckland, New Zealand. He received a Bachelor of Social Science in Human Service from the Auckland College of Education (1994–97) and a Diploma in Architectural Technology from UNITEC Auckland (2004–05). He did social work for various agencies from 1990 to 2001, but during that period he also bought land on an island off the coast of Auckland and designed and built a house there. He left his social work in 2001 to manage the construction of a large house on the same island designed by Richard Priest. In 2006 he created Chris Tate Architecture and completed his first project, Forest House (Titirangi, Auckland, 2006, published here).

CHRIS TATE wurde 1971 in Auckland, Neuseeland, geboren. Er erwarb einen Bachelor in Sozialwissenschaften am Auckland College of Education (1994–97) und ein Diplom in Architektur an der UNITEC Auckland (2004–05). Von 1990 bis 2001 war er für verschiedene Organisationen im sozialen Bereich tätig, kaufte während-dessen aber auch Land auf einer Insel vor der Küste von Auckland und entwarf und baute dort ein Haus. 2001 gab er seine Tätigkeit als Sozialarbeiter auf, um auf der-selben Insel die Aufsicht über den Bau eines großen Hauses zu übernehmen, das er für Richard Priest entworfen hatte. 2006 gründete er Chris Tate Architecture und realisierte sein erstes Projekt, das Forest House (Titirangi, Auckland, 2006, hier vorgestellt).

CHRIS TATE, né en 1971 à Auckland, en Nouvelle-Zélande, est diplômé en sciences humaines et sociales du Auckland College of Education (1994–97), et il a également un diplôme en technologie architecturale de UNITEC Auckland (2004–05). Il a participé à différentes interventions sociales pour diverses agences de 1990 à 2001, et pendant cette période s'est acheté un terrain sur une île de la côte d'Auckland où il s'est construit une maison. Il a quitté son travail dans les services sociaux pour diriger la construction d'une vaste maison conçue par Richard Priest sur la même île. En 2006, il a fondé l'agence Chris Tate Architecture et a achevé son premier projet, la maison de la forêt (Titirangi, Auckland, 2006, présenté ici).

FOREST HOUSE

Titirangi, Auckland, New Zealand, 2006

Floor area: 100 m². Client: Chris Tate. Cost: € 150 000

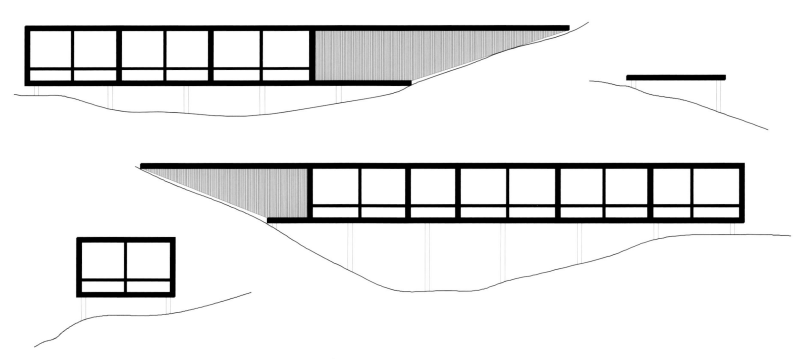

This house was built on a densely forested and steep 800-m² lot. Entering the house, visitors are required to descend 45 steps to reach the entrance. According to Chris Tate: "The site is slip sensitive, flood prone, and is protected by the local building authority as a 'Protected Environment.'" Including one bedroom, a study and a bathroom, with an open-plan living, dining, and kitchen area, the house is intended as "an interpretation of Philip Johnson's 1949 Glass House" (New Canaan, Connecticut, USA). A building platform was created on 16 poles across a gully and this glass box was set on it, cantilevered in all directions "to create a floating feeling." The precise site was selected to minimize tree removal, and New Zealand native trees were planted after construction. The house was designed to stop at a large Pururi (arched tree), saving it from being cut. A black-and-white color scheme was chosen in order to contrast with the green forest environment. Tate was allowed to build on the site because of the "low environmental impact" of the design. The floor inside the house is made of rough eucalyptus wood painted in high-gloss white.

Das Haus wurde auf ein dicht bewachsenes, steiles 800 m² großes Waldgrundstück gebaut. Besucher müssen zuerst 45 Stufen hinabsteigen, um zum Hauseingang zu gelangen. Chris Tate erklärt: „Das Grundstück ist erdrutsch- und überschwemmungsgefährdet und wurde von der örtlichen Baubehörde als Naturschutzgebiet ausgezeichnet." Das Haus mit einem Schlafzimmer, Arbeitszimmer, Bad und einem offenen Wohn-, Ess- und Küchenbereich wurde als „Interpretation von Philip Johnsons Glass House von 1949" (New Canaan, Connecticut, USA) gestaltet. Über einem Regenwasserablauf wurde eine Gebäudeplattform auf 16 Stützen aufgeständert. Hierauf wurde der Glaskubus platziert. Dieser kragt nach allen Seiten aus, um „einen schwebenden Eindruck" zu vermitteln. Die genaue Lage des Baugrunds wurde gewählt, um nicht zu viele Bäume fällen zu müssen. Nach Bauabschluss wurden heimische Bäume angepflanzt. Der Entwurf nahm Rücksicht auf einen großen herabhängenden Pururi-Baum, sodass dieser nicht gefällt werden musste. Als Kontrast zur grünen Waldumgebung entschied man sich gestalterisch für eine Schwarzweißpalette. Tate erhielt seine Baugenehmigung auch wegen des „geringen Eingriffs in die Umwelt". Der Boden im Innern des Hauses wurde aus rohem Eukalyptusholz gefertigt und glänzend weiß lackiert.

Cette maison a été édifiée sur un terrain de 800 m², incliné et abondamment planté d'arbres. Pour entrer, le visiteur doit d'abord descendre 45 marches. Selon Chris Tate : « Le site, qui pourrait être sujet à des glissements de terrain et des inondations, est classé par la réglementation locale en "environnement protégé" ». Comprenant une chambre, un bureau et une salle de bains, un séjour de plan ouvert et un espace pour la préparation et la prise des repas, la maison se veut « une interprétation de la maison de verre de Philip Johnson » (1949, New Canaan, Connecticut, États-Unis). Une plate-forme située au-dessus d'un ravin a d'abord été mise en place. Elle repose sur 16 pieux et soutient la boîte de verre, elle-même en porte-à-faux dans toutes les directions « pour créer une sensation de flottement ». L'implantation précise a été déterminée de façon à limiter le nombre d'arbres à supprimer. Des arbres d'essences locales ont été replantés après le chantier. La maison s'est volontairement arrêtée devant un grand pururi (arbre arqué) pour ne pas avoir à le couper. Le noir et le blanc ont été choisis pour contraster avec le vert de l'environnement forestier. Tate a eu le droit de construire sur ce terrain parce que le projet n'exerçait qu'un « faible impact environnemental ». Le sol intérieur est en planches brutes d'eucalyptus peintes en blanc laqué brillant.

The Forest House is indeed carefully inserted into its site, abutting the earth on one side, bridging a gully, and entirely surrounded by existing trees.

Das Forest Haus wurde außerordentlich umsichtig in sein Umfeld integriert – auf der einen Seite am Boden „andockend", überbrückt es einen Regenwasserablauf und ist rundum von Bäumen umgeben.

La « maison de la forêt » est soigneusement insérée dans son site, butant contre le relief d'un côté, franchissant un ruisseau et entièrement entourée d'arbres.

The interior of the house retains a modern if not modernist spirit, rendered more surprising by the almost invasive presence of nature all around its windows.

Das Interieur ist modern, wenn nicht modernistisch gehalten, was angesichts der geradezu invasiven Präsenz der Natur vor den Fenstern umso überraschender wirkt.

L'intérieur de la maison conserve un esprit moderne, voire moderniste, rendu plus étonnant encore par la présence presque envahissante de la nature devant les fenêtres.

TEZUKA ARCHITECTS

Tezuka Architects
1–19–9–3F Todoroki
Setagaya
Tokyo 158–0082
Japan

Tel: +81 3 3703 7056
Fax: +81 3 3703 7038
E-mail: tez@sepia.ocn.ne.jp
Web: www.tezuka-arch.com/

TAKAHARU TEZUKA, born in Tokyo, Japan, in 1964, received his degrees from the Musashi Institute of Technology (1987) and from the University of Pennsylvania (1990). He worked with Richard Rogers Partnership Ltd. (1990–94) and established Tezuka Architects the same year. He is currently a professor at Tokyo City University. Born in Kanagawa, Japan, in 1969, **YUI TEZUKA** was educated at the Musashi Institute of Technology and the Bartlett School of Architecture, University College of London. The practice has completed about a dozen private houses, and won the competition for the Matsunoyama Museum of Natural Science in 2001. Since then it has been based in Tokyo. Their work includes the Soejima Hospital (Saga-shi, Saga, 1995–96); Wood Deck House (Kamakura-shi, Kanagawa, 1999); Roof House (Hadano-shi, Kanagawa, 2000–01); Toyota L&F Hiroshima (Hiroshima-shi, Hiroshima, 2003); Echigo-Matsunoyama Museum of Natural Science (Tokamachi-shi, Niigata, 2002–03); Floating Roof House (Okayama, 2005); Fuji Kindergarten (Tachikawa, Tokyo, phase 1, 2006; phase 2, 2006–07); Temple to Catch the Forest (Yokohama, Kanagawa, 2006–07); Steel Sheet House (Tokyo, 2008–09); Pitched Roof House (Nagano, 2008–09, published here); and Woods of Net (Ninotaira, Hakone, Kanagawa/inside of the Hakone Open-Air Museum, 2009), all in Japan.

TAKAHARU TEZUKA, 1964 in Tokio geboren, studierte bis 1987 am Musashi Institute of Technology und bis 1990 an der University of Pennsylvania. Er arbeitete bei Richard Rogers Partnership Ltd. (1990–94) und gründete 1994 Tezuka Architects. Gegenwärtig ist er Professor an der Tokyo City University. Die 1969 in Kanagawa, Japan, geborene **YUI TEZUKA** studierte am Musashi Institute of Technology und der Bartlett School of Architecture, University College of London. Das Büro hat etwa ein Dutzend Privathäuser ausgeführt und 2001 den Wettbewerb für das Matsunoyama Museum of Natural Science gewonnen. Seitdem hat es seinen Sitz in Tokio. Zu seinen Projekten zählen das Soejima Hospital (Saga-shi, Saga, 1995–96), das Wood Deck House (Kamakura-shi, Kanagawa, 1999), das Roof House (Hadano-shi, Kanagawa, 2000–01), Toyota L&F Hiroshima (Hiroshima-shi, Hiroshima, 2003), das Echigo-Matsunoyama Museum of Natural Science (Tokamachi-shi, Niigata, 2002–03), das Floating Roof House (Okayama, 2005), der Kindergarten Fuji (Tachikawa, Tokio, 1. Bauabschnitt 2006; 2. Bauabschnitt 2006–07), Temple to Catch the Forest (Yokohama, Kanagawa, 2006–07), das Steel Sheet House (Tokio, 2008–09), das Pitched Roof House (Nagano, 2008–09, hier veröffentlicht) sowie Woods of Net (Ninotaira, Hakone, Kanagawa/im Hakone Open-Air Museum, 2009), alle in Japan.

TAKAHARU TEZUKA, né à Tokyo en 1964, est diplômé de l'institut de technologie Musashi (1987) et de l'université de Pennsylvanie (1990). Il a travaillé pour le Richard Rogers Partnership Ltd. (1990–94) et a fondé l'agence Tezuka Architects la même année. Il est actuellement professeur à l'université de la ville de Tokyo. Né à Kanagawa en 1964, **YUI TEZUKA** est diplômé de l'institut de technologie Musashi et de la Bartlett School of Architecture, University College, à Londres. L'agence a construit une douzaine de résidences privées et remporté en 2001 le concours du musée des sciences naturelles Matsunoyama. Installée aujourd'hui à Tokyo, elle a réalisé, entre autres et toujours au Japon : l'hôpital de Soejima (Saga-shi, Saga,1995–96) ; la maison Wood Deck (Kamakura-shi, Kanagawa, 1999) ; la maison toit (Hadano-shi, Kanagawa, 2000–01) ; Toyota L&F Hiroshima (Hiroshima-shi, Hiroshima, 2003) ; le musée de sciences naturelles Echigo-Matsunoyama (Tokamachi-shi, Niigata, 2002–03) ; la maison au toit flottant (Okayama, 2005) ; le jardin d'enfants Fuji (Tachikawa, Tokyo, phase 1, 2006 ; phase 2, 2006–07) ; Le Temple qui capte la forêt (Yokohama, Kanagawa, 2006–07) ; la maison de feuille d'acier (Tokyo, 2008–09) ; la maison au toit à deux versants (Nagano, 2008–09, présentée ici) et Woods of Net (Ninotaira, Hakone, Kanagawa/à l'intérieur du Musée de plein air Hakone, 2009).

PITCHED ROOF HOUSE

Nagano, Japan, 2008–09

Area: 107 m². Client: not disclosed. Cost: not disclosed
Collaboration: Hirofumi Ohno/OHNO JAPAN

Located on a 1059-m² site, this house employs what the architects call "an extremely simple pitched roof" that is unusual to the extent that only 40 percent of the space under the roof is enclosed as internal space. The cantilevered roof edge provides space extending out to the landscape. The architects writes: "The main theme of the house is the space under the eave. The existence of the internal space relies very much on the intermediate space. Every detail of this house is designed to achieve the columnless eave space. The folded shape of the pitched roof helps the very thin cantilevered roof to stretch almost six meters." Using full-height sliding doors for the enclosed space, it has been made possible to entirely open the interior when weather conditions permit. The architects conclude: "We believe the true nature of Japanese architecture lies in the intermediate space between outside and inside. The internal space exists, because the intermediate space exists. The client requested a simple house responding to the Japanese landscape. This is the attempt to amplify the Japanese-ness of the house to the limit that the latest technology allows."

Dieses auf einem 1059 m² großen Grundstück gelegene Haus hat ein, in den Worten der Architekten, „extrem einfaches, geneigtes Dach", was insofern ungewöhnlich ist, als nur 40 % des von ihm überdeckten Bereichs Innenräume sind. Das auskragende Dach bedeckt Flächen, die sich in die Landschaft erstrecken. Der Architekt schreibt: „Das Hauptthema dieses Hauses ist der Raum unter der Dachtraufe. Die Existenz der Innenräume beruht weitgehend auf den Zwischenbereichen. Jedes Detail dieses Hauses war darauf ausgerichtet, den stützenfreien Raum unter dem Dach zu ermöglichen. Die gefaltete Form des geneigten Daches trägt dazu bei, dass es über fast 6 m auskragen kann." Durch geschosshohe Schiebetüren können die Innenräume ganz geöffnet werden, sofern das Wetter dies zulässt. Die Architekten erklären abschließend: „Wir sind der Überzeugung, dass das eigentliche Merkmal der japanischen Architektur im Zwischenbereich zwischen außen und innen liegt. Der Innenbereich existiert, weil der Zwischenbereich existiert. Der Bauherr wünschte sich ein schlichtes Haus in Übereinstimmung mit der japanischen Landschaft. Dies ist ein Versuch, das Japanische des Hauses so weit zu führen, wie es die moderne Technik zulässt."

Implantée sur un terrain de 1059 m², cette maison fait appel ce que les architectes appellent « un toit extrêmement simple à deux versants », d'aspect curieux dans la mesure où le volume intérieur habitable n'utilise que 40 % de la surface sous toiture. L'espace sous le porte-à-faux s'étend vers le paysage. Selon l'architecte : « Le thème principal de cette maison est l'espace sous le débord du toit. L'existence de l'espace intérieur dépend en grande partie de cet espace intermédiaire. Tout est conçu pour que cette zone protégée de dessous la toiture ne comporte pas de colonnes. Le pliage du toit en deux parties permet un porte-à-faux de chaque côté de près de six mètres. » Grâce à des portes coulissantes toute hauteur qui ferment l'espace intérieur, on peut entièrement ouvrir celui-ci quand le temps le permet. « Nous pensons que la véritable nature de l'architecture japonaise tient à l'espace intermédiaire entre le dedans et le dehors. L'espace interne existe parce que l'espace intermédiaire existe. Le client souhaitait une maison simple qui réponde aux caractéristiques du paysage japonais. C'est une tentative d'amplifier le caractère nippon de cette maison jusqu'aux limites permises par les technologies les plus récentes. »

The very large roof of the house and its long, low form make it blend into the site in the image above.

Das sehr große Dach des Hauses und dessen lange, niedrige Form betten es gut in das Gelände ein (oben).

Le très grand toit surbaissé de la maison facilite sa fusion avec le paysage (ci-dessus).

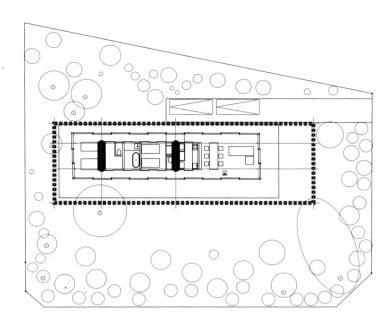

A drawing shows the predominant
shape of the roof. Below, the roof
serves to cover living areas that can
thus be exposed to the open air.

*Die Zeichnung zeigt die beherr-
schende Form des Dachs. Unten:
Das Dach dient auch zur Überdeckung
von Aufenthaltsbereichen im Freien.*

*Le dessin montre la prééminence de
la forme du toit. Ci-dessous, la toiture protège des zones du séjour qui
peuvent ainsi rester ouvertes.*

TNA

Makoto Takei + Chie Nabeshima/TNA
3-16-3-3F Taishidou
Setagaya-ku
Tokyo 154-0004
Japan

Tel: +81 3 3795 1901
Fax: +81 3 3795 1902
E-mail: mail@tna-arch.com
Web: www.tna-arch.com

Makoto Takei was born in Tokyo in 1974. He graduated from the Department of Architecture of Tokai University in 1997. Between 1997 and 1999 he was at the Tsukamoto Laboratory, Graduate School of Science and Engineering, Tokyo Institute of Technology, and worked with Atelier Bow-Wow. Between 1999 and 2000 he worked in the office of Tezuka Architects, before establishing **TNA (**Takei-Nabeshima-Architects**)** with Chie Nabeshima. Chie Nabeshima was born in Kanagawa in 1975 and graduated from the course in Habitation and Space Design, Department of Architecture and Architectural Engineering, College of Industrial Technology, Nihon University (1998), before working at Tezuka Architects (1998–2005) and co-founding TNA. Their projects include the Wood Wear House (Hayama, Kanagawa, 2005); the Color Concrete House (Yokohama, Kanagawa, 2005); the Ring House (Karuizawa, Nagano, 2006, published here); the Wood Ship Café (Hayama, Kanagawa, 2007); and the Mosaic House (Meguro-ku, Tokyo, 2007, also published here), all in Japan.

Makoto Takei, 1974 in Tokio geboren, schloss sein Architekturstudium 1997 an der Universität Tokai ab. Zwischen 1997 und 1999 war er am Tsukamoto-Labor der Graduate School of Science and Engineering am Tokyo Institute of Technology tätig und arbeitete mit dem Atelier Bow-Wow. Von 1999 bis 2000 war er für Tezuka Architects tätig, bevor er mit Chie Nabeshima das Büro **TNA** (Takei-Nabeshima-Architects) gründete. Chie Nabeshima wurde 1975 in Kanagawa geboren und schloss den Studiengang Wohnbau und Raumgestaltung am Institut für Architektur und Bauwissenschaften am College of Industrial Technology der Universität Nihon ab (1998), bevor sie für Tezuka Architects tätig war (1998–2005) und TNA mitbegründete. Zu ihren Projekten zählen das Wood Wear House (Hayama, Kanagawa, 2005), das Color Concrete House (Yokohama, Kanagawa, 2005), das Ring House (Karuizawa, Nagano, 2006, hier vorgestellt), das Wood Ship Café (Hayama, Kanagawa, 2007) sowie das Mosaic House (Meguro-ku, Tokio, 2007, ebenfalls hier vorgestellt), alle in Japan.

Makoto Takei, né à Tokyo en 1974, est diplômé du département d'architecture de l'université Tokai (1997). De 1997 à 1999, il a travaillé dans le Laboratoire Tsukamoto de l'école supérieure de sciences et d'ingénierie de l'institut de technologie de Tokyo et a collaboré avec l'Atelier Bow-Wow. De 1999 à 2000, il est architecte chez Tezuka Architects avant de créer **TNA** (Takei-Nabeshima-Architects) avec Chie Nabeshima. Chie Nabeshima, né en Kanagawa en 1975, a été diplômée de conception d'espace et de l'habitat du département d'architecture et d'ingénierie architecturale du collège de technologie industrielle de l'université Nihon (1998), elle est ensuite entrée chez Tezuka Architects (1998–2005) et de fonder TNA. Parmi leurs projets, tous situés au Japon, on peut citer la maison Wood Wear (Hayama, Kanagawa, 2005) ; la maison Color Concrete (Yokohama, Kanagawa, 2005) ; la maison Ring (Karuizawa, Nagano, 2006, présentée ici) ; le Wood Ship Café (Hayama, Kanagawa, 2007) et la maison Mosaic (Meguro-ku, Tokyo, 2007, également présentée ici).

RING HOUSE

Karuizawa, Nagano, Japan, 2006

Floor area: 102 m². Client: Hill Karuizawa
Cost: not disclosed

This unusual house was built in a forest setting. It is a laminated lumber structure with a basement and two levels above ground, for a total height of 9.37 meters. Its site covers a total of 1387 m². The forest clearly inspired the architects to design in a different way than they would have in the city. "Rather than having a single-directional view, a space where one is able to see the forest milieu from every direction and height is achieved." The "ring" referred to in the name of the house does not refer so much to its shape as to the 360° views its interiors offer. Made of wood and glass, with burnt cedar siding positioned in bands whose width and number are unrelated to floor levels, the Ring House has an enigmatic presence. Its largely empty interiors, with their birch floors, almost dissolve into the forest background creating an impression of suspended volumes or weightlessness.

Das ungewöhnliche Haus wurde in einer Waldgegend errichtet. Die Konstruktion aus laminiertem Holz mit Keller und zwei oberirdischen Geschossen hat eine Höhe von insgesamt 9,37 m. Das Grundstück ist 1387 m² groß. Der Wald inspirierte die Architekten ganz offensichtlich zu einem gänzlich anderen Designansatz, als sie ihn in der Stadt gewählt hätten. „Statt eine auf einen Punkt konzentrierte Aussicht zu haben, wurde hier ein Raum geschaffen, von dem aus das Waldumfeld aus jeder Richtung und von jeder Höhe aus zu sehen ist." Der Begriff „Ring" bezieht sich weniger auf die Form des Hauses, als auf den 360-Grad-Ausblick, den es erlaubt. Das aus Holz und Glas gebaute Ring House besitzt eine rätselhafte Präsenz. Die Verkleidung aus rußgeschwärztem Zedernholz wurde zu Bändern angeordnet, deren Breite und Anzahl jedoch nicht mit den Etagen des Hauses korrespondieren. Die überwiegend leeren Innenräume mit ihren Birkenholzböden verschmelzen geradezu mit dem Wald-hintergrund und erzeugen den Eindruck von schwebenden Volumina oder Schwerelosigkeit.

Cette étonnante maison s'élève dans un cadre forestier. De trois niveaux, dont un en sous-sol, pour une hauteur totale de 9,37 mètres, sa structure est en bois lamellé-collé. Le terrain couvre une surface de 1387 m². La forêt a évidemment inspiré aux architectes une solution différente de ce qu'ils auraient pu construire en ville. « Plutôt que de privilégier une vue dans une seule direction, nous avons abouti à un espace d'où l'on peut voir la forêt dans toutes les directions et sur différentes hauteurs. » Le « ring » ou anneau, qui a donné son nom à la maison, ne se réfère pas à la forme, mais à la vue panoramique à 360°. Les façades, en bois et en verre, sont habillées de cèdre brûlé posé en bandeaux, dont le nombre et la largeur sont indépendants des niveaux, ce qui confère à cette maison une présence énigmatique. L'intérieur aux sols de bouleau est presque vide et se dissout dans le fond de la forêt, donnant ainsi une impression de volumes suspendus ou d'absence de poids.

The house sits on a hilly site in the forest, its irregular black banded exterior giving little hint as to the real location of the floors.

Das Haus liegt auf einem hügeligen Waldgrundstück. Der mit unregelmäßigen schwarzen Bändern überzogene Außenbau verrät wenig über die tatsächliche Lage der Stockwerke.

La maison est implantée en forêt sur un terrain mouvementé. Ses façades à bandeaux noir et blanc de largeur variée ne donnent que peu d'indications sur la répartition des niveaux.

Although the plan of the house is a perfect square, the disposition of interior elements, including the bedroom or bathroom seen on this page, defy any rigorous pattern.

Obwohl der Grundriss des Hauses ein perfektes Quadrat ist, folgt die Anordnung des Innenausbaus, einschließlich Schlafzimmer und Bad auf dieser Seite, keineswegs einem strengen Muster.

Bien que le plan de la maison soit un carré parfait, la disposition des éléments intérieurs, y compris la chambre ou la salle de bains représentées ici, défient toute toute logique.

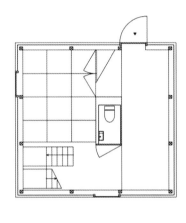
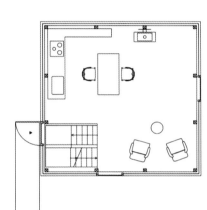
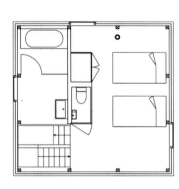

MOSAIC HOUSE

Meguro-ku, Tokyo, Japan, 2006–07

Floor area: 84.5 m². Client: not disclosed. Cost: not disclosed

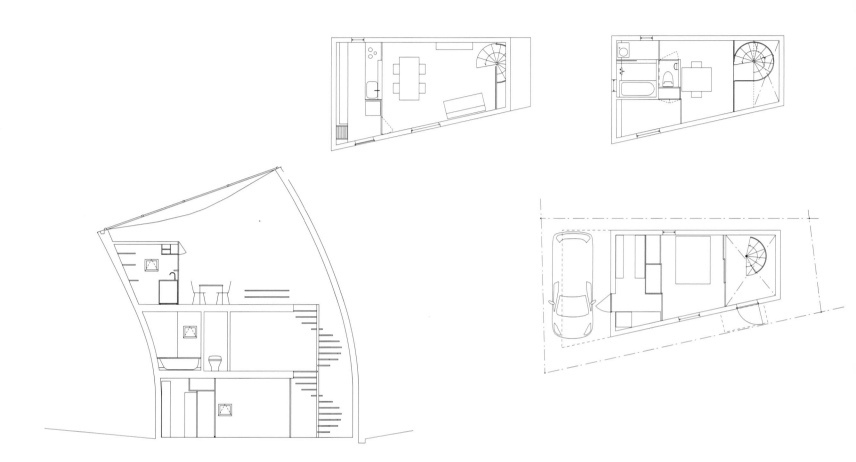

Built in a former parking lot for a couple with one child, this house is typical in its size of the numerous very small residences being designed in Japan, especially in densely built cities like Tokyo. Clad in white mosaic tile, the house appears to lean toward the "south sky like a sunflower." This orientation and the size of the skylight mean that the interior of the residence is flooded with light, despite its rather closed façades. The idea that nature can be present in the city and in architecture through such elements as light or wind is a particularly Japanese one, but one that is perfectly justified, especially in the urban matrix of Tokyo, where little space is left for nature in its more traditional representations (as in the gardens of the Imperial Palace). With this residence, or other realizations, such as their Ring House, the architects of TNA have shown a particular interest in nature and the environment, depending on location and their own sensitivity.

Die Größe des auf einem ehemaligen Parkplatz erbauten Hauses für ein Paar mit Kind ist typisch für die zahlreichen kleinen Wohnbauten, die in Japan entworfen werden, insbesondere in dicht besiedelten Städten wie Tokio. Das mit weißen Mosaikfliesen verblendete Haus neigt sich zum „südlichen Himmel wie eine Sonnenblume". Durch die Ausrichtung des Baus und die Größe des Oberlichtfensters sind die Innenräume trotz der eher geschlossenen Fassaden lichtdurchflutet. Der Gedanke, dass die Natur durch Elemente wie Licht oder Wind in Stadt und Architektur präsent sein kann, mag typisch japanisch sein, gerade in der urbanen Matrix Tokios ist er aber absolut gerechtfertigt, wo für die Natur und ihre traditionelleren Erscheinungsformen (etwa die Gärten des Kaiserpalasts) nur wenig Platz bleibt. Mit diesem Wohnhaus und anderen Projekten wie dem Ring House haben die Architekten von TNA je nach Lage der Grundstücke und mit dem ihnen eigenen Einfühlungsvermögen besonderes Interesse an Natur und Umwelt bewiesen.

Construite sur un ancien parking pour un couple et son enfant, cette maison est typiquement japonaise dans la petitesse de ses dimensions, fréquente dans les villes très densément construites comme Tokyo. Parée de mosaïque blanche, elle semble s'orienter vers le « Sud et le ciel comme un tournesol ». Cette orientation et la taille de la verrière signifient que l'intérieur est baigné de lumière malgré des façades assez fermées. L'idée que la nature puisse rester présente dans la ville et son architecture à travers des éléments tels que la lumière ou le vent est une vision très japonaise, mais parfaitement justifiée, en particulier dans la matrice urbaine tokyoïte où peu de place est laissée à la nature, même dans ses schémas traditionnels (comme les jardins du Palais impérial). Dans cette résidence et d'autres réalisations dont leur Ring House, les architectes de TNA montrent me[u]r sensibilité particulière pour la nature et l'environnement en fonction du contexte.

The house quite literally takes a bow to the sky, channeling natural light inside while shielding it from excessive heat gain.

Das Haus verneigt sich buchstäblich vor dem Himmel, lässt Tageslicht in den Bau und schützt ihn zugleich vor allzu starker Wärmeentwicklung.

La maison s'incline littéralement devant le ciel, pour lui permettre de canaliser l'éclairage naturel vers l'intérieur tout en la protégeant d'un gain solaire excessif.

Contrary to external appearances that show only a few small windows, the house is flooded with light from above.

Anders als die Außenaufnahmen vermuten lassen, die nur wenige kleine Fenster zeigen, ist das Haus von oben her lichtdurchflutet.

Contrairement aux apparences – seules quelques petites fenêtres sont visibles – la maison est baignée de lumière zénithale.

Furnished in sparse fashion, which is typical of Japan, the house has high spaces and is suffused constantly with natural light.

Das Haus ist sparsam möbliert, was für Japan typisch ist, hat hohe Räume und ist den ganzen Tag über von natürlichem Licht durchflutet.

La maison est meublée avec sobriété, à la japonaise, et ses hauts volumes bénéficient toute la journée de l'éclairage naturel.

UNSTUDIO

UNStudio
Stadhouderskade 113
1073 AX Amsterdam
The Netherlands

Tel: +31 20 570 2040
Fax: +31 20 570 2041
E-mail: info@unstudio.com
Web: www.unstudio.com

Ben van Berkel was born in Utrecht, the Netherlands, in 1957 and studied at the Rietveld Academy in Amsterdam and at the Architectural Association (AA) in London, receiving the AA Diploma with honors in 1987. After working briefly in the office of Santiago Calatrava in 1988, he set up his practice in Amsterdam with Caroline Bos. As well as the Erasmus Bridge in Rotterdam (inaugurated in 1996), **UNSTUDIO** has built the Karbouw and ACOM office buildings (1989–93), and the REMU Electricity Station (1989–93), all in Amersfoort; and housing projects and the Aedes East Gallery for Kristin Feireiss in Berlin, Germany. Projects include an extension for the Rijksmuseum Twente (Enschede, 1992–96); the Möbius House (Naarden, 1993–98); Het Valkhof Museum (Nijmegen, 1998); and NMR Laboratory (Utrecht, 2000), all in the Netherlands; a Switching Station (Innsbruck, Austria, 1998–2001); an Electricity Station (Innsbruck, Austria, 2002); VilLA NM (Upstate New York, USA, 2000–06, published here); the Mercedes-Benz Museum (Stuttgart, Germany, 2003–06); and the Arnhem Station (The Netherlands, 1986–ongoing). Recent work includes a Tea House (Groot Kantwijk, Vreeland, The Netherlands, 2005–07); a Music Theater (Graz, Austria, 1998–2008); a Research Laboratory at Groningen University (Groningen, The Netherlands, 2003–08); Star Place (Kaohsiung, Taiwan, 2006–08); and Burnham Pavilion (Chicago, Illinois, USA, 2009).

Ben van Berkel wurde 1957 in Utrecht geboren und studierte an der Rietveld-Akademie in Amsterdam sowie der Architectural Association (AA) in London, wo er 1987 das Diplom mit Auszeichnung erhielt. Nach einem kurzen Arbeitseinsatz 1988 bei Santiago Calatrava gründete er mit Caroline Bos sein eigenes Büro in Amsterdam. Neben der 1996 eingeweihten Erasmusbrücke in Rotterdam baute **UNSTUDIO** in Amersfoort die Büros für Karbouw und ACOM (1989–93) sowie das Kraftwerk REMU (1989–93), und realisierte in Berlin Wohnbauprojekte sowie die Galerie Aedes East für Kristin Feireiss. Zu den Projekten des Teams zählen ein Erweiterungsbau für das Rijksmuseum in Twente (Enschede, 1992–96), das Haus Möbius (Naarden, 1993–98), das Museum Het Valkhof (Nijmegen, 1998) und das NMR Labor (Utrecht, 2000), alle in den Niederlanden, eine Umschaltstation (Innsbruck, 1998–2001), ein Elektrizitätswerk (Innsbruck, 2002), die VilLA NM (bei New York, 2000–06, hier vorgestellt), das Mercedes-Benz Museum (Stuttgart, 2003–06) sowie der Bahnhof Arnhem (Arnhem, 1986–andauernd). Jüngere Arbeiten sind u. a. ein Teehaus (Groot Kantwijk, Vreeland, 2005–07), ein Musiktheater in Graz (1998–2008), ein Forschungslabor an der Universität Groningen (2003–08), Star Place (Kaohsiung, Taiwan, 2006–08) sowie der Burnham-Pavillon (Chicago, 2009).

Ben van Berkel, né à Utrecht en 1957, étudie à l'Académie Rietveld d'Amsterdam ainsi qu'à l'Architectural Association de Londres dont il sort diplômé avec mention en 1987. Après avoir brièvement travaillé pour Santiago Calatrava en 1988, il ouvre son agence à Amsterdam, en association avec Caroline Bos. En dehors du pont Érasme à Rotterdam (inauguré en 1996), **UNSTUDIO** a construit à Amersfoort les immeubles de bureaux Karbouw et ACOM (1989–93), la sous-station électrique REMU (1989–93), ainsi que des logements et l'Aedes East Gallery de Kristin Feireiss à Berlin. Parmi leurs projets plus récents : l'extension du Rijksmuseum Twente (Enschede, 1992–96), la maison Moebius (Naarden, 1993-98) ; le musée Het Valkhof (Nimègue, 1998) ; le laboratoire NMR (Utrecht, 2000), tous aux Pays-Bas ; une gare d'échange (Innsbruck, Autriche, 1998–2001) ; une station d'électricité (Innsbruck, 1997–2000) ; la VilLA NM (État de New York, 2000–06, présentée ici) ; le musée Mercedes Benz (Stuttgart, Allemagne, 2003–06) et la gare d'Arnhem (Pays-Bas, 1986–). Plus récemment, l'agence a réalisé une maison de thé (Groot Kantwijk, Vreeland, Pays-Bas, 2005–07) ; une salle de concert (Graz, Autriche, 1998–2008) ; un laboratoire de recherche pour l'université de Groningue (Pays-Bas, 2003–08) ; le centre commercial Star Place (Kaohsiung, Taiwan, 2006–08) et le pavillon Burnham (Chicago, Illinois, 2009).

VILLA NM

Upstate New York, USA, 2000–06

Floor area: 230 m². Client: not disclosed. Cost: not disclosed
Design Team: Ben van Berkel with Olaf Gipser and Andrew Benn, Colette Parras, Jacco van Wengerden,
Jan Debelius, Olga Vazquez-Ruano, Martin Kuitert. Local Consultant: Roemer Pierik

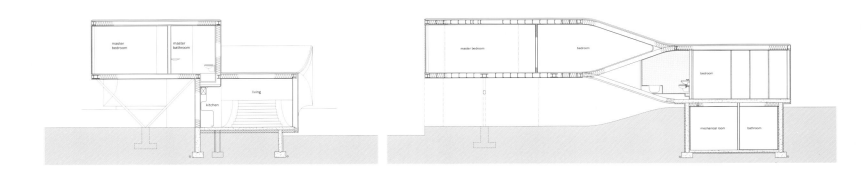

Located about two hours' drive from New York City, near Sullivan County, the area where this house was built has become popular for younger city-dwellers looking for a place to build. The sloping 7000-m² site has a 360° view of forest and meadowlands. The architects used a combination of concrete and glass with a light metal construction. One volume of the house follows the northern slope, another is "lifted above the hill" and contains a covered parking area. Bathrooms, kitchen, and fireplace are located in the vertical axis. Some rooms are partially closed off from the outside for privacy; others have large glazed surfaces. As the architects describe the house, "The volumetric transition is generated by a set of five parallel walls that rotate along a horizontal axis from vertical to horizontal. The walls become floor and vice versa. The ruled surface maintaining this transition is repeated five times in the building. Standardizing and pre-fabricating this structural element lowered the building costs without reducing the spatial quality of the interior. The interior space also takes advantage of the split-level organization. The kitchen and dining area on the ground floor are connected by a ramp to the living space above, the 1.5-meter height change allowing for a tremendous view over the valley. A similar ramp connects the living area to the master and the children's bedrooms on the second floor."

Die Gegend, in der dieses Haus errichtet wurde, etwa eine zweistündige Autofahrt von New York City entfernt unweit von Sullivan County gelegen, ist in letzter Zeit bei jüngeren Stadtbewohnern beliebt, die nach einem Bauplatz suchen. Das abschüssige, 7000 m² große Grundstück bietet eine Rundumsicht auf Wald und Wiesen. Die Architekten kombinierten Beton und Glas mit Leichtmetallbauweise. Ein Teil des Hauses folgt dem Abhang nach Norden, ein weiterer ist „über den Hügel angehoben" und enthält eine überdachte Parkfläche. Bäder, Küche und Kamin befinden sich auf der vertikalen Achse. Um Privatheit zu schaffen, sind einige Räume teilweise nach außen geschlossen, andere zeichnen sich durch große Glasflächen aus. Die Architekten beschreiben das Haus wie folgt: „Der volumetrische Übergang wird durch eine Gruppe von fünf parallelen Wänden geschaffen, die entlang einer horizontalen Achse von der Vertikale in die Horizontale verschwenkt werden. Die Wände werden zu Fußböden und umgekehrt. Dieser Übergang wiederholt sich im Gebäude fünfmal. Standardisierung und Vorfertigung dieses konstruktiven Elements senkten die Baukosten, ohne die räumliche Qualität des Innenraums zu mindern. Dieser macht sich die Anordnung auf versetzten Ebenen zunutze. Küche und Essbereich im Erdgeschoss sind durch eine Rampe mit dem darüberliegenden Wohnbereich verbunden, wobei der Höhenunterschied von 1,5 m einen fulminanten Blick über das Tal ermöglicht. Eine ähnliche Rampe verbindet den Wohnbereich mit dem Elternschlafzimmer und den Kinderzimmern im zweiten Stock."

Située à deux heures de voiture de New York, près du comté de Sullivan, la région dans laquelle cette maison a été édifiée est très prisée par les jeunes citadins qui cherchent un terrain pour construire. La parcelle de 700 m² en pente bénéficie d'une vue à 360° sur la forêt et les pâturages. Les architectes ont combiné le béton, le verre et une structure légère en métal. Un des volumes de la maison suit la pente nord, l'autre « se soulève au-dessus de la colline » et dégage la place nécessaire au garage couvert. Les salles de bains, la cuisine et la cheminée sont regroupées dans l'axe vertical. Certaines pièces présentent d'importantes parois vitrées. Selon l'architecte : « La transition volumétrique se fait grâce à un ensemble de cinq murs parallèles qui pivotent le long d'un axe horizontal de la verticale à l'horizontale. Les murs deviennent ainsi des sols et vice versa. Cette surface de transition se répète à cinq reprises. La standardisation et la préfabrication de cet élément structurel a permis d'abaisser ses coûts de construction, sans porter atteinte à la qualité spatiale intérieure. Le volume interne bénéficie également de cette organisation décalée de l'espace. La cuisine et l'aire des repas au rez-de-chaussée sont connectées par une rampe au séjour situé, la différence de hauteur de 1,5 mètres ménageant une vue splendide sur la vallée. Une rampe similaire relie le séjour à la chambre principale et à celle des enfants à l'étage. »

Taking up in many ways where the architects' Möbius House left off, the VilLA NM represents a study of the intersection of different volumes, rendering both plan and section dynamic and surprising.

Die VilLA NM, die in vieler Hinsicht da einsetzt, wo das Haus Möbius der Architekten endete, stellt eine Studie sich durchschneidender, unterschiedlicher Baukörper dar, was einen dynamischen, überraschenden Grundriss und Schnitt zur Folge hat.

Partant à plusieurs égards de là où la maison Möbius avait été laissée par les architectes, la VilLA NM représente une étude sur l'intersection de divers volumes qui dynamise à la fois les plans et les coupes.

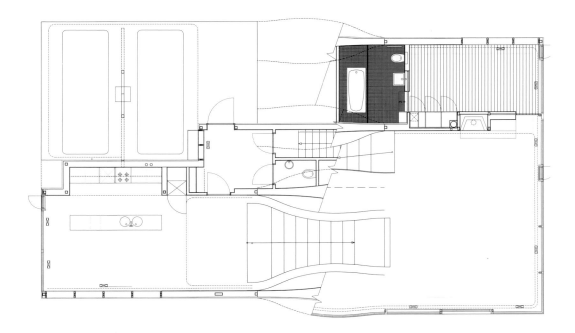

Interior spaces flow into each other, and create unusual, almost cavern-like volumes that open, as is the case above, onto a bright, fully glazed area, in this case the living room.

Innenräume gehen ineinander über und schaffen ungewöhnliche, fast höhlenartige Räumlichkeiten, die sich wie oben zum hellen, voll verglasten Wohnbereich hin öffnen.

Les espaces intérieurs s'interpénè-trent et créent des volumes inhabi-tuels, presque caverneux qui donnent, comme ci-dessus, sur la zone lumi-neuse largement ouverte du séjour.

The openings and passageways in the house are irregular, almost as if they had been designed by hand rather than carefully crafted with the most sophisticated computer programs available.

Die Öffnungen und Durchgänge im Haus sind uneinheitlich, fast als seien sie von Hand und nicht mit den kompliziertesten, verfügbaren Computerprogrammen entworfen.

Les ouvertures et les passages sont irréguliers, comme s'ils avaient été dessinés à la main plutôt que mis au point par certains des logiciels informatiques les plus sophistiqués du moment.

The architects have given the house its basic furnishings, leaving spaces that are fully defined in architectural terms. Wires replace a handrail on the stairway.

Die Architekten haben das Haus mit seiner Grundmöblierung ausgestattet und dabei in architektonischer Hinsicht komplett festgelegte Räume hinterlassen. An der Treppe ersetzen Drähte den Handlauf.

Les architectes ont meublé simplement la maison, laissant des espaces parfaitement définis en termes d'architecture. Des câbles remplacent une main courante le long de l'escalier.

WEBER + HUMMEL

Weber + Hummel
Traubenstr. 51
70176 Stuttgart
Germany

Tel: + 49 711 29 75 65
Fax: + 49 711 29 75 73
E-mail: buero@weber-hummel.de
Web: www.weber-hummel.de

GÜNTER WEBER was born in Illertissen, Germany, in 1958. He studied at the University of Stuttgart and at the ETH in Zurich (1979–86). He worked in the Sonntag architectural office in Illertissen (1986–87) and cofounded Weber + Hummel in 1991. Since 2000, he has been a Professor of Interior Design, Lighting and Architectural Design at the University of Applied Sciences (Wiesbaden). **JOACHIM HUMMEL** was born in 1960 in Bräulingen, Germany. He also studied architecture at the University of Stuttgart and at the ETH in Zurich (1979–87). He worked in the office of Günter Hermann in Stuttgart (1987–91), before cofounding Weber + Hummel. The work of the firm includes interior design for an orthodontist's practice (Burghausen, 2008); the G/S House (Ulm-Reutti, 2009); House U (Erlangen, 2008–10, published here); and the "Landhaus Bubat", the refurbishment of a listed, one-family residence (Freiburg, 2011), all in Germany.

GÜNTER WEBER wurde 1958 in Illertissen, Deutschland, geboren. Er studierte an der Universität Stuttgart und an der Eidgenössischen Technischen Hochschule in Zürich (1979–86). 1986–87 arbeitete er im Architekturbüro Sonntag in Illertissen und wurde 1991 Mitbegründer des Büros Weber + Hummel. Seit dem Jahre 2000 ist er Professor für Innenraumgestaltung, Lichttechnik und Entwerfen an der Hochschule RheinMain in Wiesbaden. **JOACHIM HUMMEL** wurde 1960 in Bräunlingen, Deutschland, geboren. Auch er studierte an der Universität Stuttgart und an der ETH in Zürich (1979–87). Bis zur Gründung von Weber + Hummel arbeitete er im Büro von Günter Hermann in Stuttgart (1987–91). Zu den Werken von Weber + Hummel zählen die Innenausstattung einer Praxis für Kieferorthopädie (Burghausen, 2008); das Haus G/S (Ulm-Reutti, 2009); das Haus U (Erlangen, 2008–10, hier vorgestellt) und das „Landhaus Bubat", der Umbau eines denkmalgeschützten Einfamilienhauses (Freiburg, 2011), alle in Deutschland.

GÜNTER WEBER, né à Illertissen (Allemagne) en 1958 a étudié à l'Université de Stuttgart et à l'ETH de Zurich (1979–86). Il a travaillé pour l'agence d'architecture Sonntag à Illertissen (1986–87) avant de fonder Weber + Hummel en 1991. Depuis 2000, il est professeur d'architecture intérieure, d'éclairage et de conception architecturale à l'Université des sciences appliquées de Wiesbaden. **JOACHIM HUMMEL**, né en 1960 à Bräulingen (Allemagne), a également étudié à l'Université de Stuttgart et à l'ETH de Zurich (1979–87). Il a travaillé pour l'agence de Günter Hermann à Stuttgart (1987–91), avant de fonder Weber + Hummel. Les réalisations de l'agence, toutes en Allemagne, comprennent entre autres : l'architecture intérieure d'un cabinet d'orthodontiste (Burghausen, 2008) ; la maison G/S (Ulm-Reutti, 2009) ; la maison U (Erlangen, 2008–10, présentée ici) et la Landhaus Bubat, reconstruction d'une résidence familiale classée (Freiburg, 2011).

HOUSE U
Erlangen, Germany, 2008–10

Area: 460 m²
Client: not disclosed. Cost: not disclosed

This is a single-family residence built on a sloped 2000-m² site near Erlangen. The structure is made up of individual pavilions connected by courtyards. Because of the large floor area required, the architects preferred the pavilion solution because it allows them to maintain a modest scale. Full-height glazed façades "create floating transitions between inside and outside." The architects participated in the interior design. Portuguese limestone and teak parquet are used for indoor flooring, with plaster and plasterboard ceiling and wall surfaces. The two-level structure is made of reinforced concrete, with an overall height of six meters. They write: "Whether you look from the guest pavilion into the 'quiet courtyard' or from the bedroom onto the Bavarian hillsides, introversion and extroversion maintain a fine balance."

Dieses Einfamilienhaus bei Erlangen wurde auf einem 2000 m² großen Hanggrundstück errichtet. Der Bau besteht aus einzelnen Pavillons, die durch Innenhöfe miteinander verbunden sind. Aufgrund der großen Wohnfläche bevorzugten die Architekten die Pavillonlösung, weil diese es ihnen ermöglichte, den Maßstab relativ klein zu halten. Geschosshoch verglaste Fassaden „erzeugen fließende Übergänge zwischen innen und außen". Die Architekten waren auch an der Innenausstattung beteiligt. Für die Fußböden im Innern wurden portugiesischer Kalkstein und Teak-Parkett gewählt, für die Decken und Wände Putz und Gipskarton. Das zweigeschossige Gebäude besteht aus Stahlbeton und hat eine Gesamthöhe von 6 m. Aus dem Bericht der Architekten: „Ob man vom Gästepavillon in den ‚stillen Innenhof' schaut oder vom Schlafraum über das bayerische Hügelland – Introvertiertheit und Extrovertiertheit halten ein ausgewogenes Gleichgewicht."

Cette maison familiale a été édifiée sur un terrain en pente, de 2000 m² situé près de Erlangen. La structure se compose de pavillons individuels reliés entre eux par des cours. C'est parce que le client souhaitait une grande surface habitable que les architectes ont opté pour la solution de pavillons permettant de maintenir une échelle d'apparence modeste. Les façades de verre pleine hauteur « créent des transitions floues entre l'intérieur et l'extérieur.» Les architectes ont participé à l'aménagement intérieur. Les sols sont en calcaire du Portugal et en teck, les murs et les plafonds en plâtre ou panneaux de plâtre. La construction est en béton armé et ses deux niveaux atteignent une hauteur de 6 mètres. « Que vous regardiez du pavillon des invités vers la » cour tranquille « ou de la chambre vers les collines bavaroises, un équilibre raffiné a été obtenu entre introversion et extroversion » commentent les architectes.

The architecture corresponds rigorously to the renderings below. A thin white band is wrapped around a glazed core, making the house appear to float in its setting.

Die Architektur entspricht exakt den unten wiedergegebenen Zeichnungen. Ein schmales, weißes Band umgibt den verglasten Kern; dadurch scheint das Haus in seinem Umfeld zu schweben.

L'architecture correspond rigoureusement aux images de synthèse ci-dessous. Le mince bandeau blanc qui entoure le noyau en verre donne l'impression que la maison flotte dans son environnement.

Although its plan is made up of geometric blocks, the house offers angles and contrasts in materials that enliven the space and its rapport with the exterior.

Obgleich das Haus aus geometrischen Blocks zusammengesetzt ist, bietet es Ecken und Materialkontraste, die den Raum und seinen Bezug zum Außenbereich beleben.

Bien que son plan soit composé de blocs géométriques, la maison multiplie les angles et les contrastes de matériaux qui animent l'espace et son rapport avec l'extérieur.

Full height glazing opens onto a
courtyard space, guaranteeing a
proximity to the outside and nature
that is in clear contrast with the white
interior spaces.

Die geschosshohe Verglasung öffnet
sich auf einen Hof und garantiert eine
Nähe zum Außenbereich und zur
Natur, die einen deutlichen Gegensatz
zu den weißen Innenräumen bildet.

Des baies vitrées pleine hauteur
ouvrent sur l'espace d'une cour,
assurant ainsi une proximité avec
l'extérieur et la nature qui contraste
fortement avec la blancheur des
espaces intérieurs.

WILLIAMS AND TSIEN

Tod Williams Billie Tsien Architects
222 Central Park South
New York, NY 10019
USA

Tel: + 1 212 582 2385
Fax: + 1 212 245 1984
E-mail: mail@twbta.com
Web: www.twbta.com

TOD WILLIAMS was born in Detroit, USA, in 1943 and got his B.A. in 1965, and his Master of Fine Arts in 1967 (Princeton University). After six years as associate architect in the office of Richard Meier in New York, he began his own practice in New York in 1974. He taught at the Cooper Union for more than 15 years, and has also taught at Harvard, Yale, the University of Virginia, and SCI-Arc. He received a mid-career Prix de Rome in 1983. **BILLIE TSIEN** was born in Ithaca, New York, in 1949. She received her B.A. at Yale (1971), and her M.Arch from UCLA (1977). She has been a painter and graphic designer (1971–75). She has taught at Parsons School of Design, SCI-Arc, Harvard, and Yale. Their built work includes Feinberg Hall (Princeton, New Jersey, 1986); New College, University of Virginia (Charlottesville, Virginia, 1992); the renovation and extension of the Phoenix Art Museum (Arizona, 1996); and the Cranbrook Natatorium (Bloomfield, Michigan, 1999). More recent projects include the American Folk Art Museum (New York, New York, 2001); the Mattin Student Art Center at Johns Hopkins University (Baltimore, Maryland, 2001); the Shelter Island House (Shelter Island, New York, 2001–03, published here); and the David Rubenstein Atrium (New York, New York, 2009). Their current work includes the new home of the celebrated Barnes Foundation in Philadelphia (2007–), all in the USA.

TOD WILLIAMS wurde 1943 in Detroit geboren und erwarb 1965 den B.Arch sowie 1967 den Master of Fine Arts an der Princeton University. Nach sechs Jahren Tätigkeit als assoziierter Architekt im Büro von Richard Meier in New York gründete er 1974 dort sein eigenes Büro. Er lehrte über 15 Jahre an der Cooper Union sowie in Harvard, Yale, an der University of Virginia und am Southern California Institute of Architecture. 1983 erhielt er den Prix de Rome. **BILLIE TSIEN** wurde 1949 in Ithaca, New York, geboren. Sie erwarb den Bachelor of Arts in Yale und den M.Arch an der University of California in Los Angeles (1977). Von 1971 bis 1975 arbeitete sie als Malerin und Grafikerin. Gelehrt hat sie an der Parsons School of Design, am Southern California Institute of Architecture SCI-ARC, in Harvard und Yale. Zu den ausgeführten Bauten des Büros zählen die Feinberg Hall der Princeton University (New Jersey, 1986); das New College der University of Virginia (Charlottesville, Virginia, 1992), die Sanierung und Erweiterung des Museum of Fine Arts in Phoenix, Arizona (1996) und das Cranbrook Natatorium (Bloomfield, Michigan, 1999). Jüngere Projekte sind das das Museum of American Folk Art in New York (2001), das Mattin Student Art Center der Johns Hopkins University (Baltimore, Maryland, 2001), das Haus Shelter Island (Shelter Island, New York, 2001–03, hier vorgestellt) und das David Rubenstein Atrium (New York, New York, 2009). Gegenwärtig planen sie den Neubau der renommierten Barnes Foundation in Philadelphia (2007–).

TOD WILLIAMS, né à Detroit en 1943, est diplômé de Princeton (1965), où il a également obtenu un master en arts visuels en 1967. Après avoir été architecte associé pendant six ans chez Richard Meier à New York, il crée son agence en 1974 dans cette ville. Il enseigne à Cooper Union pendant plus de 15 ans mais également à Harvard, Yale, à l'Université de Virginie et au Southern California Institute of Architecture. Il a reçu le Prix de Rome en 1983. **BILLIE TSIEN**, née à Ithaca (New York) en 1949, est diplômée de Yale et a obtenu un master en architecture de UCLA (1977). Elle a été peintre, et graphiste (1971–75) et a enseigné à la Parsons School of Design, au Southern California Institute of Architecture (SCI-ARC), Harvard et Yale. Parmi leurs réalisations figurent : le Hall Feinberg (Princeton, New Jersey, 1986) ; New College à l'Université de Virginie (Charlottesville, Virginie, 1992), la rénovation et l'extension du Musée des Beaux-Arts de Phoenix (Arizona, 1996) et le Cranbrook Natatorium (Bloomfield, Michigan, 1999). Plus récemment, ils ont réalisé le Musée d'art folklorique américain à New York (2001), le Mattin Centre des étudiants en art de l'Université Johns Hopkins (Baltimore, Maryland, 2001), la Maison Shelter Island (Shelter Island, New York, 2001–03, présentée ici), et le David Rubenstein Atrium (New York, New York, 2009). Ils travaillent actuellement sur le projet du nouveau siège de la fameuse Fondation Barnes à Philadelphie (2007 – en cours).

SHELTER ISLAND HOUSE

Shelter Island, New York, USA, 2001–03

Floor area: 464 m². Client: not disclosed. Cost: not disclosed
Project Architects: Paul Schulhof, Betty Chen

Located on a bluff overlooking the Atlantic Ocean, this house is on the side of Shelter Island that faces away from Sag Harbor. It is built on a cast-in-place concrete lower level and foundation. Brazilian granite panels (1.5 x 2.5 meter slabs) are used for the exterior cladding, while New York Bluestone floors and solid cherry walls were selected for the interior. Designed for a "physically active single man," the house was erected on the site of a previous residence that had burned down, leading the client to want architecture that would "engender a sense of permanence." An elevated courtyard frames an ocean view, and serves as an "outdoor room" connecting the volumes formed by the main house and the garage. A guest bedroom, kitchen, dining area, and living room are located on this level. The master bedroom is on the lower floor, together with two additional bedrooms. A game room is located beneath the garage and is connected to the house by a glass corridor. As the architects explain, "The interior furnishings are still spare because the owner spends most of his time involved in outdoor physical activity. However the house is a powerful shell: weighty, set into the ground like a large rock outcropping overlooking the sea and the sky."

Das Haus steht auf einem Steilufer über dem Atlantik, auf der Sag Harbor abgewandten Seite von Shelter Island. Es wurde auf einem Untergeschoss und Fundament aus Ortbeton errichtet. Die Außenseite ist mit brasilianischen Granitplatten (Größe 1,5 x 2,5 m) verkleidet, während im Inneren die Wahl auf Böden aus New Yorker Blausandstein und massive Kirschholzwände fiel. Das für einen „sportlich aktiven Junggesellen" entworfene Haus entstand an der Stelle eines früheren, durch Brand zerstörten Wohnhauses, was beim Auftraggeber den Wunsch nach einer Architektur mit „einem Gefühl von Dauerhaftigkeit" auslöste. Ein erhöhter Innenhof rahmt den Blick aufs Meer und dient als „Zimmer im Freien", das die Baukörper des Haupthauses und der Garage verbindet. Auf dieser Ebene befinden sich ein Gästezimmer, Küche und Essbereich sowie das Wohnzimmer. Das Hauptschlafzimmer und zwei weitere Schlafräume finden sich auf der unteren Ebene. Ein Freizeitraum liegt unterhalb der Garage und ist mit dem Haus durch einen gläsernen Korridor verbunden. Den Architekten zufolge „ist das Haus nur spärlich möbliert, weil der Eigentümer die meiste Zeit mit sportlichen Aktivitäten im Freien verbringt. In jedem Fall ist das Haus ein machtvolles Gehäuse: in den Boden gesetzt wie ein großer Felsvorsprung mit Aussicht auf Meer und Himmel.".

En bordure d'une crête qui donne sur l'océan Atlantique, cette maison se trouve sur Shelter Island face à Sag Harbor. Elle repose sur des fontations et un sous-sol en béton coulé sur place. Des dalles de 1,5 x 2,5 m en granit du Brésil ont été utilisées pour le parement des façades, la pierre « New York Bluestone » pour les sols, des panneaux en cerisier pour les murs intérieurs. Conçu pour « un célibataire ayant une activité physique importante » la maison a été érigée sur le site d'une ancienne résidence qui avait brûlé, ce qui avait conduit ce client à souhaiter une architecture qui « engendre un sens de permanence ». Une cour surélevée cadre une vue de l'océan et sert de « pièce d'extérieur » qui relie les volumes formés par la maison principale et le garage. La chambre d'amis, la cuisine et la zone de repas et le séjour sont situés à ce niveau. La suite principale se trouve au niveau inférieur ainsi que deux chambres supplémentaires. Une salle de jeux se trouve sous le garage, reliée à la maison par un couloir vitré. Comme l'explique l'architecte : « L'aménagement intérieur est encore minimal car le propriétaire consacre le plus clair de son temps à des activités sportives. Cependant la maison est une coque : pesante, posée sur le sol comme un gros affleurement de rocher donnant sur la mer et le ciel »

Concrete structures, clad with 1.5 x 2.5 meter panels of blue Brazilian granite, the house, set on a bluff overlooking the Atlantic, assumes a certain solidity as seen from the water's edge.

Vom Ufer aus gesehen vermitteln die beiden, mit 1,5 x 2,5 m großen Platten aus blauem, brasilianischem Granit verkleideten Betonbauten, die auf einem Steilufer über dem Atlantik stehen, Solidität.

Faite d'éléments en béton habillés de panneaux en granit bleu du Brésil de 1,5 x 2,5 m, la maison implantée sur un escarpement qui surplombe l'Atlantique présente, vue du bord de l'eau, une certaine massivité.

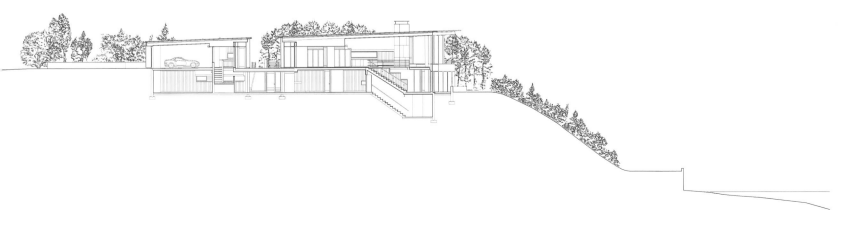

"The house," write the architects, "is a powerful shell: weighty, set into the ground like a large rock outcropping overlooking the sea and the sky."

„In jedem Fall ist das Haus", so die Architekten, „ein machtvolles Gehäuse: in den Boden gesetzt wie ein großer Felsvorsprung mit Aussicht auf Meer und Himmel."

« La maison, écrivent les architectes, est une coque pleine de force : pesante, posée sur le sol comme un gros affleurement de rocher donnant sur la mer et le ciel. »

As in many of their projects, the architects work in great detail on the juxtaposition of materials and on the finishes.

Wie bei vielen ihrer Projekte legten die Architekten großen Wert auf kontrastreiche Materialien und Oberflächen.

Comme dans beaucoup de leurs projets, les architectes accordent le plus grand soin à la juxtaposition des matériaux et aux finitions.

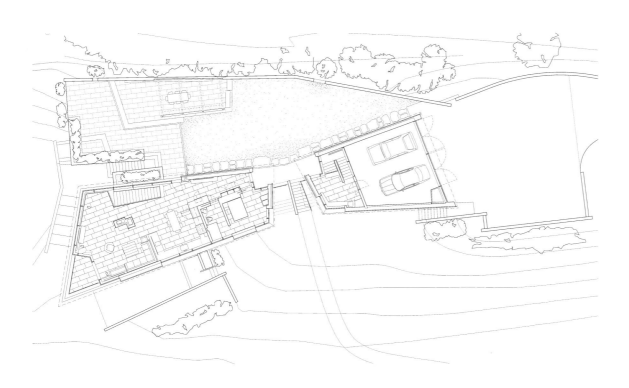

Window frames in the house are teak on the exterior and redwood on the interior. The floors are a honed bluestone and walls are either sandblasted concrete, natural plaster, or solid cherry panels. The furnishings are "spare because the owner spends most of his time in outdoor physical activity."

Die Fensterrahmen des Hauses sind außen aus Teakholz, innen aus Redwood gefertigt. Die Fußböden bestehen aus poliertem Blausandstein, die Wände entweder aus sandgestrahltem Beton, naturbelassenem Putz oder massiven Kirschbaumpaneelen. Die Möblierung ist „spärlich, weil sich der Eigentümer die meiste Zeit sportlich im Freien betätigt".

Les encadrements des fenêtres sont en teck à l'extérieur et en bois de séquoia à l'intérieur. Les sols sont grès bleu poncé et les murs en béton sablé, plâtre naturel ou panneaux en cerisier massif. Le mobilier est « peu abondant parce que le propriétaire consacre la plupart de son temps à des activités physiques de plein air. »

As seen in plans, left, the house assumes a much less cubic or block-like form than its exterior appearance indicates.

Wie aus den Grundrissen links ersichtlich, hat das Haus eine weit weniger kubische oder blockartige Form, als sein äußeres Erscheinungsbild vermuten lässt.

Les plans à gauche montrent que la forme de la maison est beaucoup moins cubique ou en « bloc » que son aspect extérieur ne le laisse supposer.

ZECC

Zecc Architecten
Westerkade 4
3511 HA Utrecht
The Netherlands

Tel: +31 30 273 12 89
Fax: +31 30 273 02 89
E-mail: info@zecc.nl
Web: www.zecc.nl

ZECC was created in 2003 in Utrecht. The director of the firm, Marnix van der Meer, was born in 1972 in Benschop, the Netherlands, and was educated at the University of Applied Sciences in Utrecht (1991–95), and at the Amsterdam Academy of Architecture (1996–2002, M.Arch), while he worked in the office of Meyer & Van Schooten Architects (Amsterdam, 1996–2002). The firm's work includes a design for 24 apartments (Vathorst, Amersfoort, 2005); remodeling of offices in Utrecht (Herenstraat 12, 2006); apartment projects in Almere (Homeruskwartier, 2007); and in 2008, designs for apartments in Groningen, Hilversum, and Vathorst, as well as a renovation and reuse project for a water tower in St. Jansklooster, all in the Netherlands. The firm had already converted a church into offices in Dieren (2005), thus the project published here, Stairway to Heaven (Utrecht, 2007), was not their first venture into this rather delicate type of intervention.

ZECC wurde 2003 in Utrecht gegründet. Marnix van der Meer, Leiter des Büros, wurde 1972 in Benschop, Niederlande, geboren und studierte an der Hogeschool Utrecht (1991–95) sowie an der Academie van Bouwkunst in Amsterdam (1996–2002, M.Arch.), während er zugleich im Büro Meyer & Van Schooten Architecten tätig war (Amsterdam, 1996–2002). Zu den Projekten von Zecc zählen u. a. 24 Wohnungen (Vathorst, Amersfoort, 2005), der Umbau von Büros in Utrecht (Herenstraat 12, 2006), Wohnungen in Almere (Homeruskwartier, 2007), Entwürfe für Wohnungen in Groningen, Hilversum und Vathorst (2008) sowie die Sanierung und Umnutzung eines Wasserturms in St. Jansklooster (2008), alle in den Niederlanden. Das Büro hatte bereits in Dieren eine Kirche zu Büroräumen umgebaut (2005), insofern ist das hier vorgestellte Projekt Stairway to Heaven (Utrecht, 2007) nicht das erste Mal, dass die Architekten mit einer solchen, eher heiklen Baumaßnahme zu tun hatten.

L'agence **ZECC** a été fondée en 2003 à Utrecht. Son directeur, Marnix van der Meer, est né en 1972 à Benschop, Pays-Bas, et a étudié à l'université des sciences appliquées d'Utrecht (1991–95) et à l'académie d'architecture d'Amsterdam (1996–2002, master), tout en travaillant déjà pour l'agence Meyer & Van Schooten Architects (Amsterdam, 1996–2002). Parmi les réalisations de Zecc, on compte 24 appartements (Vathorst, Amersfoort, 2005) ; une rénovation de bureaux à Utrecht (Herenstraat 12, 2006) ; des appartements à Almere (Homeruskwartier, 2007) ainsi qu'à Groningen, Hilversum et Vathorst en 2008 et la rénovation, avec le projet de réutilisation, d'un château d'eau à St. Jansklooster. L'agence a également transformé une église en bureaux à Dieren (2005). Le projet présenté ici, Stairway to Heaven (Utrecht, 2007), n'était donc pas leur première réalisation dans ce type d'intervention assez délicat.

STAIRWAY TO HEAVEN

Utrecht, The Netherlands, 2007

Floor area: 250 m². Clients: Robin and Valerie. Cost: not disclosed
Team: Rolf Bruggink, Marnix van der Meer

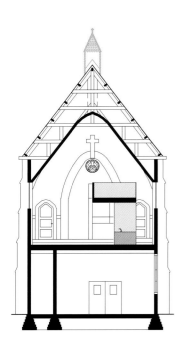

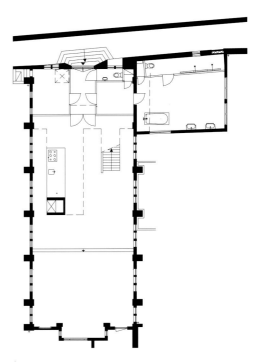

The architects have audaciously retained stained glass windows, a pipe organ and even a large candelabra as seen in the image to the right.

Die Architekten haben kühn die Buntglasfenster übernommen, ebenso wie die Kirchenorgel und sogar einen großen Kandelaber (rechte Seite).

Les architectes n'ont pas hésité à conserver les vitraux, les orgues et même un grand candélabre (photo de droite).

This very surprising project makes use of an existing church to create a residence. Though deconsecrated churches have been used for various purposes, including discotheques, the rather literal use of the church architecture, and even its religious symbolism in this instance, places the Stairway to Heaven, named after a famous song, in a category apart. According to the architects, "the balcony near the organ was maintained and extended in the form of an organizing element, free in the space. This element defines the different living spaces in the chapel." The architects explain that "specific, characterizing elements, such as relics, are maintained and used, thus a certain tension comes into existence between the old and new functions of the chapel." A "Mondrian-like" window was added in the place of stained glass in one location to permit more contact between the former church interior and the town.

Dieses sehr überraschende Projekt nutzt eine bestehende Kirche als Wohnbau. Obwohl säkularisierte Kirchen schon für die verschiedensten Zwecke genutzt wurden, sogar als Diskotheken, ist diese fast wörtliche Übernahme der Kirchenarchitektur und in einigen Fällen sogar der religiösen Symbole etwas Besonderes (seinen Namen Stairway to Heaven verdankt das Haus einem berühmten Rocksong). Den Architekten zufolge wurde „die Empore bei der Orgel erhalten und als gliederndes Element sogar frei in den Raum hinein erweitert. Das Element definiert die verschiedenen Wohnbereiche in der Kapelle". Die Architekten erklären: „Bestimmte typische Elemente, etwa Reliquien, wurden erhalten und genutzt, wodurch eine Spannung zwischen den alten und neuen Funktionen der Kapelle entsteht." Ein buntes Kirchenfenster wurde durch ein Fenster „im Stil Mondrians" ersetzt, um einen stärkeren Kontakt zwischen dem Innenraum der ehemaligen Kirche und der Stadt zu ermöglichen.

Ce très étonnant projet a consisté à transformer une ancienne église en résidence. Bien que les églises déconsacrées aient souvent été utilisées à des fins diverses, y compris celles de discothèques, le recours assez littéral à l'architecture ecclésiale, et même à son symbolisme religieux dans ce cas, place dans une catégorie à part ce « Stairway to Heaven », ainsi nommé d'après une chanson célèbre. « Le balcon près de l'orgue a été maintenu et agrandi en élément structurant, libre dans son espace. Il définit les différents espaces de vie dans la chapelle », expliquent les architectes. « Des éléments caractéristiques comme les reliques ont été conservés et utilisés, ce qui crée une certaine tension entre les fonctions nouvelles et anciennes de la chapelle », ajoutent-ils. À un certain endroit, une fenêtre « style Mondrian » a remplacé un vitrail pour permettre un plus grand contact entre l'intérieur de l'ancienne église et la ville.

A cross above a doorway or stained glass near the kitchen space recall the original function of the structure and provide an unexpected element of interior décor.

Ein Kreuz über dem Portal oder Buntglas in der Küche erinnern an die ursprüngliche Nutzung des Baus und sind zugleich ein überraschendes Element der Innenraumgestaltung.

La croix au-dessus de l'arc de pierre ou le vitrail près de la cuisine rappellent la fonction d'origine du bâtiment tout en constituant des éléments inattendus de décoration intérieure.

A simple stairway leads up to the pipe organ (right). Modern white surfaces contrast with the kind of darkness that one might expect in a church interior however.

Ein schlichte Treppe führt hinauf zur Orgel (rechts). Die modernen weißen Oberflächen sind ein Kontrast zur Dunkelheit, die man in einem Kirchenraum erwarten könnte.

Un simple escalier droit conduit à l'orgue (à droite). Les parois blanches et modernes contrastent avec l'obscurité relative à laquelle on s'attend généralement dans une église.

A simple, Mondrian-like stained glass window makes the transition between the original ecclesiastical function of the structure and its new role as a modern residence.

Ein schlichtes, mondrianeskes Buntglasfenster vollzieht den Brückenschlag zwischen der ursprünglichen kirchlichen Nutzung des Baus und seiner neuer Rolle aus Wohnraum.

Un vitrail de composition simple, dans l'esprit de Mondrian, fait le lien entre la fonction ecclésiale d'origine du bâtiment et son rôle nouveau de résidence moderne.

ZHANG LEI

AZL Atelier Zhanglei
School of Architecture
Nanjing University
Nanjing 210093
China

Tel: +86 25 5186 1368
Fax: +86 25 5186 1367
E-mail: atelierzhanglei@163.com, lzhang2000@vip.sina.com

ZHANG LEI was born in 1964 in the Jiangsu province of China. He was the founder of AZL Atelier Zhanglei, and is a Professor and Vice Dean of the School of Architecture at Nanjing University. He studied architecture at Southeast University in China (1981–88) and then at the ETH Zurich (1991–93). His major projects include the Brick Houses and the Concrete Slit House published here (Nanjing, 2006–07); the Jiangsu Software Park (Nanjing, 2006–08); the Shantang Villas (Suzhou, 2006–08); and the Fang Lljun Art Gallery (Chengdu, 2007–08), all in China.

ZHANG LEI wurde 1964 in der chinesischen Provinz Jiangsu geboren. Er war Gründer von AZL Atelier Zhanglei und ist Professor und Vizedekan der Architektur-fakultät der Universität Nanjing. Sein Architekturstudium absolvierte er an der Southeast University in China (1981–88) sowie an der ETH Zürich (1991–93). Zu seinen wichtigsten Projekten zählen die hier vorgestellten Brick Houses und das Concrete Slit House (Nanjing, 2006–07), der Jiangsu Software Park (Nanjing, 2006–08), die Shantang Villas (Suzhou, 2006–08) sowie die Fang Lljun Art Gallery (Chengdu, 2007–08), alle in China.

ZHANG LEI, né en 1964 dans la province du Jiangsu en Chine, est le fondateur d'AZL Atelier Zhanglei, et professeur et vice-doyen de l'école d'architecture de l'université de Nankin. Il a étudié l'architecture à l'université du Sud-Est en Chine (1981–88), puis à l'ETH à Zurich (1991–93). Parmi ses principales réalisations, toutes en Chine : les maisons de brique et la maison de béton fendu, présentées ici (Nankin, 2006–07) ; le parc de logiciels du Jiangsu (Nankin, 2006–08) ; les villas Shantang (Suzhou, 2006–08) et la galerie d'art Fang Lijun (Chengdu, 2007–08).

BRICK HOUSE 01

Nanjing, Jiangsu, China, 2006–07

Site area: 1650 m². Floor area: 850 m²
Client: Wang Yongjun. Cost: €68 000

Zhang Lei explains, "Brick House 01 and Brick House 02 are separate projects with two different clients who are close friends. Together with two other families they bought a property along the lake and built four houses, two other houses in between these two brick houses were designed by another local architect." Both of these large houses were built for a remarkably low cost per square meter of 80 euros. The architect acknowledges the difficulties posed by this budget, but praises the clients, who were closely involved in the entire process. Zhang Lei regards these two residences as an "evolution from the prototype of the Chinese courtyard house." He paid particular attention to the relationship of the houses to the lake that lies to the northwest of the sites. Locally produced red bricks were used for the main structures because they are the most readily available and typical construction materials in the region. The "pattern of the brick façades reflects a logic of opening, or openness," concludes Zhang Lei.

Zhang Lei erklärt: „Brick House 01 und Brick House 02 sind separate Projekte für zwei verschiedene, eng befreundete Auftraggeber. Gemeinsam mit zwei weiteren Familien hatten sie ein Grundstück am See gekauft und vier Häuser gebaut, wobei die zwei Häuser dazwischen von einem anderen ortsansässigen Architekten entworfen wurden." Die beiden großen Häuser wurden für bemerkenswert niedrige Baukosten von 80 Euro pro Quadratmeter realisiert. Der Architekt räumt ein, dass dieses Budget schwierig war, lobt jedoch die Bauherren, die in den gesamten Prozess eng eingebunden waren. Zhang Lei versteht die beiden Häuser als eine „Weiterentwicklung des Prototyps des chinesischen Hofhauses". Besondere Aufmerksamkeit galt der Beziehung der Bauten zum See nordöstlich des Grundstücks. Für die Hauptbauten wurden regional gefertigte rote Ziegelsteine verwendet, da sie am einfachsten erhältlich waren und ein für die Region typisches Baumaterial sind. Abschließend bemerkt Zhang Lei: „Das Muster der Backsteinfassaden spiegelt eine Logik der Öffnung, der Offenheit."

Zhang Lei explique que les « Brick House 01 et Brick House 02 sont des projets indépendants pour deux clients différents qui sont ses proches amis. Avec deux autres familles, ils ont acheté une propriété en bordure d'un lac et construit quatre maisons, deux étant conçues par un autre architecte local. » Ces deux grandes résidences ont été édifiées pour le prix étonnamment bas de 80 euros le m². L'architecte reconnaît les difficultés posées par un tel budget, mais félicite ses clients de s'être étroitement impliqués en permanence dans le processus du projet. Zhang Lei considère ces deux résidences comme « une évolution du prototype de la maison à cour chinoise ». Il a porté une attention particulière à la relation avec le lac qui s'étend au nord-ouest des terrains. Les constructions principales sont en briques rouges produites localement, parce qu'elles étaient plus facilement disponibles, et matériaux typiques de construction de la région. La « disposition des briques en façade reflète une logique d'ouverture, ou d'ajouré », conclut Zhang Lei.

A site plan shows the location of the two Brick Houses within an existing neighborhood. Brick House 01 is to the right on the plan (light blue) and Brick House 02 roughly in the middle of the plan.

Der Lageplan veranschaulicht die Lage der beiden Brick Houses in der bestehenden Nachbarschaft. Brick House 01 ist rechterhand zu sehen (hellblau), Brick House 02 etwa in der Mitte des Plans.

Ce plan d'ensemble montre la situation des deux « maisons de brique » dans leur environnement existant. La Brick House 01 est à droite sur le plan (en bleu clair) et la Brick House 02 au centre.

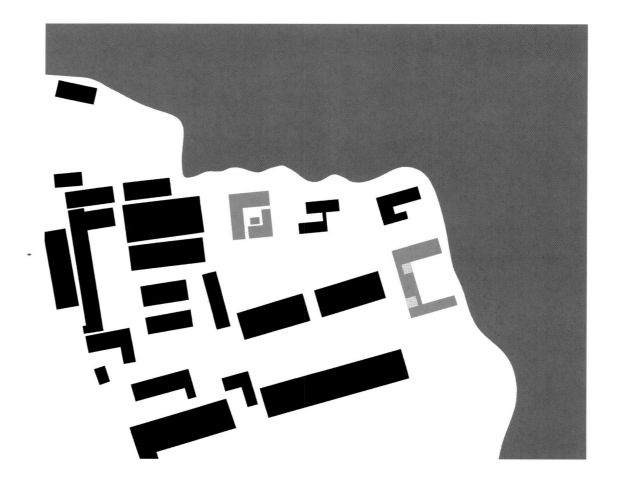

Elevations of the house show its rectilinear form and irregular pattern of openings. Above, a broad square opening, framed by the brick surface of the house, has a simple elegance. The brick pattern gives a relief and roughness to the exterior surfaces.

Aufrisse des Hauses veranschaulichen die geradlinige Form und die unregelmäßigen Wandöffnungen. Eine breite, quadratische Maueröffnung (oben), gerahmt von der Backsteinfassade, ist von schlichter Eleganz. Das Backsteinmuster verleiht den Außenfassaden reliefartige Rauheit.

Des élévations de la maison montrent sa forme orthogonale et l'implantation irrégulière des ouvertures. Ci-dessus, simple et élégante, une grande ouverture carrée cadrée de briques. Les motifs des briques confèrent un relief et une irrégularité aux surfaces extérieures.

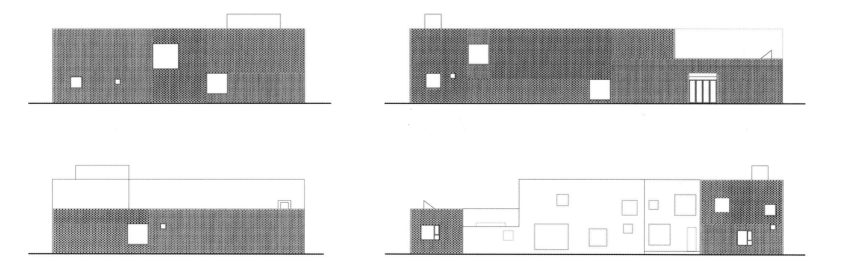

CONCRETE SLIT HOUSE

Nanjing, Jiangsu, China, 2006–07

*Site area: 320 m². Floor area: 270 m². Client: Xie Mingrui
Cost: €108 000*

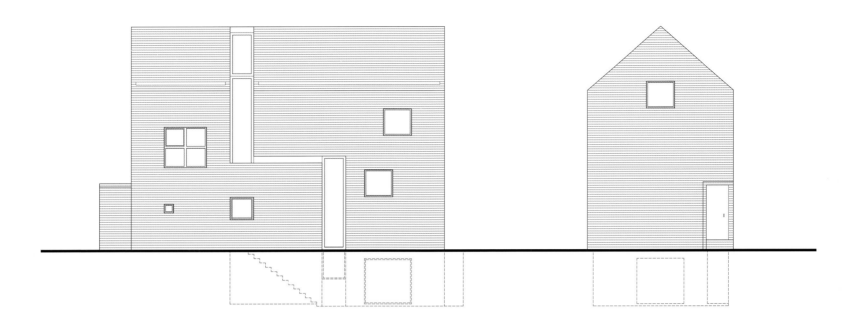

Although somewhat deformed by a wide-angle lens (right) the house is rigorously rectilinear, pierced in an unusual way by the entrance and the slit that gives the residence its name.

Trotz der leichten Verzerrung durch ein Weitwinkelobjektiv (rechts) ist das Haus streng geradlinig. Ungewöhnlich durchbrochen wird das Haus vom Eingang sowie dem Einschnitt („slit"), dem es seinen Namen verdankt.

Bien que légèrement déformée par une prise vue au grand angle, la maison est parfaitement orthogonale. Elle est percée de façon surprenante par son entrée dans l'angle et la fente (« slit ») qui lui donne son nom.

This residence, with a substantially higher construction cost per square meter than the Brick Houses (400 euros), "fits into the historical context formulated in the beginning of the 1920s in the center of Nanjing with a new form," according to Zhang Lei. Indeed, the house adapts the scale and typology of neighboring houses, while remaining decidedly different. The public areas of the house are intended to be "transparent" or open, while preserving the privacy of the spaces through "limited openings to the surroundings" in the densely built site area. This apparently contradictory result is achieved through the use of a zig-zagging slit that almost appears to cut the house in two, admitting light and views out without sacrificing privacy. Concrete was used for the entire structure, including the roof, although the exterior areas around the house offer a wooden terrace. The architect's insistence on the material can be seen as a commentary on the building boom in China. He says, "Even though we use half the world's cement, this is the first real concrete building in Nanjing, a city that has built 1300 high-rise concrete towers in the last 25 years."

Der Bau dieses Haus war mit erheblich höheren Kosten von 400 Euro pro Quadratmeter verbunden als die Brick Houses. Zhang Lei zufolge „fügt es sich mit seiner neuen Form in den historischen Kontext ein, der im Stadtzentrum von Nanjing in den 1920er-Jahren entstand". Und tatsächlich orientiert sich das Haus in Größe und Typologie an den angrenzenden Bauten, bleibt jedoch zweifellos etwas völlig anderes. Obwohl die Gemeinschaftsbereiche des Hauses „transparent" bzw. offen gestaltet wurden, wurde die Privatsphäre gewahrt, indem nur „begrenzte Öffnungen zum Umfeld" der dicht besiedelten Wohngegend eingesetzt wurden. Dieser scheinbar widersprüchliche Effekt wurde durch einen Zickzackschnitt erzielt, der das Haus geradezu in zwei Hälften zu teilen scheint. Er lässt Licht ins Haus und ermöglicht den Blick nach draußen, ohne dabei Privatsphäre zu opfern. Die gesamte Konstruktion, einschließlich des Dachs, wurde aus Beton gefertigt, wobei zum Außenbereich auch eine hölzerne Terrasse gehört. Das Beharren des Architekten auf diesem Baumaterial lässt sich als Kommentar zum chinesischen Bauboom verstehen. Er merkt an: „Obwohl wir die Hälfte des gesamten Zementverbrauchs der Welt beanspruchen, ist dies der erste wirkliche Betonbau in Nanjing, einer Stadt, die in den letzten 25 Jahren 1300 Hochhausbauten realisiert hat."

Cette résidence, qui a coûté nettement plus cher au mètre carré que les maisons de brique (400 euros), « s'intègre au contexte historique du centre de Nankin datant du début des années 1920, avec une forme pourtant nouvelle », précise Zhang Lei. La maison est en effet en harmonie avec l'échelle et la typologie des maisons voisines, tout en se montrant résolument différente. Les parties de réception sont « transparentes » ou ouvertes, en préservant l'intimité des espaces par « des ouvertures limitées sur l'environnement » de ce quartier très densément construit. Ce résultat apparemment contradictoire est atteint grâce à une fente en zigzag qui semble pratiquement couper la maison en deux, laisse passer la lumière naturelle et ouvre des perspectives, sans compromettre l'intimité de l'intérieur. La construction tout entière est en béton, y compris le toit. Une terrasse en bois a été aménagée à l'extérieur. L'insistance de l'architecte sur le choix du matériau peut être interprétée comme un commentaire sur l'explosion du secteur de la construction en Chine : « Même si nous utilisons la moitié du ciment du monde, c'est le premier bâtiment réellement en béton édifié à Nankin, une ville qui a construit 1300 tours de grande hauteur en béton au cours des 25 dernières années. »

The house adapts itself to the essential form of neighboring residences, but stands out in its austere grayness. Interiors are animated by the unexpected placement of openings and the use of wood.

Obwohl sich das Haus formal grundsätzlich in die Nachbarschaft integriert, hebt es sich durch sein strenges Grau von den übrigen Bauten ab. Die ungewöhnliche Anordnung der Wandöffnungen und die Nutzung von Holz beleben das Interieur.

La maison est adaptée à la typologie des résidences voisines, mais se détache d'elles par son austère couleur grise. Les intérieurs sont animés par la disposition inattendue des ouvertures et la présence du bois.

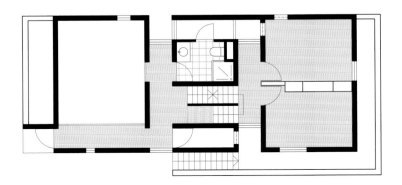

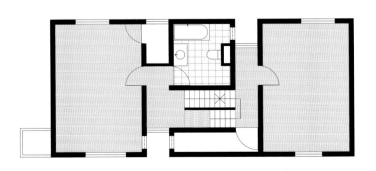

PETER ZUMTHOR

Peter Zumthor
Atelier Zumthor
Süsswinkel 20
7023 Haldenstein
Switzerland

Tel: +41 81 353 28 06
Fax: +41 81 353 30 59

PETER ZUMTHOR was born in 1943 in Basel, Switzerland. In 1958, he worked as an apprentice carpenter. He graduated from the Schule für Gestaltung in Basel in 1963 and then attended the Pratt Institute in New York, studying Architecture and Design. From 1968 to 1977, he worked as an architect for the preservation of historic monuments in the Graubünden region of Switzerland. He served as tutor at the University of Zurich in 1978 and created his own firm in the town of Haldenstein, also in the Graubünden, in 1979. He has taught at SCI-Arc in Santa Monica, the Technische Universität of Munich, Tulane University in New Orleans, and at the Academy of Architecture in Mendrisio, beginning in 1996. Peter Zumthor won the 2009 Pritzker Prize. His major buildings include the Thermal Baths in Vals (Switzerland, 1996); the Kunsthaus in Bregenz (Austria, 1997); and the Swiss Pavilion at Expo 2000 in Hanover (Germany, 2000). He also built a Single Family House (Graubünden, 1997–2003, published here); and has recently completed the St. Niklaus von Flüe Chapel (Mechernich-Wachendorf, Germany, 2003–07); the Kolumba Art Museum of the Archdiocese of Cologne (Cologne, Germany, 2003–07); and the Serpentine Gallery Summer Pavilion (Kensington Gardens, London, UK, 2011).

PETER ZUMTHOR wurde 1943 in Basel geboren. Nach einer Lehre als Möbelschreiner Ende der 1950er-Jahre besuchte er zunächst die Schule für Gestaltung in Basel (Abschluss 1963) und anschließend das Pratt Institute in New York, wo er Architektur und Design studierte. Von 1968 bis 1977 arbeitete er als Denkmalpfleger für den Kanton Graubünden. 1978 hatte er einen Lehrauftrag an der Universität Zürich, im darauffolgenden Jahr gründete er in Haldenstein in Graubünden ein eigenes Büro. Ab 1996 unterrichtete Zumthor am Southern California Institute of Architecture in Santa Monica, an der Technischen Universität München, an der Tulane University in New Orleans und an der Accademia di Architettura in Mendrisio im Tessin. Peter Zumthor wurde 2009 der Pritzker Prize verliehen. Zu seinen bedeutendsten Bauten zählen die Therme Vals im gleichnamigen Ort in der Schweiz (1996), das Kunsthaus Bregenz (Österreich, 1997) und der schweizerische Pavillon für die Expo 2000 in Hannover. Ferner hat Zumthor ein Einfamilienhaus in Graubünden (1997–2003, hier vorgestellt) ausgeführt und in jüngster Zeit eine Niklaus von Flüe gewidmete Kapelle in Mechernich-Wachendorf (2003–07), das Diözesanmuseum Kolumba in Köln fertiggestellt (2003–07) sowie den Serpentine Gallery Summer Pavilion (Kensington Gardens, London, UK, 2011).

PETER ZUMTHOR, né en 1943 à Bâle, Suisse, travaille d'abord comme apprenti-menuisier (1958). Il est diplômé de la Schule für Gestaltung de Bâle en 1963, puis étudie l'architecture et le design au Pratt Institute à New York. De 1968 à 1977, il est architecte spécialisé dans le patrimoine historique dans le canton des Grisons. Il est assistant à l'université de Zurich en 1978 et crée sa propre agence à Haldenstein, également dans les Grisons, en 1979. Il a enseigné à SCI-Arc à Santa Monica, à la Technische Universität de Munich, à Tulane University à la Nouvelle-Orléans et à l'Académie d'architecture de Mendrisio, à partir de 1996. Peter Zumthor a reçu le Prix Pritzker en 2009. Parmi ses réalisations majeures, on compte les Thermes de Vals (Suisse, 1996) ; la Kunsthaus de Bregenz (Autriche, 1997) et le pavillon suisse à Hanovre (Allemagne, 2000). Il a également construit une résidence familiale (Grisons, 1997–2003, présentée ici.) et, plus récemment, la chapelle de St. Niklaus von Flüe (Mechernich-Wachendorf, Allemagne, 2003–07), le musée d'Art Kolumba pour le diocèse de Cologne (Allemagne, 2003–07) et le pavillon de la Serpentine Gallery (Kensington Gardens, London, UK, 2011).

SINGLE-FAMILY HOUSE

Jenaz, Switzerland, 1997–2003

Floor area: not disclosed. Client: Liliane and Valentin Luzi. Cost: not disclosed

Just as he placed an emphasis on the idea of the typical wooden construction of his country in Hanover, so too, Zumthor was interested in the idea of a creating a single-family timber house in the Graubünden region. A simple, cruciform plan for a slanted, overhanging roof, the house again bridges tradition and modernity, creating an unadorned design where light and the color and form of wood are the only elements that define space. With its views of the countryside and its bow to local vernacular, albeit in the most strictly modern sense, this single-family house is a testimony to what makes Zumthor quite different from other contemporary architects, even in Switzerland. Based in a rural mountain valley, he accepted this commission from a local family where others of his level of fame might well have said they were too busy for such a "minor" project. His point seems to be that architecture is not only a public expression and one meant to contribute to the designer's reputation, but one that is practiced in a patient and modest way. Zumthor's modesty has not kept him from defining new paradigms within an apparently narrow set of precepts, although he is fully capable, as he showed in Bregenz, to work with glass and concrete as well as wood or locally quarried stone.

Ebenso wie Zumthor die Idee einer typischen Holzkonstruktion zur Vertretung seines Landes in Hannover wichtig erschien, faszinierte ihn die Vorstellung, im Kanton Graubünden ein Einfamilienhaus aus Holz zu errichten. Mit seinem schlichten, kreuzförmigen Grundriss und einem geneigten, überhängenden Dach stellt auch dieses Haus eine Verbindung zwischen Tradition und Moderne her. Bei seiner schmucklosen Gestaltung stellen Licht sowie Farbton und Form des Holzes die einzigen, den Raum bestimmenden Elemente dar. Dieses Einfamilienhaus mit seinen Ausblicken in die Landschaft und seiner Reverenz an die heimische Architektur, wenn auch im streng modernen Sinn, zeugt von dem, was Zumthor, selbst innerhalb der Schweiz, von anderen zeitgenössischen Architekten unterscheidet. Der in einem von Landwirtschaft geprägten Alpental ansässige Zumthor übernahm diesen Auftrag einer gleichfalls hier lebenden Familie, wo andere mit vergleichbarer Reputation bei einem solch unbedeutenden Projekt Arbeitsüberlastung vorgeschoben hätten. Er scheint davon überzeugt, dass Architektur nicht nur öffentlicher Ausdruck ist, der zum Ruhm seines Erzeugers beitragen soll, sondern etwas, das in verträglicher und zurückhaltender Weise betrieben wird. Zumthors Bescheidenheit hält ihn nicht davon ab, innerhalb eines scheinbar engen Regelwerks neue Paradigmen festzulegen, obgleich er, wie in Bregenz bewiesen, ebenso fähig ist, mit Glas und Beton zu arbeiten wie mit Holz oder vor Ort gebrochenem Stein.

Après avoir mis l'accent sur l'idée de la construction en bois typique de son pays à Hanovre, Zumthor s'est également intéressé à la création d'une maison monofamiliale en bois dans le canton des Grisons. De simple plan cruciforme à toit pentu à large surplomb, la maison est un pont entre tradition et modernité dans lequel la lumière, la couleur et la forme du bois sont les seuls éléments qui définissent l'espace. Donnant sur la campagne, elle est un salut au style vernaculaire local, mais dans le sens le plus strictement moderne. Elle est un témoignage de ce qui différencie Zumthor des autres architectes contemporains, même suisses. Sans doute parce qu'il s'est installé dans une vallée rurale, il a accepté cette commande d'une famille locale là où d'autres praticiens de son niveau auraient répondu être trop occupés pour un projet aussi « mineur ». Pour lui, l'architecture n'est pas seulement une expression publique qui doit contribuer à la célébrité du créateur mais quelque chose qui se pratique de façon patiente et modeste. Sa modestie ne l'a pas empêché de définir de nouveaux paradigmes dans un cadre de principes apparemment stricts, bien qu'il soit parfaitement capable, comme il l'a montré à Bregenz, de travailler aussi bien avec le verre et le béton qu'avec le bois et la pierre locale.

Interiors are marked by a careful use of wood surfaces that translate the rigor seen in the exterior images of the house. Clearly, interior and exterior form a whole.

Die Innenräume kennzeichnet eine sorgfältige Gestaltung der Holzflächen, welche die außen sichtbare Strenge des Hauses übernehmen. Innen und außen bilden eindeutig ein Ganzes.

L'intérieur est marqué par l'utilisation soignée du bois qui décline la rigueur dont témoignent les vues extérieures de la maison. L'intérieur et l'extérieur forment à l'évidence un tout.

Again using the wooden architecture and careful joinery that is typical of the Swiss Alps, Zumthor succeeds in allying past and present, giving a decidedly contemporary feeling to the interior and exterior of the house.

Zumthor, der auch in diesem Fall die für die Schweizer Alpen typische Holzarchitektur mit sorgfältiger Tischlerarbeit verbindet, gelang es, Vergangenheit und Gegenwart zu vereinen und dem Haus eine entschieden moderne Anmutung zu verleihen.

Utilisant là aussi l'architecture en bois soignée typique des Alpes suisses, Zumthor réussit à allier le passé et le présent tout en donnant un caractère résolument contemporain à l'intérieur et à l'extérieur de la maison.

On the right page, the subtle manipulation of space imagined by the architect plays on varying degrees of light, within a remarkably unified wooden interior.

Rechte Seite: Der subtile Umgang des Architekten mit dem Raum führt zu einem Spiel mit verschiedenen Lichtstärken innerhalb des bemerkenswert einheitlichen hölzernen Innenbereichs.

Page de droite, la manipulation subtile de l'espace imaginée par l'architecte joue sur les niveaux d'éclairage à l'intérieur d'un espace remarquablement unifié par l'utilisation du bois.

Full wooden surfaces give an undeniable warmth to the interiors despite their relative opacity, broken sometimes by generous glazing.

Die ganz mit Holz verkleideten Flächen verleihen den zwar relativ geschlossenen, doch manchmal durch großzügige Verglasung unterbrochenen Innenräumen eine spürbare Wärme.

Les surfaces entièrement en bois confèrent une chaleur indéniable à l'intérieur malgré son aspect relative fermé, rompu à l'occasion par de généreuses ouvertures.

INDEX OF BUILDINGS, NAMES, AND PLACES

CREDITS

Niall McLaughlin Architects, Hertfordshire 454

438 **MOS**, Pointe du Baril

442 **MOS**, Columbia County

Shim – Sutcliffe, Don Mills 552

Selgascano, Madrid 544

Johnsen Schmaling Architects, Green Lake 328

No.MAD – Eduardo Arroyo, San Lorenzo de El Escorial 466

David Hovey, Glencoe 304

Ábalos & Herreros, Madrid 18

Patkau Architects, Salt Spring Island 478

Correia / Ragazzi Arquitectos, Caniçada 144

Olson Kundig Architects, Mazama 472

Guilherme Machado Vaz, Vieira do Minho 414

Charles Deaton, Golden 158

Álvaro Leite Siza Vieira, Freguesia de Cerva 562

Alexander Gorlin, Genesee 256

Aires Mateus, Leiria 32

136 **Nancy Copley**, Accord

Will Bruder + Partners, Reno 120

408 **Daniel Libeskind**, Connecticut

642 **UNStudio**, Upstate New York

Richard Meier, Southern California 424

656 **Williams And Tsien**, Shelter Island

370 **KieranTimberlake**, Taylors Island

Michael Reynolds, Taos 514

430 **Toshiko Mori**, Casey Key

524 **Rural Studio**, Mason's Bend

Jorge Hernandez de la Garza, Oaxtepec 234

Arsenio Pérez Amaral, Tacoronte 492

Ricardo Bak Gordon, Olhão 78

Gianni Botsford Architect, Cahuita 110

Antón García-Abril Ruiz, Benahavis 226

Al Borde, Tumbaco 38

Marcio Kogan, Salvador 396

Bernardes + Jacobsen, Búzios 100

Simas and Grinspum, Paraty 556

Marcos Acayaba, Tijucopava 24

Bernardes + Jacobsen, Angra dos Reis 106

Mathias Klotz, Cachagua 388

Felipe Assadi + Francisca Pulido, Santiago 56

FAR Frohn & Rojas, Santiago 194

378 **Mathias Klotz**, Nahuel Huapi Lake

Pezo von Ellrichshausen, Coliumo Peninsula 498

Beals-Lyon / Christian Beals, Lake District 94